A YEAR IN THE LIFE OF A SHINTO SHRINE

JOHN K. NELSON

University of Washington Press

Seattle & London

A YEAR IN THE LIFE OF A SHINTO SHRINE

University of Washington Press
PO Box 50096
Seattle, WA 98145-5096, USA
www.washington.edu/uwpress

Library of Congress Cataloging-in-Publication Data
Nelson, John K.
    A year in the life of a Shinto Shrine / John K. Nelson.
        p. cm.
    Includes bibliographical references and index.
    ISBN 978-0-295-97500-9 (pbk. : alk. paper)
        1. Suwa Jinja (Nagasaki-shi, Japan). 2. Religious life—
Shinto. 3. Shinto—Customs and practices. I. Title.
BL2225.N2552S883   1996   95-23257
299'56135'095224—dc20   CIP

CONTENTS

ACKNOWLEDGMENTS

I have no difficulty in deciding who deserves the most thanks for his assistance with this book. Without the patience, courtesy, kindness, and generosity of the chief priest of Suwa Shrine, Mr. Uesugi Chisato, I would never have been able to get a look behind the doors at what a contemporary Shinto shrine is all about. At the time of this research, I was affiliated with no university or research institute, had no funding agency, and possessed only what little status a teaching job at a local women's college afforded. And yet Chief Priest Uesugi encouraged my interest at all times, spent many hours with me in conversation, but never once suggested that there was somewhere a book to be written about my new discoveries. This is all the more remarkable considering the amount of flak he must have weathered on my behalf. Anyone who has been to Japan and is aware of how conspicuous foreigners are in nearly any context knows that my presence at the shrine's many in-house events could be likened to that of a crow among doves. I expected the residents of Nagasaki to react negatively to the presence in "their" shrine of a citizen from the country that dropped an atomic bomb on them, and fully anticipated outbursts of hostility. However, at no time did I receive the slightest impression that anyone was bothered or outraged by my ongoing interest in shrine activities. I would therefore like to thank the people of Nagasaki for their tolerance and understanding, but must also attribute this congenial atmosphere to the efforts of Chief Priest Uesugi, who not only introduced me at numerous receptions held after rituals but also explained my background and interests. The shrine community of Japan is extremely fortunate to have a person of Chief Priest Uesugi's international outlook, wide experience, and deep understanding of Shinto, and I sincerely hope that he will continue to be a leading voice for many years to come.

Over a period of many months, the other priests at the shrine began to warm up (or became resigned) to my presence, so I would also like to express my gratitude to them for the courtesy I was shown, particularly by Mr. Ureshino, Mr. Matsumoto, and Mr. Otaguro, all of whom assisted me when time permitted. Mr. Nishida

Yasunori of Nagasaki Photo Service helped with photographs and encouragement. By the time of my departure from Nagasaki, I felt like a member in good standing of the Suwa "clan" and was greatly honored by a farewell party that included a photo session where I was permitted to don formal priest's robes and where my wife wore the twelve-layered kimono of Heian times.

Once back in the States, Professor George Williams of California State University, Chico, helped me understand that a book of this sort was needed and encouraged me to be the one to write it. Of the same institution, I would also like to thank Professor Emeritus Herbert Joseph, Professor Thomas Johnson, Professor Ray Barnett, and Mr. Geert Hendriks for their insights and enthusiasm. At the University of California at Berkeley, I would like to extend my appreciation to Professor Emeritus George De Vos for his initial interest in this project, to Professor Emeritus Delmer Brown for his ongoing encouragement and high expectations, and to Professor Nelson Graburn for his keen and discerning standards as well as for his support.

The potential within the original manuscript was first noticed by the late Don Cioeta at the University of Washington Press. I am very grateful for his initial encouragement and suggestions. Naomi Pascal inherited the project and moved it along through the review process, where it benefited greatly from the comments of an anonymous reader. My thanks also go to Pamela Bruton for the great care she took in copyediting the text, to Shannon Crum and Anne Alexander of the University of Texas at Austin for the maps, and to Nishida Yasunori for several of the photographs.

Finally, I owe a considerable karmic debt to my partner, Miko, and to my son, Junet, both of whom provided reassurance and support and whose understanding of the writing process permitted me the time and energy to complete this book during difficult times of transition. Having a child in Japan opens doors that could never be touched in other ways, so I am particularly grateful for Junet's good humor and inquisitiveness about participating in certain shrine events. I hope that in the future he will come to understand and enjoy Japan in some of the ways that his parents have.

CONVENTIONS

As is the custom for books employing Japanese terms and names, I will give Japanese words in italics except for those Japanese terms that are familiar to English speakers, and I will give Japanese names with the family followed by the given name. I use "Shinto" without the macron over the final *o* as is the practice for other words more or less familiar to Western readers (e.g., Tokyo, Kyoto, sumo), but elsewhere follow standard romanizations.

One of the more noticeable features of the text is my capitalization of the word "Kami" as well as not placing it in italics. My reasons for doing so are twofold: first, to give it the same kind of visual status within the text as the word "God" might have in a Christian context and, second, to thus divest it of the special attention italics often are meant to give a word or concept. The Kami are as fundamental to a shrine as are its rituals, so I feel justified in treating their textual representation in a matter-of-fact, though respectful, way.

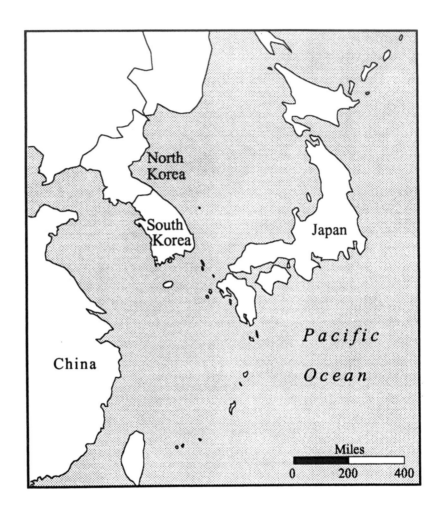

Map of Japan

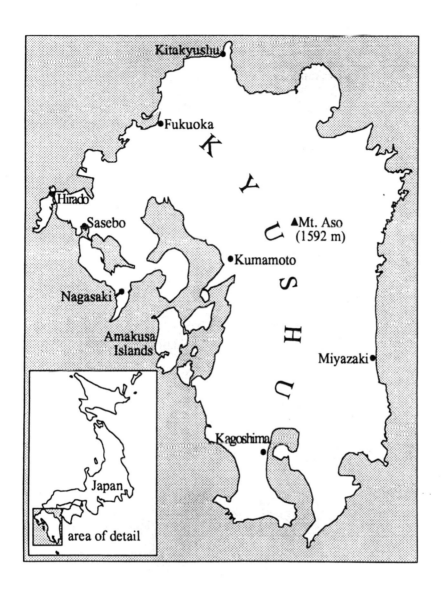

Map of Kyushu Island

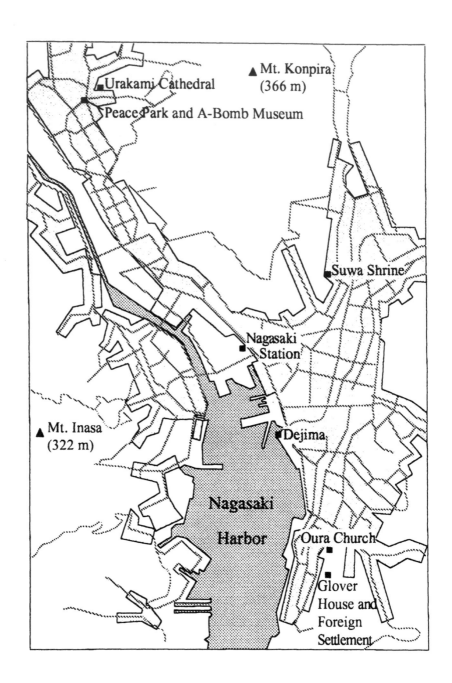

Map of Nagasaki

A
YEAR
IN
THE
LIFE
OF
A
SHINTO
SHRINE

I

FRAMES

AND

FOCUSES

Shinto is sacred rope wrapped around a huge tree or mossy stone, little shrines scattered seemingly at random throughout both city and country landscapes, festivals that can be solemn and raucous simultaneously—yet these are only the more readily accessible characteristics of a tradition considered to be "ethereal" and "inscrutable" because it does not *act* the way religions usually do. What we today call Shinto has been at the heart of Japanese culture for almost as long as there has been a political entity distinguishing itself as Japan, or Nihon, "Land of the Sun Source." Through fourteen centuries of recorded history this mixture of rituals, institutions, magical practices, charms, and so forth continues to participate in the framing of Japan both to the outside world and to the Japanese themselves. From "structural impediments" affecting the ongoing trade imbalance with the United States, to Japanese sensitivity about international criticism of its economic policies, to the outlay of public funds at the death of one emperor and the enthronement of his son—Shinto-based orientations and values, like some great aquifer, lie at the core of Japanese culture, society, and character, nourishing and furthering the lives of both individuals and institutions in subtle, yet often quite tangible, ways.

As the twentieth century comes to a close, it is increasingly difficult to find societies like Japan where cosmologies from the past are still thought immediately relevant to the present-day activities of modern men and women. Where but in Japan will a corporation begin construction of a state-of-the-art laser refraction laboratory with an ancient ritual to calm the spirit of the earth? Where else can we find so many individuals who feel a need to take their brand new Honda or Toyota sedan to a shrine to have it blessed before subjecting it to the vicissitudes of city and highway driving? From the new emperor in his Tokyo palace down to the poorest farmer in his thatched-roof house in Iwate, Shinto cosmologies have been like the glass of a window through which the phenomenal world and human existence have been viewed for over two thousand years. Yet, due to a lack of charismatic teachers and intellectually stimulating theological texts, of which Shinto has had very few, those in the West who have made an effort to understand Japan and its people have never really grasped Shinto's influence upon social, cultural, and, especially, political norms.

So perhaps it is reasonable to ask, why bother about Shinto at all, or about one of its shrines, if so little attention has been given to its postwar presence until now? Buddhism has always been much more appealing, both intellectually and aesthetically, to those interested in Japanese culture and the application of certain key ideas to Western contexts. Then again, what about neo-Confucianism, with its philosophy of correct conduct for the individual and its interpenetration of society's civil and political elements? Surely it has a more timely relevance to contemporary life than the vague, oftentimes contradictory, "semimystical" wanderings and practices of Shinto?

But then, recent political and social events speak otherwise. There remains to be explained the curious behavior of a modern industrialized society's fixation upon its past through the institution of a heavily subsidized Imperial household. When Emperor Hirohito died in 1989, the government allocated nearly $73 million for funeral rites and then another $90-odd million for enthronement proceedings for the new emperor, his son, rites that were essentially Shinto in origin, design, and orientation. These events become even more fascinating and complicated when one considers that Japan's constitution expressly forbids any interaction of government and this ancient system of ritual practices. It would be analogous to a death in Britain's royal family being observed with Celtic symbolism and Druid pomp—leading to the question why a connection should exist between such historically diverse periods at all as well as why it is promoted by government, the national media, and various organizations. We might also ask why a majority of Japanese continue to find an emotionally satisfying but intellectually unarticulated resonance with many of these traditions. One need only turn out at New Year's to see a demonstration of this infatuation with "tradition" by millions of people who, in the bitter cold of midnight, come to pray for health, wealth, and happiness at a Shinto shrine. Are there definable social and cultural trends that can be studied, explained, and analyzed, or should we take at his word one of the early Japanese theorists, Yamazaki Ansai, who advised in his writings, "One should not bring reason to the explanation of Shinto"?[1]

To answer these questions and address the hoard of ensuing concerns which follow in their wakes is one of the goals of this book. Rather than casting about in the oceans of information and history relevant to Japan as a whole, I hope to convince the reader there is no better place to look than into the "life" of a contemporary Shinto shrine (such as Suwa Jinja of Nagasaki) for issues of "tradition," "modernity," and "individual versus group agency" and, of course, for matters of religious and spiritual import. I use the word "life" with some care, to emphasize that a shrine is an entity constantly adapting to its environment, requiring infusions of nurturing substances (human energy, intelligence, money) by means of which it aims to achieve an influence and purpose extending far beyond its physical limitations. By examining its traditions and rituals, the people who make it work, and their interactions with the community at large, I hope to show how we can discover a local manifestation of a more general but equally remarkable path—one which begins in the prehistory of Japan, weaves its way through and then into the fused institutions of government, clergy, and state of the early historical period, withstands being paved over with militaristic ideology on a number of occasions, and finally continues through the corridors of the most modern electronics laboratory of the late twentieth century, still very much a part of the cultural codes a nation and its people utilize to meet the challenges of today as well as of the next millennium. Shinto, or the "way of the Kami," can never be accused of nonaccommodation.

Yet, in part due to the lessons learned from its long history, Shinto does not give up its secrets easily, nor does it allow easy access to accurate encapsulations, whether theoretical or descriptive. Until the 1940s, both native and foreign writers attempted with varying degrees of success to convey to the international community the religious dynamism behind Japan's rapid modernization. But in the restrictive political climate of the time, where professors could be fired and even imprisoned for going against state ideology, a highly managed and selected image was all that could be offered as a starting point for handling the hot potato of Shinto's influence on secular and state affairs.[2] With the end of World War II and the liberalization of governmental policies controlling access to historical documents and research materials, plus the increase in international scholars able to read and write Japanese, a number of important and influential works have given a new impetus to examining the role of Shinto in social and cultural realms.[3] Nevertheless, there has yet to be published a substantive "inside" account of what goes on at a shrine, and it is to this end that the following chapters add more features to the slowly forming portrait of this fascinating subject.

It is not the intention of this book to present a detailed analysis of the Shinto tradition or a wide-ranging overview of its various ritual practices, nor does it opt for a single methodology of presentation (symbolic, structural, neo-Marxist, phenomenological, and so on). Instead, by showing how a contemporary shrine functions throughout the course of a year, it is hoped that the dominant "moods and motivations" which fuel its activities, compel its priests and participants, and situate it within the community at large will gradually emerge. The reasons for this approach are many but stem from two basic concerns. First, by minimizing the use of technical terms and theorizing and by presenting a more human side to shrine activities, it is hoped that the discussion will interest a wider audience than scholarly publications normally aim for. Second, if there is any progress made in the following chapters in divesting from the image of Shinto its long-ascribed parameters of "mysticism" and "inscrutability," as something so thoroughly "Japanese" that no non-Japanese can ever hope to understand it, then all the translating, research, interviews, and travel will be a satisfying contribution to increased cultural understanding. The customs of any society different from one's own may seem highly esoteric and remote at first encounter, but I hope to show how Shinto ritual practices—from their origins to their present-day expressions running the length and width of the entire Japanese archipelago (and recently to several other countries as well)—are pragmatically designed to benefit not only the individual but his or her community and nation as well. Just how this comes about is a fascinating journey of adaptation and resourcefulness, with a few timely lessons for the Western world as well.

* * *

There are a few terms and concepts central to any discussion of Shinto and its ritual practices which, like a giant sumo wrestler (a sport rich with Shinto symbolism; see Cuyler 1979), need to be grappled with from the onset. Just as the names of the wrestlers are announced at the beginning of a match, let me similarly introduce what kind of "Shinto" I am talking about, followed by "politics," "religion," "tradition," and "culture," all to be dispensed with in five brief bouts.

Like Christianity, Buddhism, or Islam, "Shinto" is not a unified, monolithic entity that has a single center and system all its own. There is "folk" Shinto practiced by private individuals without any institutional setting other than what they think is appropriate for a time, place, and situation. There is, or more accurately was, "state" Shinto, the now illegal government-sponsored ethical and educational ideology which effectively united the Japanese people for the Second World War. At its center was "Imperial household" Shinto, with its veneration of the deity Amaterasu as the omnipotent force animating both the "unbroken" line of emperors and the Japanese people. The emperor still conducts household rituals both at his palace in Tokyo and more infrequently at the Ise shrines, although these activities are supposedly separated from any connection with the state. Finally and most importantly for the limited focus of this book, there is the phenomenon of "shrine" Shinto, whereby ancient religious institutions, some of which have origins in prehistory, have managed to convey to the present day a body of ritual practices essentially agricultural in design and animistic in content yet which somehow manage to attract participation from among urban-dwelling Japanese. When I use the word "Shinto," I am referring to the last type without distinguishing it each time by the prefix "shrine" and hope that this convenience will not cause confusion.

Now to the four terms. Pick up almost any scholarly work on Shinto and chances are that the discussion will begin with the line "Shinto is Japan's indigenous religion."[4] Immediately we are in water made hot by the friction of politics against the historical record, because it is unclear what context the word "indigenous" (meaning "native," "endemic," "aboriginal") refers to. Not only is there considerable controversy about just who the original Japanese actually were as well as where they came from, the fact remains that before their arrival, the islands were already occupied by several ethnically diverse tribal groups, one of which may have been the predecessor of the Ainu peoples, a group decidedly not Japanese.[5] The divinities of these groups were probably very different from what we now call the Shinto Kami, although it is likely they both share a similar function in helping human beings cope with the forces of the natural world. To imply, however, that Shinto is "indigenous" without offering any context for the remark is similar to calling pasta indigenously Italian or Buddhism indigenously Chinese. Writing of this sort implicitly authenticates claims of the Imperial household that there is an "unbroken" line of emperors reaching back to prehistoric times and that the first *real* Japanese were their ancestors of the Yamato clan.

Thus, readers are advised to be aware (as well as beware!) of what is commonly called the "subtext" of certain statements, opinions, and "facts" when reading about Shinto. Even though appearing with the full force of a writer's academic credentials or an informant's authority as an "insider," many pronouncements about Shinto rituals and beliefs need to be placed within contexts best described as political, since, as is their custom, individuals the world over are constantly busy with a million ways of legitimating, authenticating, and sometimes obfuscating their real intentions. We should not be surprised by this occurring in a religious institution any more than in an educational or a political one, but a reader needs to keep a sharp eye open for broader or alternative interpretations. Perhaps, with such a statement, I am undermining my own descriptions and efforts to convey what I witnessed during the course of a year at a contemporary shrine; still, I feel better for having said it, since to avoid politics when studying ritual practices is all but impossible.

Consideration must next be given to one of the most slippery and emotionally charged words in the English language: "religion." Ask a Japanese whether or not he or she has one and most likely you will receive an answer in the negative, though that very morning the person may have placed offerings of rice, water, and flowers upon a family altar. This seeming contradiction is partially due to the nuances associated with the way "religion" is translated into Japanese via the word *shūkyō*, with the first character for *shū* meaning "sect" and the *kyō* standing for "doctrine." Most Japanese do not belong to or actively participate in a specific sect and know little about the complexities of religious doctrine; thus their answer is perfectly logical. It is absolutely crucial to understand that "religious belonging and the practice of religion in Japan are not primarily conditioned by notions of belief," a phenomenon resulting in Japanese religion's overarching theme of "action, custom, and etiquette" (Reader 1991, 9 and, citing Omura, 14). From an anthropological perspective that compares cultures worldwide, belief is one of the least important characteristics of religious activity. Were we to judge the ritual practices of other societies solely on a Judeo-Christian basis of whether or not their participants believe in them, it is likely we would find a majority of the world's people to be without religion (a common ideology of many overzealous Christian missionaries). It is far more useful to look at the surrounding social environment within which apparently religious activities occur. There, one may find that an individual's ritual participation is motivated by status, economic, or political considerations, not to mention the possibility that custom encourages certain modes of behavior an outside observer might label as "religious" or as motivated by belief.

Thus, it is important to try and think of "religion" not in a Western, institutionalized sense—with gilded cupolas, Sunday schools, and sacred texts—but more as "a system of symbols which acts to establish powerful, pervasive, and long-lasting moods and motivations . . . [which serve as] screens through which experience is interpreted and [as] guides for action" (Geertz 1973, 90). For the early Japanese, "religion" was inseparable from daily life. It had a multidimensional character that permeated everything people did—from making a fire to cooking food, from hunting to raising crops, from engaging in trade or battle with other communities to interpersonal relationships that might result in marriage, cooperation, or formal worship of the clan's divinities. It was not so much the way in which individuals were *advised* to live, it was instead how they were *obligated* to live.[6] All this has changed of course with the arrival of the modern period, but one frequently encounters vestiges of this older cosmology within contemporary Japan—particularly its political character of community-building nationalism, its philosophical character grounded in everyday realities, and its ethnical characteristic of "purity" and "brightness" (Muraoka 1964, 23)—and we must try to understand why it still has a power to motivate action and participation.

How one goes about handling the interaction of a religion's dual dynamics—one personal and subjective and the other institutional and objective—is one of the challenges of writing a book like this. It seems presumptuous to assume that I can accurately convey the private, affective, individual experiences of those participating in Shinto rituals, but the reader will find numerous cases where I attempt to do exactly that. Anticipating a little healthy skepticism, may I say that, in addition to my own interpretations and discoveries based on attending fifty-five rituals, I made a considerable effort to ask people afterward how they felt or what they got out of a particular service, then incorporated these responses into my rendering of the event. Though the language of this book freely employs imagery, metaphor, different voices, and what may be characterized as a somewhat confessional approach, what transpires in these chapters is in no way compromised by the modes of representation. My purpose in employing a variety of narrative techniques is to help readers overcome cultural distances so that, had they been in my place, a similar experiencing of the event would have been within their grasp. Rather than using this book primarily for reference, I am interested in having people actually follow the flow of shrine events page by sequential page and have therefore made every effort to keep the text free of theoretical arguments, academic vocabulary, and digressions, which (with the exception of this opening chapter) are handled in the notes at the end of the book.

Let me finally turn to the conceptual pair of "tradition" and "culture," which will frequently appear in the following pages. When looking at people in other countries and the ways they go about ordering the world, some of what they do strikes us as odd, irrelevant, bizarre, or even downright wrong. Recently, however, what with the speed of communication and the penetrating glare of the camera, as long as there is a certain physical and mental buffer between "us" and "them," we do our best to diplomatically tolerate the customs of other societies by saying, "Oh well, that's just one of their cultural traditions and (thus) it can't be helped that they enjoy eating locusts —or breast-feed their children till age four—or make their houses out of dung." Which is to say condescendingly that those "poor" people are bound and gagged by the twin thugs of culture and tradition because neither is flexible enough to adapt to social change.

I opt for a different perspective throughout this book, one reflecting my basically anthropological leanings assisted by the works of historians and sociologists as well. When I use "tradition," it is in the way that Edward Shils (1981) or Eric Hobsbawm and Terence Ranger (1987) intend, namely, that what meets the eye as being a culture's time-honored custom may in fact be an entirely new, radically novel event designed to create communal spirit, participation, or even political and financial capital. As we will see for the Dolls' Day festival and for Okunchi and when TV cameras are present at Suwa Shrine, tradition is not necessarily a heavy weight from the past that an institution lugs around from year to year, slowing down its more progressive members and deterring full participation in contemporary society. Instead, paraphrasing Hobsbawm, when a tradition seeks to instill certain values and behavioral norms by stressing a series of repetitive ritual or symbolic practices which automatically imply continuity with the past, it can best be thought of as a creative process "invented" to fit the complexities of the social moment. However, this is not to imply that it is impromptu, unstudied, illusory, or fictitious; to the contrary, an "invented" tradition is a highly sophisticated design that fulfills three broad purposes. First, by establishing or symbolizing membership of real or artificial groups, it promotes social cohesion among dispersed individuals, families, or classes. Second, by establishing or legitimizing status, institutions, or relations of authority, it conveys and centralizes a symbolic power that can later be translated into political terms. Finally, as mentioned above, by its efforts to socialize individuals' awareness and acceptance of certain beliefs, values, or conventions of behavior, it encourages a continuity of compliance with existing social and cultural orders.[7]

Time and again we will find a conjunction of all three of these influences operating from within Shinto rituals as communities, even whole nations, are blessed by the Kami, as people seek out the shrine to legitimize important events in their lives, and as real efforts are made to educate modern men and women that their local shrine is both conveying and innovating traditions "sacred" to the fabric of Japanese culture. And yet, there is one more dimension to the picture that, if ignored, leaves the whole portrait without its frame. One could probably guess that since I am arguing for "tradition" to be seen as an ongoing process, so should the larger sphere of reference that gives it the meanings and symbols to work with in the first place: that of culture. Richard Fox succinctly states the case for a new understanding of culture: "Culture is not a heavy weight of tradition, a set of configurations, or a basic personality constellation that coerces and compels individuals. It is instead a set of understandings and a consciousness under active construction by which individuals interpret the world around them . . . it is a tool kit or set of scenarios that individuals use to implement or stage daily life" (1990, 11).

The key concept we will need in placing Shinto ritual within Japanese culture and society (and vice versa) is not so much the analogy of a "tool kit" or "scenario" but rather the notion that culture is actively being made into sets of understandings that people use to make sense of their world. Clifford Geertz (1973) and others have shown that as problems arise, as opportunities appear, or as transitions sweep the known and familiar into new and dynamic shapes, culture not only *compels* people to make sense of and adapt to what is happening but also *enables* a flexibility of approach as novel or sometimes radical methods are created and applied to the situation at hand. Thus, while the outward form of a cultural tradition (such as a Shinto ritual) may appear continuous with the past and be advertised as "a thousand years old" by its priestly practitioners, its inward content may change depending on a variety of factors, ranging from the ideas of the head priest, to the need to increase community participation, or even to the weather. In all cases, what we have to be sensitive to is the way that culture gets practiced (Fox 1990, 11) by means of human intention, power, and, in light of the following discussions, the strong focusing capacity that religiously based symbols can have upon people who may not have the slightest interest in the particulars of their meaning. Yet time and again in Japanese society, we find it is these same "disinterested" people who, when circumstances demand, actively and creatively employ cultural traditions as ways to pattern and organize their own lives, buying into an ordering of the cosmos that provides support in ways their own imaginations or efforts cannot consistently manage. From that simple rite of purification for a new car or construction site, to an elaborate celebration in the middle of a city's skyscrapers in honor of the rice harvest, people look to their culture for "tools" to build meaning and look to their local Shinto shrines as places where skilled "craftsmen" shape the universe into familiar designs. Thus oriented at a number of general levels, we are now ready to enter the local climate of Nagasaki and see how these themes have manifested themselves in the cycle of events that compose the "life of a shrine."

2

HISTORICAL MOMENTUMS

Since we will be in Nagasaki for the rest of this book, and since "place" is so crucial to both the origins and contemporary manifestations of shrine Shinto, it is important to focus on some of the historical background of the "where" and "when" of Suwa Shrine. What will emerge as a particular style of Shinto practice is rooted in historical precedents in which political, economic, and cultural innovations have always had a bearing on the way the shrine operates. To expect religious institutions to somehow remain free of these concerns is to misunderstand the embeddedness of a religious tradition within the social worlds that surround it. A religion may take aim at social, physical, or political situations and offer formulas or doctrines said to address, balance, or transcend these worldly concerns, but the relationship between ends and means is always symbiotic. The complexity and diversity of our attempts to find meaning, avoid suffering, and gain power in this lifetime ensure a continuing engagement with both new and established religious traditions that, for better or worse, provide venues for achieving these goals.

When talking about what has gone into making a place (or its institutions and people) significant, a struggle is required to distinguish the "past" from "history," or at least to take note that there can be a difference. Harold Isaacs considers the "past" to be a created ideology designed to motivate societies, inspire classes, or control individuals. "History," on the other hand, is the discipline that aims at "cleansing the story of mankind from deceiving visions" (1975, 120). Leaving debates about historiography and historicity aside for now, we will see that the "past history" of Suwa Shrine is as full of multiple interpretations as is the place it presently occupies in the lives and psyches of the people of Nagasaki.

Most shrines in Japan trace their origins back to either a mythological or semihistorical incident (as at Ise and Izumo), as acknowledgment of the sacred essence of a place (the Nachi Falls, Mount Fuji, the seaside cave of Udo) or as reverence for the "divine" qualities of an actual historical personage (as at Kyoto's Kitano Tenmangū Shrine, in honor of persecuted scholar Sugawara no Michizane, or at the Tōshōgū Shrine at Nikko, built for Tokugawa Ieyasu). But in the case of Suwa Shrine (I will hereafter use both the English word "shrine" and the Japanese *jinja* to refer to the same entity), its founding is in a special, often-overlooked category. Neither mythically nor ancestrally based, the reason Suwa Shrine exists at all is partially due to the influence of Christianity in southern Japan in the sixteenth and seventeenth centuries and the subsequent struggle by the authorities to win back the loyalties and obedience of the local populace. A brief capsulization of an extremely complicated story will help to set the stage for the shrine's founding in 1625. To help frame the following discussion, a brief directive from Foucault seems appropriate: "History has no meaning, though this is not to say that it is absurd or incoherent. On the contrary, it is intelligible and should be susceptible of analysis down to the smallest detail— but this must be in accordance with the intelligibility of struggles, of strategies, and tactics" (1980, 80). As long as we keep in mind that we are dealing primarily with the strategies and tactics of political, rather than spiritual, affairs, we can avoid glossing over the true beginnings of what has become one of Nagasaki's most powerful religious institutions.

Midway through the 1500s, during a time of civil war in Japan, three Portuguese adventurers found their way via a Chinese ship to the island of Tanegashima, south of Kyushu.[1] The Japanese authorities were naturally curious about these travelers but they were equally fascinated by their arquebus rifles, which were purchased, copied, and manufactured in record time. Saltpeter and gunpowder were soon needed but so were more rifles, apparently because the strategic impact of this new technology was significant in deciding the outcome in clashes among warring clans. Rifles were bought as fast as they could be made available in the hope that these weapons would favorably influence a dramatic shift in the balance of power, territorial claims, and trading networks. As Portuguese ships began to ply the waters between their colony in Macao and the southern island of Kyushu, Jesuit priests, led first by Francis Xavier, used their papal and royal connections to link this trade to missionizing activities. If a local lord wanted the Portuguese to use a port city in his fief, whereby he would reap substantial profits, he had to permit

the Jesuits the freedom to preach and establish small churches and permanent communities. Not surprisingly, competition among the lords was fierce for this "privilege." The local people, largely fishermen and poor farmers but also samurai as well, were often forced by their rulers to adopt the Catholic faith as a way of increasing the likelihood of attracting Portuguese trading vessels.

It was a mutually convenient, mutually exploitative relationship that developed initially. However, in spite of the Jesuit goal of converting the ruling class first, many agricultural and fishing communities saw in the transcendent message of loyalty to an omnipotent god a way to liberate themselves from centuries of oppression and submission. Converts learned to view traditional institutions such as temples and shrines as having been in collusion with the feudal lords, who had so long kept them in abject poverty. Inspired by the zealous preaching of certain Jesuit priests (and, later, those from Franciscan and Augustinian orders, who came from Spanish Manila), the new religion's fervor spilled over into violent action, as numerous temples and shrines throughout what is today Nagasaki and Kumamoto Prefectures were put to the torch. Christianity, or the approximation the Jesuits were able to transmit of its practices and dogma, became the people's main religion for several decades in this part of Japan, reaching 750,000 adherents by 1605.[2] That it was tolerated at all, however, needs to be seen in the larger context of local profits as well as of the hegemonic maneuvering among the powerful warlords in the north.

After the years of civil war, the first ruler to succeed in temporarily unifying Japan under one military government was Oda Nobunaga. He knew very well that the growing assertiveness of Nagasaki-area Christians was a small price to pay in exchange for the rewards of trade with a Western power, bringing in firearms and Chinese silk in particular but also medicines, spices, and mechanical devices such as clocks. However, upon Nobunaga's untimely assassination in 1582, his successor, Hideyoshi, slowly changed the government's policy regarding the Jesuits and their religious freedom. Due partly to his deep suspicion of foreigners and a fear of domination growing from the widening sphere of sacred and secular influence exerted by the Portuguese, he used a relatively minor infraction of the law to decree all proselytization to cease. By this time, however, trade with the Portuguese had grown to such proportions that any curtailment of mission activities would have a severe impact on the revenues of Hideyoshi's treasury, just when he needed vast sums of money to finance an invasion of Korea. He realized how deeply entrenched the

Portuguese were becoming (would Nagasaki become another Goa or Macao?), but he was not able to intimidate them until another incident forced his hand in 1596. After the wreck of a Spanish galleon, the ship's captain had boasted to his captors that the priests and the trade they helped to facilitate were part of an organized master plan to encroach upon Japanese territory and bring this part of Asia under Spanish influence. As a result, six Franciscans, seventeen of their Japanese neophytes, and three Japanese Jesuits (included by mistake, according to Boxer 1951) were paraded from Kyoto to Nagasaki and there crucified in February of 1597. Nagasaki was confiscated by the central government (although foreign residence was still permitted) and throughout the country, some 120 churches were destroyed and their priests ordered to move to Nagasaki.

Still, it was a long way from Hideyoshi's court in Kyoto to Nagasaki, and in spite of the 1597 decree which prohibited Christianity, Hideyoshi's disastrous Korean campaign and the sympathy of local administrators allowed the "Kirishitans" to hold on well after his death in 1598 and into the early years of the Tokugawa era. Tokugawa Ieyasu, however, having witnessed the entire progression of Christian entrenchment from 1560 onward, was shrewd in his dealings with the Christians. He still permitted the missions to function and trade to grow, but he allowed in the English, Dutch, and Spanish to increase competition and keep prices low. Due in part to the advice of the Englishman Will Adams, whose Protestant worldview saw the Catholics as "papist pirates" and who warned of (using today's terms) their role as "fifth columnists," Ieyasu gradually became more hostile to the Portuguese and Spanish interests. An expulsion order of 1614 was only sporadically enforced, but after Ieyasu's death, his son Hidetada actively promoted the suppression of the Christian faith all through Japan beginning in 1616. In 1619, for example, over fifty Japanese Christians were executed in Kyoto and Nagasaki, although no foreign-born Christian perished until 1622. Priests who refused to leave or recant were imprisoned, Japanese converts were likewise exiled, imprisoned, and (beginning with the administration of Iemitsu, the third Tokugawa shogun, in 1623) tortured. Also in 1622, monetary rewards were offered for informing upon or turning in hidden Christians. Thus a century-long campaign to stamp out the "barbarians' belief" began in earnest.[3]

There was no doubt by this time that, after years of conflicting policies, the government meant business regarding the total suppression of Christian activities, yet it also needed ways to exert its authority in nonmilitary ways over the people of Nagasaki. After all, fully ten years before the edicts that would close the country for almost two hundred years, this city's tactical importance was already established as the one port through which to deal with the outside world. It was argued that further persecutions, military intervention, or heavy-handed intimidation would only heighten local levels of tension and mistrust, giving the foreign merchants and diplomats (who were thought to be waiting for the chance to implement what they had learned from the mistakes of the Portuguese and Spanish) the confidence needed to challenge the Tokugawa with armadas pulled in from Indonesia or India.

But the Tokugawa rulers were not mere dictators, having developed a certain flair for crafty manipulations that diffused potentially explosive situations. Using what skills in social engineering they had at their disposal (thanks in part to scholars like Hayashi Razan, versed in neo-Confucian principles of "benevolent" rule), the government began a policy which stressed that a revival of traditional Japanese beliefs and institutions was essential in restoring centralized control to the Nagasaki region.[4] Since the Christian values of individual worth were so obviously inflammatory and hostile to the plans of stability which the Tokugawas had charted as essential to national peace, a return to communal values promoted by Buddhist and Shinto temple/shrine complexes could only enhance local and regional compliance with the "beneficence" of the government's authority. It began contributing heavily to the reconstruction of destroyed temples and shrines throughout the area, but nowhere more so than in the center of Nagasaki. The first temple to be rebuilt was Shōkaku-ji in 1604, but due to acts of sabotage during its construction, additional rebuilding plans went slowly. Still, plans were set in motion around 1610 for an institution that would embody the myths of the founding of the Japanese nation and promote vigilance, purity, and unity. Named after one of the deities of valor and duty, Suwa-no-kami, the shrine would be strategically located on the side of a mountain overlooking the lower regions leading out to the harbor. Its official date of conception is listed in the shrine's annals as 1614 (the same year as Ieyasu's edict against Christianity), and a small structure is thought to have been completed soon after, but frequent harassment by Christian urban guerillas and the lack of a powerful personality to guide development kept the idea of a central shrine little more than an idea.

The man who would become the first priest of Suwa Shrine, Aoki

Kensei, came to Nagasaki in 1623 from Saga Prefecture.[5] Up to that point he had been a wandering monk in the tradition of Shugendō, famous for its *yamabushi* ascetic-priests, who were given license by the military government to roam freely and dispense cures, charms against demons, and Buddhist doctrine influenced by Shingōn metaphysics and ritual practices. Although there is no evidence that he was directly employed by the Tokugawa government, the missionary zeal with which he attempted to revive Shinto in Nagasaki, and the logistic as well as financial support these efforts received, indicate a close working relationship. One of his first reports to the government listed the number of shrines and temples that had been destroyed by the Christians starting around 1567. He tried to find people to aid him in his rebuilding efforts and solicited help from local carpenters and administrators, but even at the height of the persecutions he made little progress. Deciding to go to Kyoto, he sought advice and legitimation from leaders of Yoshida Shinto, a powerful institution that stressed a revitalized religious nativism. They invested him with the authority to rebuild shrines in Nagasaki but stopped short of naming him a priest.

In 1624, he and his sons went to work against considerable odds. The government's policy at this time, while sympathetic to Aoki, was focused more on rebuilding Buddhist temples as instruments of the state wherein a population of former Christians could be registered and their activities monitored under the *danka* system. Nonetheless, Aoki procured materials, hired workmen, and guarded the construction from sabotage until the completion of a modest structure in 1625. One of the first rituals held was the dramatic *yutate-sai* (described in chapter 10), in which priests plunge their hands into scalding water to ward off demons, a theatrical staple of the *yamabushi* tradition. Unfortunately, despite the added entertainment value of a sumo match that followed the ritual, it is reported that no one came.

Soon after this initial attempt, Aoki and his sons again went to Kyoto and explained their frustrating situation, returning this time with full status as Yoshida-sect priests. Aoki would serve as chief priest, his second son as *kannushi* (senior priest), and his first son as *shasō*, a type of Buddhist monk whose ritual duties involved both Shinto and Buddhist deities and concerns.[6] We can imagine that Aoki must have felt like a trapeze artist on a high wire forced to juggle balls of differing sizes and weights at the same time. He was surrounded and harassed by closet Christians hostile to the very idea of a shrine while the military government was breathing down his neck and trying to manipulate policy from far-off central Japan. There were also relations with the strange-looking but important "barbarians," surely the oddest ball to juggle. They too were part of the audience he felt obliged to impress with the power of Japan's "native" tradition. Because of all these factors, plus the shrine's Kami to serve at the same time, it is likely he spent many long nights trying to fashion ways to implement the restrictive *and* expressive set of social codes and conventions the new shrine was to embody—and to somehow avoid falling into a space where there was no safety net.

In 1633, the government instituted harsher measures designed to resolve the Christian/foreigner problem by effectively closing the country's ports to all sailing vessels, whether arriving or departing. To oversee this radical policy, a specially tailored system of administration for the Nagasaki area, known elsewhere in Japan since Heian times as *bugyō*, had been installed a year earlier. It was generally the case in this system that a single representative of the government would be placed in charge of a particular region; in the hot spot of Nagasaki, however, two high officials were given the task of implementing and enforcing policy. Part of the reason behind this extraordinary dual posting of officials was the government's inability to determine to what extent it had been successful in eradicating Christianity. Its new laws were being followed and assertions came readily from the people that their minds and religious habits had changed, but social practices common elsewhere in Japan lagged behind. At the shrine, Aoki quietly confirmed what the *bugyō* authorities already knew: there were far too few people visiting Suwa Jinja to perform the gestures of worship (*omairi*).

The year 1634 was in many ways a major historical landmark not only for the city and shrine but for the nation as well. The closed-country (*sakoku*) edict of 1633 was fully enforced in 1634, followed by another declaration in 1635. These directives ordered that any Japanese returning from overseas was to be put to death, while the second order extended capital punishment to those trying to leave as well. Additionally, all foreign residents and commercial activities were now restricted to a single, small artificial island in the Nagasaki harbor known as Dejima. Constructed with funds collected from local merchants, the island symbolized the subjugation of the once proud and defiant local leaders to the authority of the Tokugawa regime. Amazingly enough, trade still continued, even though forced to operate in a repressive and increasingly hostile environment.

Increased governmental presence was felt at the shrine as well, which in many ways answered the long-standing petitions of Aoki and sons. The shrine was exempted from paying property taxes, received funds for ritual and administrative operating expenses, and underwent a building expansion. Prior to 1634, the government had merely "encouraged" but not enforced public participation in shrine events. Now, it issued a decree requiring all residents of the city to register at the shrine as parishioners (*ujiko*) and be counted. Those who did not, by simple logic of association, were suspected Christians and therefore subversives subject to arrest, imprisonment, torture, and execution if they failed to renounce their faith. Additionally, three wealthy businessmen and community leaders were chosen and handsomely paid to supervise shrine rituals and pressure public participation, a policy which continued until the end of the Tokugawa (Edo) period (Morita 1990, 22).

The state also appropriated for official shrine management a local fall festival known as *kunchi*. Beginning with the celebration of 1634, the deities of Suwa Jinja were put into portable shrines (*mikoshi*) and carried through the streets of the city to a harbor-side location where, in a "normal" Japanese city, the population would come readily to seek closer access to the powers of these Kami. While priests today interpret this event as a benevolent act (subjecting the Kami to the profane world) on the part of their predecessors, many citizens of the time must have seen it quite differently—as another heavy-handed provocation by the Tokugawa administration that required, like the decree to register at the shrine, public compliance (Suwa Shrine Shamusho n.d., 22). Although the size of the Nagasaki crowds is not reported, we do learn that the portable shrines were carried by farmers, that city merchants made special floats and participated in a parade, and that courtesans from the entertainment district danced in front of the Kami (Morita 1990, 23). As we will see later in this book, the Okunchi festival, manifesting a continuing dynamic of secular and sacred concerns, prospers to this day as one of the most vibrant *matsuri* in all of Japan.

By subjecting the people's festival to the control of Suwa Shrine, the government sought not only to link this event to traditional religious sources (the Shinto predilection for autumn or harvest celebrations of gratitude to the Kami) but also to give it a more fitting stage to impress the Dutch and Chinese, whose shipping trade was a needed source of hard currency. The local residents were still permitted their odd assortment of dances and merrymaking, but to show everyone (locals and foreigners alike) the importance of the shrine, it was decreed that from 1638 onward the main event of the annual festival would be that most subtle and glorious achievement of Japanese culture and sensibility, Noh drama. No other shrine in the nation (save for Tōshōgū Shrine at Nikko, which was built as the tomb for Ieyasu, the founder of the Tokugawa dynasty) received such direct supervision and funds from the government as did Suwa Shrine during the years 1634–85.[7]

Faced with intervention of this magnitude and persistence, the citizens of Nagasaki had little choice but to accept the new shrine and the practices associated with it. As time passed and the memory of the Christian era grew less immediate, the shrine became a place where baby dedications, coming-of-age ceremonies, exorcisms, purifications, and other functions were regularly performed. Apart from a few catastrophic floods, typhoons, epidemics, famines, and one particularly disastrous fire that destroyed most of the Noh masks, kimonos, and props in 1856, the history of the shrine was fairly peaceful throughout the entire Tokugawa period. Chief priests came and went, and civil administrators met with varying degrees of success in keeping foreigners and locals separated (or committed seppuku if they failed, as happened to the magistrate when the British ship *Phaeton* sailed into the poorly guarded harbor in 1808 and threatened a bombardment if provisions were not supplied) or were promoted to positions that let them escape the wilds of this frontier post.

The opening of the country during the Meiji era (1868) brought an economic and cultural boom to Nagasaki,[8] but it was not until the summer of 1945 that world history again took notice of the city. The militarists responsible for the long succession of events that turned Japan from a feudal society into an imperialistic monolith with half of Asia under its control had used, as one of their tools, the symbols and mythology of Shinto to try and convince the Japanese people they were destined for greatness by the Kami. They had many precedents from the close association of the state with Shinto to draw upon, among the most obvious being Hideyoshi's adoption of Shinto ideology to counter Spanish and Portuguese missionary activities and the religious legitimation of his temporary conquest of Korea. Once again, from the 1890s onward, Shinto was used to provide a ritual and mythological structure whereby the "mystic idea of an entire people supernaturally bound together by the common heritage of a national soul defined a unique Japanese political order and social morality superior to the West" (Wagatsuma 1975, 320). Japan was said to be destined to become the "protector" of Asian nations and drive out the imperialistic West by means of a "sacred" war. It took only a few seconds to finally destroy this illusion, though its demise also cost the lives of over 140,000 people in Hiroshima and 70,000 people in Nagasaki.[9]

In Nagasaki, people found their own interpretations for the horrific bombing. When talking to survivors of August 9, 1945, one frequently hears a fatalistic acceptance of this dreadful outcome. After all, people will sadly say, Japan started the war and thus could expect to be severely punished for its actions, the same way entire clans in Japan have been wiped out after having failed to achieve their objectives. Shortly after the bombing, however, another, more positive explanation was in vogue. The northern part of the city is separated from its central and southern parts by Mount Konpira, and because of Suwa Shrine's location in the central part of the city on the mountain's southern flank, the shrine received virtually no major damage from the bomb. On the other hand, the northern area's famous Urakami Cathedral and surrounding Catholic neighborhoods (flourishing since the middle Meiji period's policy allowed religious freedom) were at the very center of the devastation. To people desperate for understanding, the fact that the Americans, known to be a Christian nation, had dropped this terrible weapon on the largest cathedral in all of Asia and left the city's main Shinto shrine untouched was a significant omen. According to a firsthand account, a street preacher named Honda had walked far and wide, exhorting the dazed public to remember that it was the protection of the Kami of the shrine which had saved two-thirds of the city from total ruin. The message must have been well taken because it was only one year after the bombing and end of the war that the shrine's major festival, the Okunchi *matsuri*, was permitted by the Occupation and received citywide support.

Since the beginning of the Meiji period, the government had imposed a separation of Buddhism from Shinto so that the latter tradition could be more easily manipulated into a nationalistic ideology of service to the state's agendas. As a result, the rituals and orientations of Buddhism, focused on salvation and the cessation of suffering, dominated concerns people had regarding their ancestors, death, and mortuary propriety. In the weeks and months after the war's abrupt end, people went to the city's surviving temples to pray for the souls of family and friends killed in the war and by the atomic bombing. While Shinto institutions in many parts of the country were shunned because of their complicity in the doomed war effort, Suwa Shrine seems to have weathered this disaffection better than most shrines, perhaps because of ideologues like Honda.

For the first time in its eventful history, the postwar shrine emerged from under the watchful eye of military rulers. It began an appeal to citizens in need of strength, luck, health, new opportunities, a spouse, a first pregnancy, protection from sickness and natural disasters, and the perseverance necessary to rebuild shattered lives. We can imagine the comfort a visit to the shrine must have provided at that time — to come from a shantytown structure or damaged dwelling (90 percent of the city's buildings received some damage from the bomb) into a green enclave of large trees, and there have a drink of pure spring water before and after asking for blessings. A visitor then could clearly see how the shrine had been spared destruction, with its hundred-year-old gates and three sanctuaries still stately and elegant in their function of providing housing for the Kami. All of these impressions must have been like ointment for the scorched souls of the people. As the city rebuilt, the priests from Suwa Shrine were a visible presence out in the neighborhoods, consecrating land and purifying existing structures of the death and suffering that had so recently filled them. People saw again how the shrine could be an elemental pivot for so many stages of their lives, and how everything from the food they ate to the buildings they lived within, from natural forces impossible to understand to the kitchen fire merrily heating water for tea, all had some aspect of Shinto tradition as a higher, broader, or subtler point of reference.

The postwar years, while impressive in their achievements of industrialization and reconstruction, have taken their toll on practices, beliefs, and values that used to more closely bind individuals to their local shrine.[10] But again, because Nagasaki is so far removed from the centers of economic activity in Tokyo and Osaka, this trend has not been as harsh as it might have been on the viability of Suwa Shrine as a center for communal activity. We will later see in more detail how certain individuals have had a profound effect on the economic and even psychological health of the shrine since the 1980s, restoring its early stature as the center and nurturer of practices thought conducive to social cohesion. As long as Japanese culture and society continue to recognize occasions that call for some expression of gratitude to the spirits of the land, to the ancestors, or to the historical figures who helped shape the nation,[11] it is likely the 350-year history of Suwa Shrine will provide a rich repertoire from which a variety of actors can attempt to shape, in the words of one of the priests, "the foundations for future generations to build their lives upon."

3

THE KAMI

For many foreigners who have worked and lived in Japan for lengthy periods, the society and culture have become as familiar and comfortable as any they know. Years of residency often yield fluency of language, skill in what at first appears the almost mystical domain of social etiquette, and wide knowledge of esoteric facts and historical currents concerning contemporary society. Certain characteristics of modern life in Japan—the marvelous trains, telephones, quality of goods, and so on—become highly predictable and constant to native and newcomer alike. Yet when it comes to fully comprehending how or why their Japanese friends or neighbors act or feel the way they do, surprises abound, often because the relations between causes and effects answer to non-Western expectations about the world. The often-bestowed compliment "You're more Japanese than a Japanese!" seems at times to be little more than a polite rejoinder that reminds one how difficult indeed is a true empathetic assessment of what being Japanese (in all its variety) actually means. Is it really possible, for example, to discern why a well-educated man or woman would turn to a spirit exorcist to resolve a family crisis or why a distraught woman would kill her entire family, before taking her own life, to prevent their future "suffering" or why the mere mention of the emperor can often transform the most mild-mannered, rational businessman into a righteous ideologue espousing the sanctity of the Japanese nation? Nowhere are modernity's supporting pillars of intellect and reason more threatened by deep-seated emotional or psychological fissures than in trying to present to Western readers socially and culturally accurate information about the center of Shinto practices: those "spirits," "forces," "powers," "divinities" (the list could go on) known as Kami.

But before taking the plunge, let me relate a personal experience that might help establish a few images useful as reference points in the discussion that will follow.

On the outskirts of southern Kyoto lies the shrine of Fushimi

Inari, where my intention as a first-time tourist to Japan was to climb to the top of a sacred mountain belonging to a spirit involved with rice and fire. As I passed through the grounds of the old shrine at the base of the mountain, it was obvious where the trail began—thousands upon thousands of vermilion-painted torii archways formed a shadowy tunnel twisting up the wooded side of the mountain. Though I knew next to nothing about the history of the place or even of the "religion" called Shinto, I was nevertheless astounded at the extravagance of religious devotion enabling the donation of so many archways.

After nearly thirty minutes of steady climbing, pausing here and there to watch a variety of worshippers make offerings of large smoky candles at wayside altars, I began to look forward to the coming glimpse of sky once the archways, less dense now than at the beginning of the trail, came to an end. I was not sure what I would find, but earlier climbs on other mountains associated with religious institutions had shown there was usually some small building housing or honoring the divinity, along with a sweeping view of the lowlands— a view which was, after all, my main purpose in making the ascent in the first place. The trail finally culminated with a huge stone torii nearly twenty feet high and I walked out under the open sky again, but the building I had expected was oddly absent. I felt disappointed because now I would lack a good photograph to distinguish this mountaintop from the others I had been to.

Even when I looked closely at the spot where other climbers had clustered—some of them in business suits, others in mountaineering knickers and hiking boots, and still others in skirts and high heels— I could not discern why they were drawn to what appeared to be a simple stone cairn. It was not until I was standing behind them that I finally saw atop the stones a round mirror tilted slightly toward the sky, reflecting the late-afternoon's silver-rimmed clouds as they rode a wind from the Inland Sea toward the blue mountains bordering Lake Biwa. Then suddenly it dawned on me—so *this* is what Shinto holds as divine! Not a text or dubious miracles or what someone maybe said or a particular structure but the *actual phenomena* of the world itself. If seen from a more level vantage point, the mirror of this open-air altar would show the climber's own face, as well as the path he or she had just traveled to enter the shrine (which was, as it turned out in this particular case, the *entire mountain*). My understanding was intellectual, of course, and not emotional in a way that might have led me to enact the same intense petitioning as the

Japanese I watched bowing, chanting, and, in some instances, weeping before the mirror, but I felt I had some tiny grasp of what the Kami might signify and what part of the nebulous social and cultural reality called Shinto might be about.

I look back on this experience now with a mixture of embarrassment and acknowledgment, the former as it applies to my naivete about what I was seeing and the latter to my curiosity (which is still far from being satisfied). Let me try for a moment to deal with ideas of what constitutes the sacred in a somewhat reified and "idealized" Shinto cosmology—the kind that priests are fond of talking about but which common folks rarely consider except in moments of crisis or obvious transition. The practitioners of Shinto hold that anything we can see or sense that is full of power, mysterious, marvelous, uncontrolled, strange, or simply beyond our abilities of comprehension is what constitutes the Kami. Therefore, to translate the word as "god" or "deity" is not quite what the Japanese, from ancient times until now, have in mind. And, to be precise, it is nothing they have "in mind" at all; instead, it would be more accurate to consider the concept of Kami as one "enculturated" rather than intellectualized; these vague comprehensions (if indeed they are even that) exist at a nonverbal, alogical depth for most people. The old attitudes about Kami were originally structured on the experience of extraordinary events, which could have been anything from large, strangely formed trees or rocks that aroused a feeling of dread, to lightning issuing from storm clouds, to a white deer, or even to the ecstasy of dances done for magical benefits (Holtom 1965, 24). The early people felt that themselves, the land they lived upon, the mountains, rivers, trees, valleys, mist, and animals that surrounded them were all born of the Kami and thus intimately related. There was simply no such thing as an "inanimate" universe.

This is not to say, however, that this relationship was all bliss and harmony. More often than not, there was considerable anxiety involved in wondering whether the human and "heavenly" worlds were in the state of balance necessary to ensure that the crops would grow, game be plentiful, babies be born, and intruders kept at bay. The Kami were felt to have both a beneficent, refined nature, their *nigimitama*, and a coarse or violent one, their *aramitama*—how else to explain all the dualities in the phenomenal world? As in numerous other systems of ritual practice and their accompanying beliefs throughout the world, a particular Kami was invoked at the beginning of a ritual and offered the praise and gratitude of the community; it was then offered food and drink before the priest made known the specific request motivating the ritual in the first place.

As society developed and gained a degree of refinement (due to a variety of sources) in the ideas its members held about men and women and the world they lived in, a mythology was put in place that gave many of these forces names and structured genealogies in a humanized pantheon. Part of the need for this was political, as the early Yamato rulers sought to justify and legitimize their reigns to other clans as well as to the powerful kingdoms in Korea and China. The *Kojiki* (Philippi 1968) and the *Nihongi* (*Nihon-shoki*) (Aston 1978), two of the oldest records of these myths, describe what happened to individual Kami as the world was being created, followed by the exploits of the first human descendants of the Kami, the early emperors and their courts. Because the deities "developed" distinct personalities and will, human existence, by extension, is neither aimless nor haphazard but is related to the sacred pattern created by the volition of the Kami. In Shinto, this "will" is anything but explicit; nonetheless, certain values and ideas—among them *harae* (purification), *makoto* (sincerity), and *kansha* (gratitude)—although they may be emphasized differently according to a head priest's philosophy, are nevertheless thought to be synonymous with the "way of the Kami."

Izanagi and Izanami are the mythical couple said to have created much of the world, with their offspring acting as children will, fighting and arguing among themselves to see who would control what. Amaterasu (who issued from Izanagi's left eye) attained the highest status among their many progeny. She was a divinity of the sun, but perhaps more importantly in a society where traditionally kinship determined everything, Amaterasu became the divine source of the imperial Yamato clan and thus, depending on the prevailing ideological winds of different periods, of the entire Japanese nation. It is thought that as early as the eighth century c.e., most of the educated or political elite of the various clans accepted Amaterasu as the central deity in the Yamato clan's pantheon (a status developed in part as a response to the recently imported personality cult of the Buddha).[1]

But even before the precedent for divine ancestry of the Imperial clan was established, smaller, less-powerful clans had formed kinship groups that worshipped their own deities. Until roughly the end of the Heian period (1192), the function of these Kami was to protect and nurture the community, the *ujiko*. They became the most important Kami of the recently emerged pantheon simply because they were so localized. Any problem of the community, any aspiration of its members (as in prayers for a good rice crop) and any joy or feeling of gratitude for blessings received were taken before the "Kami of the people," the *ujigami*, where ritual specialists were in place to ensure the transmission of local concerns to the "heavenly" sphere. Eventually, the *ujigami* came to mean not just the Kami of one clan but of the locale itself or a section of it. They were still its guardians and benefactors but they fulfilled this role for everyone who dwelled within the area. A more appropriate term, as suggested by Hori Ichiro (1968), might be *hito-gami* (person-kami), which overtly acknowledges the strong personal character of the Kami and indicates that its authority is directly reflected in the status of its priests or shamans. According to Hori, the *hito-gami* system has greatly influenced present-day ritual events and *matsuri*, as well as the system of Shinto priests taking over the family shrine based on hereditary status.[2] While today most young priests attend one of the two main training universities—Kokugakuin in Tokyo or Kōgakkan in Mie Prefecture near Ise—many of the older generation were simply born at the right time and in the right place to inherit substantial landholdings, respect from the community, and the right to mediate with the Kami.

Shinto mythology speaks of the "eight hundred myriads of Kami" (or "eight million Kami"), and each community has Kami specific to the place. However, they all are thought to be subordinate parts of Amaterasu, the Supreme Sun Kami, whose principal shrine is at Ise. It is a temptation to see this as an Asian version of omnipotent monotheism, but, to use the *Kojiki* as a guide, Amaterasu herself is but an intermediary for a number of the Heavenly Kami (whom we never meet in any form other than by this name), whom she must obey. Confused? No doubt the average Japanese would be too if he or she ever thought about it.[3] Let us turn now to see how all this relates to the Kami that are specific to Suwa Shrine.

The principal Kami of Suwa Jinja—Suwa-no-Kami, Morisaki, and Sumiyoshi—are, in the words of Chief Priest Uesugi, "points of access to the more encompassing powers of Amaterasu." Think of the tributaries of a great river system, he suggests, like the Nile or Mississippi, and perhaps it will be easier to see how the Kami specific to a local shrine, even one as large as Izumo or Meiji, all lead and connect the worshipper to the more pervasive currents of power which are supposedly beyond the scope of human comprehension.

Whether the Kami are local or "heavenly," the prayers directed to them and the ritual observances performed on their behalf are all intended to harmonize human life with the changing environments of outer and inner worlds. Whereas Buddhism tends to stress how an individual soul relates to and transcends a cosmos of illusion and suffering, the Shinto Kami are thought to assist with strategies for and solutions to the more immediately pressing needs of adapting to this world and all of its complexities, dualities, and ambiguities. They are thought to help human beings harmonize with elemental balances of the natural cycle of life which are nowadays so frequently taken for granted. Equinoxes, marriages, seasonal changes, aging, childbirth, floods, typhoons, epidemics, the full moon of autumn, and the first sunrise of the new year—all resonate within the ever-changing features and personalities of the Shinto Kami.

Each Kami of a specific place naturally has a special characteristic that, somewhat surprisingly, may or may not directly reflect some aspect of the actual economic base of the community. In a mountainous farming area the chances of finding a Kami whose primary efficacy is linked to the sea are very remote; but that does not necessarily exclude the Kami from having another aspect of its character stressed. The same heavenly being thought responsible for bringing fishermen a bountiful catch may be revered in the mountains, not for its ability to bring fish into waiting nets, but for its fecundity in making rice grow. As to how Kami that at first seem "foreign" to their local community got there, one must remember the considerable political turmoil that has characterized Japan for centuries, and how often lands and protective deities changed hands. One should also note that there are myths of Kami traveling from one area to another, and that wandering preachers (*hijiri*), whose expertise was rarely challenged by locals, also spread beliefs.[4]

Long before the founding of Suwa Shrine in 1614, it is thought there was most likely another, smaller Suwa shrine in a neighborhood of the same name which was, like so many others, destroyed by Christian zealots during their reign of power.[5] The shrine's "holy of holies" (*go-shintai*), which the Kami was believed to temporarily invest with its presence during a ritual, was somehow removed from the rubble and secretly ensconced by one of the *ujiko*. It was this object of veneration—possibly a statue, a stone, or a piece of paper wrapped within layers of silk cloth (no priest has ever gone on record as having seen it)—which was rescued from obscurity by the Tokugawa in 1614 as part of their efforts to wrest the region away from Christian control. As such, the already existing presence of Suwa-no-Kami was a stroke of luck in perfect alignment with their designs for Nagasaki, for this deity is the benefactor of valor and vigilance. What better traits to have present in a city that would soon be functioning as the only open port to the Western world? The namesake Kami of Suwa Shrine would instill within the population the need to be like good samurai in their dealings with foreign traders: loyal always to the Tokugawa masters they served.

At the same time Suwa-no-Kami was installed, the deity called Morisaki was placed alongside it in the main sanctuary. Although Suwa-no-Kami is undoubtedly old, Morisaki-no-Kami would have to be called ancient. Long before there were feudal rulers and foreign traders with designs on the harbor that later came to be called Nagasaki, when there was only a very small cluster of fishermen of no consequence to anyone, a low hill at the shallow end of the harbor was home to a small shrine of great antiquity. It served as a place to pay homage to the prolific vitality of all life, one of the dominant currents running through the entirety of Shinto ritual practices. The local people most likely worshipped the fundamental forces of regeneration and fertility, as we have seen evidenced in Izanagi and Izanami's successful procreative efforts, which formed the islands of the Japanese archipelago, as well as numerous Kami representing the environmental and climactic forces necessary to promote other life.[6]

When the Portuguese were granted permission by the local lord of nearby Omura to establish a trading post and church in this same long harbor in the early 1500s, they chose the hilltop of Morisaki Shrine upon which to build a house for their "tutelary deity," where it might command a strategic view of the entire harbor. The local villagers knew these strange foreigners were acting with the sanction of their feudal lords and therefore could not protest the loss of a small shrine; however, the story goes that once again someone managed to save the sacred *go-shintai* and shield it until it could be housed in a newly built shrine a century later.

Here the story takes a curious and, to my knowledge, unique twist. According to a 1992 documentary produced by the local Kyushu Broadcasting System (KBS) in which priests and local historians appear, when the *go-shintai* of Morisaki is placed into its temporary shrine for the procession of the Okunchi festival, it is far and away the largest and heaviest of the three sacred essences. Chief Priest Uesugi as well mentioned this characteristic to me in an interview; to him the *go-shintai* was, without a doubt, a statue of some sort. The KBS documentary proposes that when the Tokugawa government began its persecution of Christian churches in the early 1600s, the Portuguese church built at the head of the harbor was one of the first to be burned. But, just as the shrine's sacred essence was rescued earlier when the shrine was destroyed by the Portuguese, this time a relic of the church was kept for safekeeping. Since the large Christian population had to be brought once again under the government's thumb, the church's statue was somehow enshrined alongside the Kami called Morisaki, which thus encouraged Christian participation in shrine affairs. With a long-standing cultural tendency to view both Kami and Buddhas as aspects of the Japanese religious universe, the pairing of a Christian effigy with a Kami would certainly not be improbable.

A few years after 1634, when the main shrine was enlarged, a third deity was included to add a realm of influence specifically concerning the sea. The multiple Kami of Sumiyoshi, once the object of special worship by the legendary empress Jingū, are considered great protectors of seafarers, fishermen, and travelers in general, as well as having functions related to purification. Thus, the three together form a trinity that has the breadth and scope to gain an audience from all segments of the community: the ruling classes and samurai prayed to the martial vigilance of Suwa, the farmers to Morisaki's benign fecundity, and the fishermen and traders to Sumiyoshi.

Accordingly, each Kami has a special festival, one attentive and sympathetic to its character. Morisaki-no-Kami's festival, for instance, is celebrated in the spring to honor the transformations so important for producing crops. Sumiyoshi-no-Kami's festival belongs to the summer, when the seas are warmed by southern currents and run full of mackerel, bream, tuna, and shrimp, but also when purifications are in order to combat the potential for epidemics or pestilence brought on by the rainy season. And since Suwa is the principal Kami and therefore closer (in theory) to the great Amaterasu, its festival date is in the fall, offered as thanksgiving for the successful harvest just completed and the abundance of material and spiritual gains granted by both it and the other two Kami during the year. Interestingly enough, no longer is emphasis given to the spirit of *bu*, or "martial valor," which is supposed to be a part of Suwa-no-Kami's essential character. And although the other two Kami have their own festivals, they both accompany Suwa-no-Kami at all times during its primary festival as a kind of "emotional bodyguard" (according to one of the priests) to keep this now-subordinated aspect of its personality in check.

All of this sounds highly polytheistic and, strictly speaking, is just that, yet these various Kami are thought of as working together in harmony, so that, according to Floyd Ross (1965), the universe is just as unified as in the religions claiming to be monotheistic. As Chief Priest Uesugi will elaborate upon later, the local Kami are familiar to the populace, invoking feelings of intimacy not possible were the Sun Goddess, Amaterasu, to be imposed in their midst. All Kami, likewise all men and women, are considered to be related to each other in the broadest sense as well as in a metaphorical vein: all are traveling together upon a course linking growth, development, creativity, and improvement. It is in the best interests of both humans and the Kami to be on friendly, "speaking" terms in the marvelously varied world they share. Maintaining this rather precarious balance has remained central to Japanese religious practices for at least fourteen centuries. One might think that after all this time the priests would have resolved and systematized the way people think about the Kami, or even the way they present these concepts in public. But the fact that they have not speaks volumes for a strategic Japanese predilection for ambiguity, contextual referents of meaning, and a rather anarchic freedom (from a Western theological perspective) to call forth only those Kami that best suit the situation. Call it animism, polytheism, or any number of handy categorizations, the Kami remain intimately connected to "this" world but are, at essence, decidedly "other," operating with a form-denying fluidity and ethical flexibility we poor humans can only mythologize and venerate, dreaming of such power.

4

RITUAL

AND

CEREMONY:

AN

OVERVIEW

Of all the aspects of Japan that are stereotyped in the West—the inscrutability of the people, the strict hierarchy of society, the difficult language, or the "economic animal" syndrome of an aggressive and protective capitalism—one of the cultural traits actually deserving a certain fame is the Japanese love for formal recognition of events. Whether it is starting kindergarten, buying a new car, joining a company, or getting married, a formalized acknowledgment of significant moments and transitions is deeply a part of what it means to be Japanese. Not to have an appropriate ritual upon the seventh anniversary of Grandfather's death would be a grave oversight; likewise, to deny a newborn baby a dedicatory ritual at a shrine would be an opportunity missed that could be potentially influential to his or her life.

It is believed that the human need for some kind of formal, often public acknowledgment of significant events is one of the fundamental forces of our development as social beings. At the same time, ritual allows us to transcend our individual selves to gain a sense of participation with the greater environment of the forces controlling our singular and communal destinies. And since ritual is primarily action, requiring motor skills to achieve its expression, we have what Evan Zuesse calls the "prestige of the body," which is the vehicle for religious experience. It is through physical actions and experiences that consciousness is more immediately and irresistably engaged, a state bestowing a far stronger sense of reality than mere mental philosophizing. It may be said of preliterate ritual practices such as Shinto that their beliefs were more "acted out than thought out" (Zuesse 1979, 406).

But when participating in a formal ceremony or ritual, what is really happening? Are we, as Freud believed, trying to relieve certain psychological tensions (such as anxiety, aggression, or despair) that are unable to find conscious voices in daily life? Or are these rituals a way of directly strengthening social sentiments and the cohesiveness of the group, allowing its fundamental needs (economic, biological, sexual) to be symbolically dramatized, while at the same time resolving the group's conflicts with the environment, historical experience, and even the personality types that form the community?[1]

Both of these approaches, while having certain limited, though relevant, applicability, fall short of thoroughly explaining what ritual and ceremonies mean to the Japanese who periodically adopts Shinto or Buddhist practices. First of all, when offerings are presented to the Kami or bows are made in front of the family or shrine's altar, we are concerned with a nonverbal system of communication in which the actions themselves are significant statements of basic cultural themes. To apply the ideas of the late Victor Turner (1973), what the Japanese hold to be true about the nature of the world, society, and their relationships with greater powers (as well as each other) is not only controlled but promoted and even stimulated via the business of ritual expression.

The reader might have noticed a gradual shift away from using the word "ceremony" to talk about what goes on in formal presentations of offerings and prayers to the deities at a shrine. At the risk of sounding pedantic, let me elaborate a bit on different ways of distinguishing between "ceremony" and "ritual" and why this separation might be important. A "ritual," in its broadest secular sense, is usually taken to mean anything done in a habitual manner, like brushing your teeth before bed or having a cup of coffee in the morning, or it is used to describe what members of the animal kingdom do to attract the attention of the opposite sex when mating season has arrived. But we are concerned here with those gestures, words, and objects that are used in activities performed in a place somehow removed or separated from the everyday world. These activities are usually ordered in a specific sequence that is designed to influence forces on behalf of the participants' goals and interests—which, in traditional Japan, could range from having a successful harvest, to ease in childbirth, to victory in an upcoming battle.

To be brief, let us consider "ceremony" as "elaborate conventional forms for the expression of feelings, not confined to religious occasions" (Monica Wilson in Goody 1961, 159). It is, according to

Gilbert Lewis, a "species of ritual with emphasis on the symbolic acknowledgment of a social situation rather than on the efficacy of the procedures in modifying that situation. It does not sustain the situation or effect a change in it" (1980, 21).[2] Ritual, on the other hand, is usually set apart as "a body of custom specifically associated with religious performance" (Leach 1968, 521)[3] and is standardized, repetitive, and symbolically representative of a people's social interdependence (Kertzer 1988, 9).[4] Through ritual, to sketch but a few of its effects, the past can become part of the present, distant deities can be summoned to one's own neighborhood, acts and institutions (ranging from sword making to politics) can be sanctified, or social and psychological moods can be expressed as part of the order of the cosmos. Ritual has a definite purpose and is concerned with reaffirming relationships held to be vital to the continuation of physical, sociopolitical, or individual worlds. It may also be directed toward altering the world at large or the perceptions of its participants about the forces of the world they are experiencing. Barbara Myerhoff remarks that no primitive society is so unempirical as to expect to cause rain by dancing a rain dance; the very fact that the ritual has been properly conducted is enough to alter or alleviate those socially generated tensions underlying the enactment in the first place (1984, 170). Subsequent rainmaking rituals may have to be held if no rain is immediately forthcoming, but to say that a ritual's efficacy depends entirely on some change in the atmosphere or environment overlooks the social dimension of ritual.

Although classification by an outside observer frequently imposes irrelevant structures on local practices and beliefs, Turner's typology of ritual (1973) is useful for untangling the oftentimes dazzling complexity of rituals according to purpose. First, there are those that are *seasonal* in nature, honoring a specific moment of the climatic cycle, activities involved in planting or harvesting a crop, or perhaps the move to different pastures for nonagrarian peoples, upon which depends the livelihood of the community. Second, some rituals are *contingent* upon moments of individual or collective crisis or transition, such as birth, puberty, marriage, or death, as well as those placating or exorcising physical or spiritual afflictions. Three other groups cover observances that deal with *divinatory* services (a practice monopolized by the Urabe and Nakatomi families in Japan for many centuries); *protective* rituals performed by the authorities to ensure the health and fertility of human beings, animals, and crops in their territories; and *ancestral* rituals that require the daily offering of food and libations as a way of honoring those who have already become part of the realm of spirits. Needless to say, the classes are not exclusive, and certain rituals may partake of characteristics from more than one class.

The kinds of objective symbols used in a ritual, that is, those that are visual or in some other way discernible to the senses, may serve to further transmit a ritual's particular themes to the participants. For example, the wand of purification's white paper streamers (at the left of fig. 10) appear at the beginning of most Shinto rites, so one might think that their overall importance in stressing physical and spiritual cleanliness could be considered to be dominant. The priests, how-ever, see the wand as a preliminary preparation, so its role in the main ritual occasion may not be emphasized in any particular way. Other objects, such as the food offerings, the bells used by the *miko* (female shrine attendants) in their dance before the Kami, or the round mirror representing the sun deity on the altar (to name a few), are ritually presented in different settings throughout the year and with differing combinations of thematic linkages. And yet, by and large, there are few occasions when a particular meaning is promoted or imposed upon the participants, leaving them with considerable interpretive freedom to find and apply meaning only when it matters. In the words of Raymond Firth, there are, strictly speaking, no inherently symbolic objects; there are only symbolic relationships (1973, 245).[5] That shrine Shinto permits the casual participant to individually negotiate many of these relationships is, I think, part of the reason for its postwar success.

What this interaction means for the shrine's parishioners is that those members who have been exposed to parts of the shrine's ritual cycle gradually experience—through repetition, variation, and con-trast of symbols and themes—the subtle ways Shinto rituals mold and manipulate certain values, behavioral rules, and even the mental categories upon which much experience is grounded. Even more im-portantly, as Turner mentioned, they learn in what cultural settings and with what degree of intensity the themes of ritual should apply. Ritual is not just a concentration of framed messages about values, norms, and guidelines for everyday action which show how couples should interact or how farmers should treat their fields if they want their rice to grow. Instead, ritual is also "a fusion of the powers be-lieved to be inherent in the persons, objects, relationships, events and histories which are represented by the ceremony itself." Continuing to follow Turner, what we are talking about here is "a mobilization of energies as well as messages. The objects and activities . . . are not merely things that stand for other things or something abstract, they participate in the powers and virtues they represent" (1969, 59).

Applied to what goes on in the course of a year's cycle of activities at a major Shinto institution such as Suwa Shrine, certainly all of these aspects (and more) are very much a part of the events designed to benefit the individual and community. What is so fascinating about Japanese culture and society is that even as it approaches the twenty-first century, many of its important ritual practices resemble in structure and expression those dating to the Heian period (794-1192 C.E.).[6] Until only recently, the stigma attached to Shinto's forced association with the militarists of the war years has kept its historical traditions and practices veiled from being seen for what they truly are: part of the foundation upon which an entire cultural gestalt is based. One can never say they have a "feel" for things Japanese without having noticed the permeation of Shintoesque orientations in everything from day-to-day life to major ritual and ceremonial observances. The Japanese love of bathing, for instance (a penchant which would seemingly qualify them as being the world's cleanest people), could be argued as having derived from notions of purity and impurity formerly held by elites before engaging in ritual activity. Likewise, the piles of salt in front of houses and businesses, the unstained countertops of white cedar which any authentic sushi restaurant must have, as well as the value attached to a variety of foods thought to have "cleansing" properties for the human body all evoke notions of purity, simplicity, or the purgation of defilement so highly valued in Shinto.[7]

From the accounts of envoys from China in the third century, archeological excavations, and the mythological narratives in the *Kojiki* and *Nihon-shoki*, we can be fairly certain that the earliest rituals in Japan were those done to thank the Kami for a plentiful food supply, to beseech protection for communities, animals, or crops, and to honor the departed souls of clan leaders and members. However, it was not until the Asuka and Nara periods, in the sixth and seventh centuries, that the leading priestly families began to formalize and codify ritual procedures, due to competition from Buddhism for the attention of the aristocracy. In fact, as every book on Shinto should tell you, there was no special word to distinguish it as being what we might call a "religion" at all. It was simply the way things were done, the way they'd always been done since anyone could remember, with affairs of the ruling council or leader strictly linked to affairs of the Kami. According to Joseph Kitagawa (1987, 118–20), keeping close contact with the Kami and attending to their needs was a cardinal criterion of being an effective chieftain in early Japan. The word *matsurau*, or "attending to" the Kami, became identified with *matsuru*, "to venerate or enshrine," providing two concepts that have been central to Imperial as well as military governments ever since: *matsurigoto* and *saisei-itchi*. Both can be translated roughly as meaning a unity of religion and government. Not only do these terms evoke an element of the state's obedience to the dictates of the Kami, but they also imply a reciprocal relationship that serves to sanctify and legitimate the state's actions, particularly when identifying itself with the nation so as to promote solidarity and continuity in times of crises.

The rituals that can be observed today at any major shrine are, according to many priests, fairly continuous with those of the Heian period, which is thought of as an idealized or "golden" age of Shinto. This was a time when Imperial and state patronage included the donation of land and estates to shrines and temples, when priestly families and lineages had high social status, and when relative political stability and calm enabled the aristocracy to devote their energies to refining aesthetic and literary sensibilities via poetry, song, painting, and rituals. For many priests of today, this period set the ideological and aesthetic standards for them to aspire to. Certainly the robes, headgear and footgear, architectural surroundings, and cosmic orientations of modern-day rituals can be seen as windows through which participants can glimpse the imagined elegance and formality of the Fujiwara court. It must be added, however, that few of the "old rituals" survived intact after the Meiji government's radical revamping and restructuring of Shinto so that it could serve as a national creed (see Hardacre 1989).

Should you visit a shrine for the first time and happen upon a ritual in progress within the Hall of Worship, the following four movements will help you structure the flow of what transpires in most contemporary Shinto ritual events:[8]

1. *Purification:* Whether it consists of simply rinsing the hands and mouth with water or with waving a wand of white paper streamers in the air over the heads of priests, trays of offerings, or that gleaming new car brought to the shrine for blessing, this first step is the preparation essential for making the environment and the individuals within it ready to petition, receive, and entertain the Kami's presence.

2. *Presentations:* As one kneels upon the tatami within the Hall of Worship, one sees a high table laden with various kinds of fruit, vegetables, seaweed, and rice cakes, which surround the core offerings of uncooked rice grains, salt, water, and two bottles of sake. Whether the observance is merely for the benefit of one person or aspires to the good of the entire nation, the core offerings to the Kami are a part of every shrine ritual. Sometimes simple, sometimes including over one hundred styles of food at the Grand Shrine of Ise, it is safe to say that a ritual without food offerings is unthinkable in Shinto practice.

3. *Petitions:* Scholars have debated whether the food offerings or the formal prayers are more important, but ask any chief priest and he will immediately answer that the *norito*, or "words spoken to the Kami," are the main part of any ritual. Beautiful, correct words, intoned with reverence and awe, bring about good influences. This is one of the oldest attitudes of Japanese religious practices (or of any ritualized system of practices, including Catholic and Hindu), deriving from an ancient belief in *kotodama*, a spiritual power residing in words. Priests often claim this tradition as being wholly Shinto, but evidence points to considerable influence from Buddhist prayers, mantras, and magical sound syllables, reaching all the way to the Vedic tradition of the Indus Valley.

4. *Participation:* After the long droning chant of the prayer, the *miko* commence a slow circular movement before the main altar, which marks the beginning of the last phase of the ritual. Upon completion of this sacred entertainment, the opportunity for participation is often extended to everyone in attendance when leafy sprigs from the sacred *sakaki* tree (native only to Japan) are distributed. Each person follows the example of the head priest in slowly coming forward, bowing, and then placing the little branch on a small table as a means of linking the individual to the divine. After the actual service is over and the priests have filed out of the hall, the partaking of a small sip of rice wine, called *o-miki*, further invests the worshipper with the blessings of the Kami. On important occasions, a large number of guests may be invited into a special banquet hall to have, at the shrine's expense, a symbolic communion, the *naorai*, that also serves as a feast of transition back to secular life. As we will see in the next chapter, the parts of a ritual flow together seamlessly—movements of a symphony dedicated to the deities.

It is thought that originally a ritual consisted of only two fundamental parts: the offerings, prayers, and sacred *kagura* dance were all considered presentations to demonstrate the sincerity of the petitioners, followed by the *naorai* feast. Later, however, a final stage was added for very special occasions: the parading of a palanquin shrine or float through the streets of the community. Since the festival, usually a seasonal one, was a vehicle to renew communal consciousness as well as regenerate divine power within the land and hearts of the community, it was perhaps a strategic development that carried it out of the shrine and into the streets (Ishikawa 1987, 101; Yanagawa 1988; Sonoda 1988b). By doing so, the bond was strengthened between the parishioners (*ujiko*) and their heavenly guardians (*ujigami*). Festivals such as these returned the celebrants to a mythical time, when the Kami and their creations were fresh and bursting with the vigor of creative energies. One need only witness a single festival of this sort to see how much enjoyment people take, sometimes accelerating into a wild abandonment, when participating in the cycles of Shinto observances.

Yet many know that in the same way rain depends on clouds for its formation, so does the color and excitement spilling through their streets intertwine with the solemn and dignified hush of the initial ritual at the shrine. Ask the man or woman on the street what their religion is and most likely they will say they don't have one. But that is not to say they lack a wealth of cultural traditions which are, in many cases, rooted in ritual. Like new shoots of rice, these practices grow upward into maturity, using (when appropriate) whatever thematic, symbolic, or social nutrients are provided by the rich and multilayered soil of life in Japan.

5

FINDING THE MEASURE

The month of March in much of Japan, from Nagasaki to as far north as Tokyo, is a month of transitions: the wet, cold winds of winter are more frequently tempered by sunny days, which stir the blossoming of magnolias, dogwoods, forsythia, and plum trees. Following their example, the business world's fiscal year comes to a close at the end of March and gears up for a fresh surge; likewise the school year winds down for two or three weeks (unlike the three-month lull in the United States) until a new one begins in early April. Similar new beginnings, from careers to special-interest classes to marriages, are all thought to come to fruition at or around the beginning of spring.

At Suwa Shrine, the schedule of events for March has just been issued from the office of the Gūji (the chief priest), and with it is the list of which priests will be serving in the rituals. It is an event both anticipated and dreaded, because in seeing who gets to do what a great deal is subtly imparted about the progress the younger priests are making in their excruciatingly slow climb up the hierarchy of rank, which, in many ways, mirrors that of a Japanese company. For one diligent "employee" of some six years' standing, whom for reasons of privacy we will call Noda-san, this particular March signals a long awaited transition in his ritual duties.

Even before the list was posted, Noda-san had been thinking it was his turn to participate in one of the "lead" roles in a rite instead of always playing the flute for the dance of the *miko*. Of the three main observances in March, he sees his name in the role of attendant (*shidori*, also *tengi*) for the March 21 service in honor of the equinox, and a smile crosses his face. His role is not as important as conveying food offerings to one of the senior priests, but nonetheless, to hold the sacred prayer that will be read by the chief priest and to deliver it at the proper moment, in correct manner and posture, is certainly better than playing the flute again . . . although that too, as he reminds himself, is also in service to the Kami.

As the equinox approaches and Noda-san begins reviewing his role (no formal practice sessions are ever held—after six years of attendance, he is expected to have the actions and order of the ritual absorbed), he decides that this time will be different from the service he participated in three months ago as an acolyte. For one thing, his status has changed from being a bachelor to a married man, and with that comes new responsibilities concerning the preparatory period before the festival. This time, for instance, in addition to having his hair washed and trimmed, his fingernails and toenails cut, his face well shaved, and his body bathed and bladder empty before the ritual begins, Noda-san has confided that he plans to sleep separately from his pretty wife. It is not strictly required, he tells me, that abstinence of this sort be practiced before a relatively minor ritual (unlike the times all the priests have to stay at the shrine before the Okunchi festival in October and again in November for the festival of New Rice), but he wants to try it for the state of mind it affords— a closer approximation to what the top priests at major shrines like Ise or Izumo experience more frequently, and what countless generations of priests before him used to undergo each time they served the Kami.

On days of a ritual, the subordinate priests like Noda-san have to be at the shrine around 7 A.M. to sweep the steps and make sure the hand-washing basin (*temizuya*) has clean towels, that the gathering hall for those members of the community who are invited guests is tidy and that the ashtrays are empty, that the *miko* have ready the serving utensils for the sake and gifts for the parishioners, and that his own robes are presentable. After all this is done, he has time for perhaps an hour of work in the office on the report he's preparing for the Gūji about the cost-effectiveness of last month's lottery drawing at the Setsubun exorcism festival (see chapter 7). But as 9:30 approaches and he leaves his seat in front of the computer, his mind drifts more and more toward the action beginning precisely at 10:00 and the state of preparedness he must now enter into.

The robes appropriate for the ritual are of the less formal type, the *jo-e*, and are simply worn over the plain white cotton kimono and light blue slit-skirt *hakama* he wears every day. The very wide and long white sleeves of the *jo-e* do not quite touch the ground, and with the black *eboshi* headpiece, the clogs made of black-lacquered paulownia wood, and his trusty flat wooden *shaku*, which he holds like a scepter, he looks quite striking, as if he turned a wrong corner in a palace or shrine of a thousand years ago and emerged resplendent for today's ritual at Nagasaki's Suwa Shrine.

At exactly 9:50, he walks up the flight of steps from the changing room, and it is there the joking and banter with his fellow priests ends. They have been teasing him about his "joining the elite" by being chosen as a bearer, and that it won't be long before he'll be the Gūji's right-hand flunky, and, "Psst," whispers one of his friends who has taken over the role of flute player for today, "be oh so careful not to fart during the ritual." But as he leaves the room ahead of them as protocol demands, their tone becomes supportive, and they say with real sincerity, "Do a good job! [*Ganbatte yo!*]."

Noda-san checks again the white pouch he has slung over his shoulder to make sure the *norito* prayer is within and then proceeds to the entry of the reception hall, from which the Gūji will emerge in five minutes. Before taking his place in the row of waiting priests, he walks over to a wooden bucket flanked by two of the *miko* attendants who will be dancing today and receives from one a dipper of water. First his left, then his right, hand is rinsed, then a fresh dipperful is poured into his left hand and lifted to his mouth, and he takes great care to spit the now defiled water into the little tray of cedar branches at his feet without spotting his shiny clogs. A fan-shaped napkin is presented for him to wipe his hands and mouth, and to prevent the faux pas of mixing together two different kinds of impurities and thus giving them a fresh place to spawn, a separate receptacle is provided for the wad of paper. Noda-san bows in thanks for their service, and they do the same in deference to his rank for today, and finally he takes his place, fifth in line from the Gūji.

As frequently and somewhat magically occurs on a festival day, the morning is clear and sunny, even though during the past week it rained every day. The azalea and camelia bushes near the covered walkway to the main shrine are gleaming with webs of crystalline droplets. It suddenly strikes him that, save for the concrete stepping-stones, everything in this area reflects traditional Japanese aesthetics: the buildings are all wood, the sound of water falling into the sacred pond is the music of haiku, and even the various blues, vermilions, and violets of the priests' and *miko*'s garments are synonymous with a thousand years of culture and refinement. As higher ranking priests clip-clop by in their splendid clogs, pausing for the hand and mouth cleansing before assuming their places in the line, it becomes clear once again why he has chosen to follow in his father's footsteps as a priest and why these rituals are so essential: it is here the vertical energy of heaven and the horizontal energies of human beings intersect. This place where he is standing is precisely upon the path of the Kami: *shin* (kami) *tō* (way).

Suddenly everyone slightly tenses and the atmosphere changes. Without looking, Noda-san knows the Gūji has emerged. He too performs purification duties at the little bucket and then takes his place, silently surveying the scene to make sure all is correct in posture, gesture, appearance, and mood. To look at him directly would be extremely ill-mannered and impudent, so for the remaining two minutes, Noda-san lowers his eyes to the ground before him and listens to the wrens in the branches of the huge camphor trees nearby. They seem to announce to one and all that on this unusually mild morning of early spring, the priests of Suwa Shrine have entered into sacred time and are ready to receive a visit from the Kami.

At precisely 10:00, as a nearby Catholic school bell tolls, from within the Hall of Worship comes the accelerating drumroll that signals the start of the service.[1] Noda-san steps forward, walks the three steps to the end of the line where the Guji is waiting, and makes the first of the many bows he will perform, head lowered ever so slightly to the earth, from which springs life and fecundity—each bow restoring him to a state of humility and balance. Then, leading the procession like the prow of a ship, he cuts through the air so that the Gūji and others can follow in his calm wake and enter the sacred enclosure used for purification, the "festival garden," which is not really a garden at all. Everyone's clogs resound noisily off the uneven pebbles and stones which cover the area, and the group divides in two—the Gūji with the *miko* behind him to the right, and everyone else to the left, all facing each other across the small expanse of gray rocks with the altar at one end and the invited guests at the other.

Long before there were beautiful buildings erected to provide a dwelling for the spirit of the Kami, an enclosure like this *was* the first shrine, demarcated from the rest of the world due to its propensity to receive the Kami. It gave early societies a center around which to orient and integrate their civil, social, administrative, and ethical affairs. This place was the absolute reality, the "localized sacred," which transcended, yet at the same time manifested itself in, the world. With a tree at its far end for the Kami to alight upon and invest with their numinous power, it was here that the community gained access, via the petitions and summonings of the head priests and shamans, to the blessings and protection they needed for their crops and villages.

Mori-san, a gentle-hearted bull of a man who is the most senior
of the priests below the Gūji, lumbers forth to just in front of the
altar to initiate an ancient call for purification. His words are the
first anyone has spoken in the past ten minutes:

To the venerated kami Amaterasu Omikami, created by the
water purification of Izanagi after his descent and defilement in
the land of the underworld, please hear our prayers and grant us
a similar purification as we humbly beseech you now.

Next, his colleague Takeshita-san steps forward in a brisk motion
to remove the white paper streamer purification wand, the *haraigushi*,
from the altar and, after bowing before the altar, turns toward the
Gūji. Takeshita-san holds the wand well in front of his body, cradled
by his left hand and firmly gripped by his right, the first manifestation of the yin (passive)/yang(active) principle that came from
Chinese Taoism to guide much of Shinto ritual. Noda-san remembers being taught in the training university how certain fundamental
opposites, such as day/night, order/disorder, and sun/moon, in addition to the male/female distinction, are correlated with the symbolism of much of Shinto ritual. As the Gūji and *miko* bow, Takeshita-
san subtly reverses his hands so that his right is now closest to the
white paper streamers; then he noisily flourishes it first over his left
shoulder, then the right, then again the left. The wand is thought to
work like a magnet, drawing out whatever pollutions and impurities
may have accumulated (either knowingly or subconsciously) within
the spirits and bodies of the worshippers. He will cleanse his fellow
priests, the invited guests, and finally any worshipper standing in the
background who has happened to visit the shrine today, each with
the same slow swishing of the wand.[2]

No sooner is he finished, and the wand replaced on the altar (much
to the dismay of several of the more learned priests who believe
it should be either burned or cast into water each time), than the
Gūji's secretary and third-ranking priest of the shrine, Ureshino-
san, follows with a less dramatic but perhaps more significant form
of cleansing ritual: a single leaf is dipped in a small unglazed cup of
water, and drops of water are scattered in the same left, right, left
motion. Left indicates a beginning—alpha, or *ah* in Japanese—and
right is a reaching to the outer realms of omega, *uhn*,[3] then back to
the left for a fresh beginning, now cleansed and ready to serve, receive, and become one with the Kami if the chance arises. Though
there was discussion in the last monthly general shrine meeting about

no longer adding salt to the water so as to protect the costly silk robes from occasionally spotting, the more traditionally minded priests believe that the cleansing aspect of water is enhanced by the salt (although, as Noda-san pointed out over coffee one afternoon, in the original myth, Izanagi washed himself in a river, not the ocean—but then, he said with a shrug, "Who listens to a 'six-year-old priest'?").

Suddenly, it is Noda-san's turn to assume center stage in the rock-strewn courtyard, but he is about three seconds slow. By the time Ureshino-san returned to his place, Noda-san should already have been moving over to the Gūji to again bow and lead the procession into the *haiden*, Hall of Worship. But this slight lull, imperceptible to anyone not actually performing the ritual, is met with equanimity by the Gūji, who neither glares nor scowls, instead almost meekly lowers his head and matches Noda-san's pace as he clatters across the sacred area to the more sensuous embrace of fragrances and textures emanating from the cypress wood and tatami of the Hall of Worship.

This transition from the outside sanctuary to the inner, according to Noda-san, always imparts a feeling of arrival—like returning home again after a lengthy absence (even though he just swept the place this morning). His place on the raised tier, where he sits *seiza* fashion (kneeling and sitting back on the heels) at the end of the row of priests on one side of the stage opposite the Gūji and the two *miko* who will dance, makes his profile the only one really accessible to the few guests and to the casual visitors, who are thrilled at their stroke of luck to have had their shrine visit coincide with a ritual.

In his role as attendant Noda-san must not only deliver the *norito* prayer to the Gūji at the proper time but also announce to all assembled what is about to happen. He is a kind of extremely formal master of ceremonies, although his status is the lowest of anyone on the raised stage (save for the *miko*, who, because they are unmarried women, but not necessarily virgins, and dancers, are in a different realm altogether). He now turns slightly and in a firm voice invites everyone to join with the Gūji as he calls on the Kami with the first silent bow.

For the Gūji to do this simply from where he sits at the far end of the stage from Noda-san would be impolite; he must rise from his knees, walk two steps forward, turn at a right angle to face the altar for the first time, walk another two steps forward, then go down on his knees on the hardwood floor and inch forward again (left knee, right knee, left again, in the same cosmic waltz as the wand of purification) until he is settled with his wooden scepter before him and his eyes on the sacred mirror representing the Sun Goddess, Amaterasu. Now he is ready and leads all in attendance in one slow wavelike bow (the priests must take great care not to raise their heads before the Gūji does). Once again upright, he reverses each step of the journey and silently returns to his seat, never looking up, never changing the expression on his face, his task of summoning the Kami's attention completed. Were this a more important ritual taking place in the upper level of the shrine in the Hall of Offerings, he would have ascended a flight of stairs and opened the curtain to the Inner Sanctuary. But here, on the lower level of the inner shrine that is closest to the public, recognition of the Gūji's role and belief in the Kami's willingness to cooperate when called suffices and sustains this pivotal part of the ritual.

Though no one really knows at what exact point the Kami arrives after being summoned to the uppermost of the three levels of the sanctuary, it is now proper to show gratitude to its hidden presence by making offerings of food and drink. Second in importance only to the actual words spoken directly to the Kami, making the correct kinds and varieties of *shinsen* offerings is left to the senior priests. Noda-san knows that it will still be a while (though precisely how long is for the Gūji to decide) before he will be allowed to participate in a festival at that level. The three priests who performed the preparatory purifications all rise and take positions in relation to the altar according to rank. In charge of actually positioning the octagonal trays on the altar is the chief senior priest; the number-three man, Takeshita-san, is out of sight in the small kitchen making the last adjustments to the trays before bringing them out. From his new vantage point, Noda-san can see how each tray is carried high and with the utmost dignity, and how each priest of the chain bows both before receiving it and before he passes it on, always making certain that the spread fingers of the giver touch those of the receiver. Yin, yang, giving, receiving, the fingers on top touch those below — the energy of ritual propriety flows along the chain of priests to the altar.

The first tray is uncooked rice, followed by a tray of rice cakes with a plum flower on top. It is fitting that rice should be first since it is considered in Shinto to be the initial gift of the Kami to help make the lives of human beings easier. Next comes red snapper with its tail arranged as if flexed, then on another tray is seasoned seaweed, then thick seaweed as brittle as old leather, and pressed fish cakes. These are the gifts from the sea. Offerings from the mountains follow, with white radish and bamboo shoots on one tray and potatoes, cabbage, and apples on another. Then, containers of salt and water are carried in. The last tray contains sacred rice wine, *o-miki*, to help wash down the feast and set the mood for the rest of the service.

Music was one of the charms used to lure an offended and angry Sun Goddess from the cave in which she had hidden herself. The Kami have always delighted in music, but not just any music of course. Immediately behind Noda-san on the lower level of grass mats are three musician-priests in green silk robes, one blowing mightily on a side flute, one on a miniature kind of oboe, and one on a seventeen-chambered bamboo-tube harmonium. Out of the corner of his eye Noda-san notices some young women, obviously tourists, who are hearing the traditional court music for the first time, if one can judge by their pained wincing. But had it not been for *gagaku* music like this, the Sun Goddess might still be in her cave and the world in darkness, for it was this alluring magic accompanying a comic (and somewhat lewd) dance that pricked her curiosity to peek out of the cave, see herself reflected in a mirror, and thus (with a helpful tug from a nearby deity) restore light to the world.

The offerings have been presented and the priests now sit on the floor in their respective serving positions, waiting for the music to end. Noda-san recalls that one of the first things he learned about Shinto rituals from his father was how to flex his leg muscles while sitting *seiza* fashion so he would be able to stand up when required and fulfill some important duty. He remembers that during the Coming of Age ritual for twenty-year-olds a month ago, the poor kids' legs became paralyzed after twenty minutes of formal *seiza*-style sitting. When they tried to stand up and make their offerings toward the end of the ritual, a young woman and a young man toppled over helplessly like bowling pins. Next year, he thought, it would be good to tell them before the service the secret to standing up after sitting on their heels for half an hour.

The last "chord" is still resonating in the dim, natural light of the Hall of Worship when Noda-san rises to deliver the *norito* to the Gūji. The highly polished natural finish of the *hinoki* wood underfoot is cool and smooth, like sliding on gossamer, as he takes a few quick steps and goes down to his knees before the Gūji, presenting the folded scroll with a bow. The Gūji places it behind his wooden scepter, bows, then waits for an inwardly relieved Noda-san to be reseated before he slowly inches forward, rises, and assumes the same position he did for the first opening bow, only this time he is closer to the altar, on a raised tatami dais three inches above the floor. Noda-san then turns slightly to the audience and announces that the *norito* will now be read and that it is proper for everyone to bow. It becomes very quiet—the Gūji clears his throat a couple times, breathes deeply, and begins in a murmur that steadily rises in pitch and volume:

> In the dread presence and before the sacred shrine of
>   Suwa-no-ō-mi-kami, the chief of the shrine, Uesugi Chisato,
>   on the twenty-first day of the third month,
>   with trembling makes utterance:
> By the command of the Sovereign Ancestral Male and Female
>   Deities,
>   who divinely remain in the High Heavenly Plain,
> Do we come cleansed and purified into thy great presence
> And make offerings on this day of heavenly alignment:
>   of food offerings; soft rice and rough rice,
>   of drink offerings, raising high the soaring necks of the
>   countless wine vessels, filled to the brim,
>   arranging in full rows the bellies of the wine jars;
>   of the fruits of the mountains and plains,
>   the sweet herbs and the bitter herbs,
>   as well as the fruits of the blue ocean,
>   the wide-finned and the narrow-finned fishes,
>   the seaweeds of the deep and of the shore,
> All these various offerings we place and raise high
> Like a long mountain range, and present them.
> And, as the full and glorious sun of this day of life and
>   plenty rises,
>   do thou hear to the end these words of praise,
>   in tranquility and peace.
> Since they thus serve thee, grant to protect and favor widely
>   both your followers and the people of this community.
> Keep them contented in heart and sound in body.
> Make their homes peaceful and their occupations prosperous.
> Thus, with reverence and dread, we declare the ending
>   of the words of praise.[4]

The Gūji's final words, ending with a vowel that slides down an octave in pitch and lasts a full five seconds, never fails to cause a chill to travel up Noda-san's spine, he confides later. Even though some of the language of an invocational prayer may not directly communicate to the average person just in off the street, its poetry, rhythm, and imagery are accessible enough to convey a sense of communion with the Kami, which is at the center of this or any other ritual. A well-delivered *norito*, such as Uesugi Gūji can do so effectively, reinforces the worshipper's hopes and gives him or her confidence and fortitude with which to manage the tremendous uncertainties of life. The *norito* relaxes anxieties and doubts because one knows the Kami has heard it and will carry its supplications into realms beyond one's meager powers of comprehension and awareness, realms which transcend and yet suffuse the realities one calls home, business, family, and feelings.

Noda-san waits until the Gūji is seated again before he moves at a more relaxed speed to receive the scroll into his pouch, being careful to hold it with his hands in a different position. After all, its power has been conveyed into the presence of the Kami, so there is no longer any reason to handle it as if it might detonate at any moment.

No sooner is he seated than the huge drum strikes, signaling the *miko* to rise and begin their dance of "worshipful" entertainment for the Kami. As the drum's "ton-ta-ta-ton!" sets one's stomach vibrating, the flute's somewhat melancholic tone—which Noda-san has played a hundred times at weddings, family purifications, and baby dedications—still seems to him like some kind of living, flying spirit that alights on the shoulders of the *miko*. The two young women walk with arms outstretched, their right hands holding the bell-wands (*suzu*) and their left hands cradling the colored streamers attached to the handles. One of the newer and prettier *miko* is dancing today, and she's already quite skilled in her grace of movement and timing; the slight rosy flush of shyness mixed with excitement on her fair cheeks only enhances her beauty as a creator of mood and reverent entertainment.

Like Noda-san, the *miko* wear white kimonos and bloomers, although their bloomers are vermilion, and for this ritual, they also wear long-sleeved, pink silk outer robes accented with the shrine's oak leaf crest. Their long hair is tightly pinned back from their foreheads, with a single ponytail bound in a tubular piece of white paper hanging neatly in the center of their backs. They are lovely to look at and even more so when responding to the music with their slow dreamlike circles, the precisely timed tintinnabulation of their bells, and their serenely downcast eyes. All other Japanese dances, from the various formal schools to Noh and Kabuki, find their roots in the sacred *kagura* dance of the shrine, which, to Noda-san, is always over too soon. The *miko* bow deeply before the altar, turn to their right, and glide back to their seats on the same side of the stage as the Gūji, making the little half steps and shuffles as if of a single mind.

It was a dance similar to this which, along with the *gagaku* music, lured Amaterasu out of her cave, although according to the ancient texts, the first *kagura* dances also resorted to a little striptease when the dancing maiden became divinely possessed and lifted up her robes. A faint smile crosses Noda-san's face as he recalls a late-night drinking session with one of the other priests who was extolling a return to the original archetypes: "With the newly resurrected ancient *kagura* that follows the *exact* letter of the myths and with attractive *miko*, why, the shrine would never have to worry about community involvement and financial support again!"

Noda-san's last official duty of this equinoctial ritual is to deliver to the Gūji the offering he will make on behalf of all the shrine's priests and employees: the sprig of waxy green leaves, called *tamagushi*, from the sacred *sakaki* tree. The two Chinese ideograms used for this offering—the first meaning "soul" and the second "linkage"—appear to say all there is to say about its purpose. As the Gūji makes another slow trip to his dais before the altar, the stem of the *tamagushi* branch is pointed to his body's center: the heart/soul (located in the abdominal region), the *hara*. But as he lays it upon the offering table, he turns the stem toward the altar, a completion of the circle that brought the Kami to humanity via the tree of the original sacred enclosure.

Noda-san has joined the other priests, and they all, though still sitting, squarely face the altar. The Gūji is representing everyone in the entire shrine, so that when he bows twice, his head nearly touching the floor, the priests also bow. When the Gūji lays down his wooden scepter in preparation to clap twice, yin and yang, Noda-san and the others mimic his actions, though their bows and claps must be a fraction of a second behind the Gūji's, creating a wavelike effect as the sound washes out from the altar into the hall and over the worshippers. A final low bow (the musicians and *miko* have remained bowing the entire time) and the priests' souls are again, via the wondrous movements of this ritual, believed to be connected to the Kami.

After the assembled guests and participants have followed suit and performed their bows and claps, Noda-san uses the interval to glance at the faces slightly below him to determine who will make the first offering of the sacred sprig, who the second, and so on until everyone has had a chance. To slight anyone's social status or age would be a wrong not easily forgotten, even in a relatively unimportant ritual like this one. Obviously, the first sprig must go to the three elderly men who are the shrine's chairmen for the planning of the major fall festival, the second to the women representing the laywomen's group which meets at the shrine twice a month, and the final ones evenly distributed to groups of three and four. It always surprises him that, even in this day and age of indifference and increasing isolation due to TV, industrialization, and the anomie of modern life in general, most people still know how to hold the little branch, come forward, and make their bows and claps in a fairly respectful manner. Even the tall foreign tourist was a good sport about it during last month's festival, though his knees cracked frightfully when he rose from the hardwood floor.

When the slow rounds have been made, the small table laden with branches is placed beside the Gūji's table. With the smiles received as he passed out the branches still warm in his memory, Noda-san loudly announces to the audience, "*Tessen!*" which tells them that the offerings just made, as well as those made at the start of the service, will now be withdrawn (to prevent their despoilment). The musicians again produce their eerie music, and the three senior priests remove the offerings in the same way they placed them: hand to hand, bow to bow, the rice first and the sacred rice wine last.

The only step remaining is for Noda-san to slowly stand, again cross the smooth stage and bow before the Gūji, then lead him to a mat placed in the eastern corner of the hall. Were the shrine in the far north of Japan, he would go to the southern corner; were it in California, to the west—whatever orientation is appropriate to direct his bows to the shrine of Amaterasu at Ise. Two bows, two claps, a final bow of renewal, and the service is at its "official" close, but not quite yet completed.

What remains is a private partaking of a sip of the special rice wine that has been offered to the Kami. The soul has been linked to the deities by the *norito* prayer and *tamagushi* offerings; now it is the body's turn to experience through the wine a communion with the Kami. Those invited guests in attendance will be meeting with the Gūji in a few moments to enjoy a few drinks and snacks that now symbolize the *naorai*, a post-ritual banquet that creates a transition between the sacred and secular worlds. The uninvited participants are now waiting in line to have the *miko* pour a bit of *o-miki* wine into a small dishlike cup, but Noda-san, the senior priests, and the musicians, pressed with official duties, will have to find a quiet moment on their own to enjoy the sweet and fragrant "ambrosia of the Kami."

Back in the changing rooms, as Noda-san carefully folds his robes, places the tall hat into its protective box, and examines the lacquer of his clogs before storing them, the other priests are alternately complimenting and teasing him about his performance. Depending on their rank, he ventures a defense or laughs along with them, making it a point nevertheless to remember what each one says with the intent of further refining his actions and understanding. "If he stays out of trouble and brings his pretty wife around sometime for us to meet, maybe we'll let him present the sacred food offerings next time—what do you think, Senior Priest Ureshino?"

"Well maybe, but only if he buys me a drink tonight after work." So much for Noda-san's plans of watching a video at home with his wife and telling her all about the ritual for the observation of the vernal equinox.

6

HEAD PRIEST
UESUGI

My initial encounter with the head priest of
Suwa Shrine occurred in a rather unlikely place. I was having dinner
at Nagasaki's only Indian restaurant and my companion, a resident
of the city for several years, took delight in pointing out to me a
rather unassuming man sitting at the counter as being the chief of
the city's main Shinto shrine. Succumbing to those stereotypes assigned to aspects of Japanese culture by naive foreigners, I was surprised to see someone who I supposed should be "holy" at all times,
not only out on the town in a smart business suit and silk tie, but
also enjoying with gusto a spicy curry dinner. After all, didn't the
temples and shrines still have stone monuments at their gates warning away persons who had indulged in spicy or "stinky" vegetables,
meat, or similar strong "potions"?

Later during my first year in Nagasaki, one of my neighbors,
Mr. Sasaki Yō, an Episcopal priest, presented me with a free ticket
to the huge fall festival known nationally as Okunchi, which began
on the grounds of Suwa Shrine (see chapter 15). The tickets had
come from Head Priest Uesugi himself as a way of saying thank you
for my neighbor's participation in the yearly commemorative service
in honor of the victims of the atomic bombing, a service probably
unique in all the world in that it combines Christian, Buddhist, and
Shinto elements in tribute to the more than 70,000 people killed on
August 9, 1945.[1] I was immensely impressed by the pageantry and
organization of Okunchi and decided to begin a systematic study of
the shrine's public and private rituals if I could only gain a proper
introduction. Again, my kindly neighbor intervened and arranged a
formal meeting for the three of us. After our initial conversation, we
were given a splendid tour of the shrine and were even allowed to
enter the Hall of Offerings, a gesture that was quite an honor for the
Episcopal priest, as he later told me.

I soon learned that the head priest was not a native of Nagasaki but a recent arrival like myself—someone whose values and experiences were of a different order from those common to the area. While the international and national image of the city is of a cosmopolitan center of commerce that has had long-standing contacts with the outside world, the truth is that the Tokugawa government was so conspicuous and heavy-handed in its administration of this contact that the average person felt quite intimidated. Add to this the continued strategic importance assigned to Nagasaki by military rulers right up to 1945, its geographic isolation at the extreme southern tip of Japan, plus a steady series of natural disasters such as floods, typhoons, and an occasional earthquake, and you have a formula for developing a highly conservative cultural gestalt—where, as Head Priest Uesugi learned, the old ways are the best ways simply because everyone accepts them. What follows are his words, without the usual question-and-answer format of most interviews. I should also add that, although brief, the information presented was gathered during the course of casual questioning after more formal "lessons" he very graciously bestowed upon me after I had witnessed a ritual and was bursting with questions. Needless to say, without his interest in conveying to me the meanings (as he saw them) of Shinto practice and belief, this book would never have been written.

*　　*　　*

"There really isn't much interesting about my life. My family is one of the oldest in a town called Furukawa, deep in the mountains of central Japan, in Nagano Prefecture. My father was a merchant and collector of the guardian dog statues you see at the entrance to shrine precincts—in fact, we established the only museum of its kind in Japan. Even though we weren't connected with a shrine, we were a family that carefully observed all the important Shinto rites at home. As a young man, I wanted to be a part of the spirit of the times and so went to Tokyo to attend Kokugakuin University, where I received an education in a lot more than Shinto.

"I guess you could say that I was the recipient, victim, and survivor of the education I received. Even until the end of the war, the school never relinquished its purpose to produce men and women who were willing to give their lives for the glory of the Japanese empire. In fact, I was in training as a kamikaze pilot when the war ended. I was ready to send my plane into a ship that perhaps your father was on—isn't that incredible to think about now? Well, I was absolutely devastated that the war ended and I was unable to give my life in the service of the emperor, but I guess I was meant for other things.

"I went back to Furukawa after the war to help with the family business and take over as the administrator of the museum. After the initial tough years passed and Japan's recovery began, I once again wanted to be in Tokyo and so took a job in the office of the Central Association of Shinto Shrines—the coordinating body that helps give a structure to the thousands of independent shrines throughout Japan. I worked hard and developed a good business skill, which was essential for survival after the war, and eventually became head of the office. I also became a full-fledged priest and began my rise through the ranks.

"When the call came from the board of regents in Nagasaki for a new head priest in 1981, I saw it as a golden opportunity to try to combine my knowledge of Shinto with my business skills since I knew they were going to remodel their old shrine. But when I got down here and saw the architect's plans for a ferroconcrete structure I said no, absolutely no. We would find a way to make a shrine that preserved the lines and aesthetics of the old building and traditional Shinto styles. It was hard going but, as you've seen, the shrine is all *hinoki* wood, with only a few places compromising to a modern need for convenience or comfort. People who come here seem genuinely impressed and pleased to be able to worship in such a beautiful shrine.

"Still, I know there were many people who would have rather let the old building just fall to pieces instead of changing it in any way. Several of the older priests felt they had to resign instead of adapting to the reality that something just had to be done. Fortunately, the regents always supported me and I was successful in raising the necessary funds to finance the construction ($650,000), but it was hard going during those first few years and I'm afraid I stepped on a lot of toes.

"There are two or three more things I'd like to accomplish in Nagasaki but eventually I'd like to transfer to a shrine where I can take things a little easier, and maybe write a book or two, or teach at a university. Most Gūji are in a position to delegate their authority to the assistant gūji but, and this is an unfortunate situation, I'm just not ready to do that. Of course, I want to see the traditions I've begun here carried on in a more or less continuous manner—just like any parent with his child—but, after all the hard work I've put in, to surrender so much control is not my way. This is one of the most troubling problems I'm currently facing and I'm not sure how it's going to be resolved.

"The problem is that people older than me are too old and that there just aren't many other people my own age to assume positions of authority and responsibility. So many of my own generation were lost in the war. Do you know that after the war there were so few men around that the government gave us permission to have more than one wife so we could replenish the population? So when I talk about the role I'm fulfilling now, it's not because I see my-self as being especially skilled or adept, it's just because there isn't anyone else.

"I suppose anyone can feel the gaps between generations in Japan, but for someone like myself, coming from Tokyo to here, it is even more obvious. I'm thinking now of the *shinjinrui*, or "new human beings," that the popular media are so fond of talk-ing about—and I don't mean the street dancers in Harajuku or the motorcycle gangs. I'm referring to the effect that the ero-sion of values and traditions is having on the young people today. It's especially obvious at the shrine when we get a group of new female attendants who are seventeen or eighteen. They have to be taught everything—not only the offertory dances they do in a ritual but how to act in public to begin with! Many of them don't know how to use chopsticks correctly or how to address people with the correct words instead of mumbling some half-audible answer. I re-member one time, when I brought a group of twelve guests back to the banquet hall for the feast following a major ceremony, the *miko* had put out twelve place settings but that was all. No cushions to sit on, no hand towels, not even any ashtrays. I had to ask for all these things to be brought out, which, done before the eyes of the guests, was very rude. You can be sure that never happened again. I know that most people don't need to act with the same degree of decorum for guests as a shrine does, but some understanding of social etiquette is essential for living in this culture.

"We hear a lot of talk these days about how Japan is regarded as one of the world's advanced societies—and that may be true materially—but culture is something which can't be classified as being high or low. One of my friends went to Africa to write a re-port as part of his job in the media and came away with the idea that although material progress is obvious, cultural progress can't be quantified. A culture's values cannot be classified on a scale. People might think that Africans are primitive because they don't have electricity or water systems, but that isn't a valid way to judge whether they are or are not primitive. They have a richness of spirit—something the Japanese had in olden times but which seems to be rapidly vanishing today. China, India, and Korea, as well as other countries, had it too, but China, in particular, after six trips there, is somewhere I don't care to go again because the revolution they had completely altered the flow of cultural traditions and values.

"Since I've got a daughter in Frankfurt, I've made a number of trips to Europe as well. You might remember when Ureshino-san and I went to Portugal last fall at the invitation of the government to conduct a couple of Shinto rituals as part of Lisbon's Japanese culture fair. I remember several people asking afterward about whether the rites we conducted imitate Catholic ceremonies, and they were quite astonished when I told them Shinto is nearly 2,000 years old. They knew that their countrymen came to Japan in the 1500s and played an important role in the development of Nagasaki as a port, but I guess they never imagined that there was anything there before that. I don't know what they thought, and these were supposedly educated people!

"But that got me thinking about the religions that existed in Europe before the advent of Christianity, religions which existed within the limitations of the natural environment. All these beliefs have the same basic ideas concerning the sanctity of the environment and man's place in relation to powers greater than himself. However, there is one big difference in the case of Shinto and that is there has never been blood sacrifice of any kind. The Imperial court of the Nara era (ca. 700 C.E.) spoke Korean, and one of the famous female empresses was rumored to have been a Korean, but even with that considerable closeness to Korea and China the idea of sacrifice didn't catch hold.

"That says a lot about Shinto I think. It is unique among all the world's beliefs because it is so closely allied to the actual geography of these islands that make up Japan. Perhaps that's why it's been able to survive all these centuries, that as long as the land and ocean are as they are, in the nonurban areas at least, then there will be a foundation for the nation's continued growth. It's a natural extension of the natural features of Japan—maybe that's the best way to say it. I see my role as a chief priest and community leader as a great privilege and great responsibility, one I probably take too seriously!"

SPRING

7

BEANS VERSUS DEMONS

Spring in Japan encourages a temporary indulgence in those images long associated with the country and its culture in general. As Osaka- and Tokyo-based television stations report on the slow northward advance of cherry blossom season, one is inundated with images of flower-laden branches of *sakura* trees from late January (Okinawa) to May (Hokkaido), usually with a venerated castle, a picturesque temple, or Fuji-esque mountains in the background. In Shinto practice, however, there are other associations with the season that precede those of flowering trees and warming temperatures. To talk about the "Shinto spring" is to evoke older orientations to the natural cycle of seasons based upon the lunar calendar instead of the romanticized postcard images generated by the mass media. The "birth of spring" (*risshun*) occurs after the close of the period of "minor cold" (*shokan*) in early February—despite the fact that what really begins is the season of the greatest cold (*daikan*), when physical, rather than spiritual, comfort urges one to huddle around the stove, keep one's feet under the *kotatsu* foot-warming table, or plunge into a steaming bath.

An important transition such as this, which marked the beginning of a new agricultural year, simply could not pass without some kind of ritual observance that provided an awareness of the greater forces the community needed to hold in balance in order to survive and prosper and that helped manage the anxiety associated with agricultural production. Many of these rites have their roots in Shinto's millennium-long cooperation with Buddhism. As preparation for the planting season and the rest of the agricultural year, a variety of exorcisms and purifications were performed and remain today vital organs in the body of Shinto ritual practice. Who would want to compromise the clean slate of a new season by trailing behind oneself shadows of illness, misfortune, or misdeed, or by neglecting to utilize protective charms against future troubles? Since these are monumental concerns not only for the individual but for the community as well—especially those early habitations dependent on intense inter-family cooperation for the cultivation and irrigation of rice fields—*matsuri* festivals of protection against evil's many manifestations became one of the highlights of the shrine/temple ritual cycle.

Each institution has its own way of handling these concerns, but three principal methods were generally available for the local priests or shamans to employ.[1] First, a practice continues to this day of designating a scapegoat, animate or inanimate, which receives all accumulated evil and bad luck (see the Oharae ritual's use of paper dolls in chapter 12). Although there are theories that human scapegoats were periodically sacrificed when influence from China was at its height in the sixth and eighth centuries, little archeological evidence has been found to suggest this might have been anything but a temporary practice. In fact, along with Buddhism, Shinto sees the shedding of blood as a vile act that cries out for purification through the power of the Kami. Another method available for dealing with impurities is a wide range of combative practices that employ offensive weapons and techniques to attack evil forces. This may entail slicing through evils with a sword or, as we shall see in chapter 10, employing boiling water to dispel impurities.[2]

The third and, in many ways, most exciting means of exorcising evil influences occurs when they are personified in the body of a demon (*oni*), who must then be prevented from rampaging through the village and further polluting the local environment. Sometimes the demons are very visible, as in the Tohoku region in the far north, where they literally storm into houses and terrify the children until they promise to be good for the coming year, or when the demons try to invade a shrine or temple only to be repelled by valiant priests, who shoot arrows at them. Other times, they are invisible forces menacing the well-being of the community. In all cases, preventive and protective measures must be undertaken by the religious authorities to not only assuage the anxieties of individuals but also empower them in their struggle against seemingly capricious ills and spiritual defilements so common to the profane world.

The Setsubun festival is one of the year's most important, not because it is solemn and intense in its exorcism of whatever raging demons are besieging the community, but rather because it is noisy and lively, illuminated by bonfires and punctuated with the sound of laughter and excited screams as magical talismans are hurled into the void of the night sky. *Setsubun* means "change of seasons," but as its mythic charter prescribes, the festival's purpose is purification and the ending of evil. Instead of offering the polished explanation of one of the senior priests concerning how the festival developed in response to a terrible plague and famine in the seventh century, I prefer a ruddy-faced grandmother's recounting of the story as we stood warming our hands beside a bonfire of last year's amulets and New Year's decorations:

> So you want to know why we're having this Setsubun festival tonight when it's so cold? All right, I'll tell you what I learned from my grandfather and you can believe it if you want to. Long, long ago, a terrible demon lived in a cave near Lake Misoro in Kumano Prefecture. This was a particularly bad demon because not only did it commit all sorts of crimes during the day, it also came out at night to snatch young girls and do things to them I can't tell you about because you're a man and it wouldn't be proper [giggles]. Brave warriors tried to kill it, but they themselves were killed or defeated. Mountain ascetics tried to exorcise it with various spells and incantations, but its evil was too strong for even the sacred sutras they were using. Then one day, seven wise men, who were sent by the emperor himself, arrived at the cave and pooled their great learning to fight that demon. You might think they had some special magical prayer but no, what they did was to throw parched *beans* into the cave, and then they blocked the entrance with the heads of *sardines* and the leaves of the *hiragi* tree [Japanese holly]. Don't ask me why it was beans and sardines and not something else — because they were *magic* and kept that demon in the cave forever. So we still throw the beans even though most people don't put up the sardine head anymore . . . and there you have it!

With this myth as a charter for auspicious actions based upon the magical efficacy of beans and sardines, popular custom appropriated the practice of casting soybeans in the direction designated as the lucky quarter for the year, and then *twice* that many in the unlucky direction. But an action without some kind of incantation would seem like a meal without rice, and so from school classrooms to corporate headquarters to temples and shrines throughout Japan, people shout, "Out with all demons! Come in good fortune!! [*Oni wa soto! Fuku wa uchi!*]." There are many variations on this practice, one of which holds that the proper way to cast out impurities is to wrap a number of beans equal to one's age, plus an extra bean, into a white paper and then leave it at a busy crossroads. When it is stepped on by some inadvertent messenger of the deities, the person who placed the little bundle becomes free of accumulated evils. There are also those who, after having scattered a number of beans equal to their age, then painstakingly pick each one up, roast them, and happily devour each talisman of good fortune.

At Suwa Shrine, preparations for the Setsubun festival begin shortly after New Year's Day as a call goes out to members of the community born under the new zodiacal sign who have somehow distinguished themselves (or are distinguishable due to their economic, media, or sports presence). In Edo and prewar times, the luminaries were always men and often only a single individual was so honored, but at Suwa Shrine in the late 1980s women are also included among those standing on a raised stage who throw out the magical beans to an excited crowd while the master of ceremonies chants *"Oni wa soto! Fuku wa uchi!"* from loudspeakers at an earsplitting volume. The crowd of young and old unceremoniously scramble for the beans, holding up sacks and open umbrellas—anything that will allow them to catch a few and thus keep away harm during the coming year. Additionally, as pointed out by the myth-spinning grandmother we met earlier, if one eats three Setsubun-beans during a thunderstorm, one will not be hit by lightning!

This particular year, however, a different kind of preparation, unlike any undertaken before, has been under way for weeks. Through their contacts in city hall and in the local television and news media, the priests at Suwa Shrine learned that during this year's Setsubun festival there would be a radar ship from the U.S. Seventh Fleet anchored in Nagasaki's fine and deep harbor. Would it not foster international goodwill—and be educational at the same time—to make a special effort to invite the sailors and officers of the U.S. Navy to participate in the shrine's festival? After all, the reasoning went, the war ended over forty years ago; what better way to have a meeting of cultures than through an ancient ritual conducted for the purpose of warding off evil (which is, after all, what armies are all about)? And, since the addition of a lottery, a local talent show, and speeches from dignitaries have recently made the evening into real entertainment, the lonely sailors so far from home would probably enjoy it a great deal. Of course, the television stations would want to cover something as significant as this, so think also of the free publicity the shrine would get while promoting international understanding. Why, it might even make the NHK national news!

But some of the older and younger priests were not so sure. How can we justify, they argued, a special invitation to members of the U.S. military when their fathers were the ones who dropped the atomic bomb on Nagasaki? The Red Cross Hospital for Victims of the Bombing is still full of those suffering from radiation-related diseases—and we've never gone out of our way to invite *them*, or inquire very much into their spiritual needs. And wouldn't it be especially inappropriate in the eyes of many of the bomb survivors to be *inviting* the "evil" of the military into the shrine at the very time we are supposed to be exorcising all evils impeding the new year? The debate went on for some time until an unexpected event occurred.

A week before the arrival of the radar ship, many religious leaders from Nagasaki's Buddhist temples, Christian churches, and several shrines received invitations to a formal reception given jointly by the ship's chaplain and captain "to foster international goodwill and peace." Everyone was quite surprised and a little perplexed, because now, how could the shrine ignore their obligation to reciprocate and not invite the officers and crew to the Setsubun festival? In the eyes of the older priests, educated in prewar codes of honor and etiquette, there was simply no alternative other than to send a representative to the reception and offer a return invitation. Those community members who objected (like the local antinuclear peace group, which consistently demonstrates against the arrival of American military ships) would simply have to see things in the proper social context of host (shrine) and guest (the ship). To withhold one's hospitality simply because of the political or historical background of the guest was out of the question. Weren't the officers and crew scheduled to visit the Peace Park and lay a wreath at the monument for the more than 70,000 killed at the time of the atomic bombing?

The chief priest was, of course, at the center of all these debates and took it upon himself to attend the reception as the shrine's representative. A former navy officer himself who was being trained to fly on a mission when the war ended, he said later that what motivated his attendance at the reception was a complicated mix of professional camaraderie as a former officer, curiosity to see the inside of a U.S. ship, and a genuine desire to further international and shrine interests for peace. Although it was cold and pouring rain, he came dressed in an immaculate suit and topcoat, complete with a tweed hat, and presented an appearance no different from one of the senior executives of a major corporation. In his briefcase, however, were not the plans for an overseas factory but 250 one-page, single-spaced information sheets in English about Shinto shrines, the worship of Kami, and Suwa Shrine's past, all of which ended with a special invitation to the ship's crew to attend the Setsubun festival on the coming night. Directions followed on how to reach the shrine.

Although the U.S. Navy had thoughtfully arranged the reception for the local religious leaders, they had not considered that few, if any, of them would be able to speak English. With no translator present, after a welcoming toast and lots of well-meaning smiles, the gathering soon fragmented into Japanese and American contingents —the naval officers occasionally breaking into loud laughter on one side of the dingy "banquet" room, and the Japanese priests and ministers (who were not all that well acquainted with each other) quietly conversing on the other about the terrible weather and if Suwa Shrine could hold its traditional Setsubun festival the coming night.

Within half an hour the party was over, but not before the chief priest had summoned what little English he knew and presented to the ship's now slightly inebriated captain the neat stack of information/invitation sheets for his officers and crew. "We'd be so happy for you to come," he said with difficulty, "For you and your crew, this will be a nice party at our shrine." The captain diplomatically answered that on behalf of his men and ship he gratefully accepted the offer and thanked the chief priest for his invitation. He then turned to one of the orderlies in the room and said, "Sailor, see to it that these are distributed via Mr. McCann," before shaking the priest's hand one more time and then excusing himself to return to his place in what seemed, when viewed from the back, a wall of blue uniforms.

Mission accomplished, the chief priest made his way down the three flights of narrow steps within the ship, then, pelted with stinging rain, down the outdoor gangway and into a waiting taxi. As he rode back to the shrine, several things occurred to him: what if *all* the sailors came? The shrine didn't have nearly enough sake for everyone at once. And what if they came from bars already drunk? There could be fights and an incident with the police, and that would defeat the whole purpose of inviting them in the first place, not to mention the political setback he'd face within the power structure of the shrine. Still, he felt that it was the right thing to have done and, having carried out his mission, pushed whatever misgivings he had into a far corner of his mind.

The next day was overcast and cold, but the rain stopped, affording the younger priests enough time to scurry around and supervise construction of the stage for the evening's activities. There would first be an opening welcome by the chief priest, then a tossing of the magical beans by one group of *toshi-bito* (or people born in the year of the Snake), a sword dance, a speech by the head of one of the shrine's volunteer organizations, another bean-tossing (one every half hour for three hours), followed by a dance by two of Nagasaki's well-known geisha, who would then assist the chief priest in conducting a lottery for several gold coins as well as for lesser prizes. The areas where people would throw their depleted New Year decorations to be burned were swept and ringed by four bamboo poles topped with sacred rope (*shimenawa*), and the bottles of sake to be discreetly consumed by the fire departments watching these bonfires were made ready. In the same outbuilding where the fire department's sake bottles were stored were several extra cases now ready for the American sailors who would be in attendance. Everyone had been instructed to be as patient and friendly as possible, especially since the media would be present.

But an odd thing happened. After the bonfires had been lit and heaped high with the once-magic wooden arrows, straw talismans, and other decorations, the hour to begin the Setsubun activities came and went with no sign of a single American serviceman. A brief ritual before the shrine's Kami altar was conducted to consecrate the evening's program and charge with efficacy the beans to be cast over the crowd. Once the *toshi-bito*, dressed in their splendid kimonos, were assembled and the beans distributed, the first round of exorcism was due to begin. "*Oni wa soto! Fuku wa uchi!*" was shouted over and over, as thousands of beans were cast from the brightly lit stage, arching briefly through the night sky before falling in some lucky person's hat, upturned hands, or open sack. "Grandmother! I got *five* that time!" "Dad, put the boy on your shoulders and then he can catch one!" "Hey you, stop jumping in front of me and stealing my beans!" The crowd was larger than last year's and filled the courtyard of the shrine's middle terrace with families, young and old couples alike, lost children crying for their mothers, a few high school students en route to evening cram schools (or, still in uniform, coming home), groups of single office girls buying fortunes and vying for the lucky beans that keep unfavorable suitors at bay, plus individuals with every variety of still and video camera imaginable—in short, all the typical participants of a Suwa Shrine public festival!

As for the American sailors, nothing more was ever said about them, although I wondered what had happened. Had the "Mr. McCann" responsible for distributing the information handouts been, as I feared, the trash can? Did the captain know his men well enough to mistrust their behavior at a religious festival and thus never informed them about it? Or was it more a political and military decision in that he didn't want his trained technicians fraternizing with the citizens of a city once so devastated by an atomic bomb that lingering hatreds might boil into acts of terrorism and violence at the slightest provocation? How would he explain *that* to his superiors? And all for the chance to see some silly ritual to keep away demons, which, as anyone with education knows, don't even exist!

8

In any organization or institution, there are those tireless individuals who seem to be everywhere at once: the person who arranges a meeting, serves as its chairperson or master of ceremonies, and then puts away the folding chairs afterward. Matsumoto-san, a priest of the *negi* rank, is one such person at Suwa Jinja, someone whose energy seems to fuel and sustain much of what goes on. He can be found working on the considerable coordination required to enact the monthly rituals, visiting the preschool adjacent to the shrine, or madly typing on a computer in the business office, the *shamusho*. A scene typical of his prodigious energy and responsibilities was the final Okunchi festival procession that I witnessed. It fell upon his shoulders to be the one obligated to organize a procession consisting of nearly five hundred people who were to follow the three Kami of Suwa Shrine as they traveled through the city to a temporary structure near the waterfront. From the senior priests riding horses, to squads of dancers representing the various neighborhoods participating that year, to the three sacred palanquins and their bearers, to mothers and children in kimonos (many of the latter whining and crying in the steamy October sun)—there he was moving quickly in his white kimono and blue *hakama* bloomers, sometimes gently cajoling a group to start moving, other times barking out orders to a group of young male bearers who had already been sampling the festival sake.

As one trying to photograph as much of the long procession as I could, I kept at its head during the first half mile, watching group after resplendent group pass by. And since someone had to be last but no one really wanted the "status" associated with the position, who should be at the end but Matsumoto-san, rather forlornly banging on a drum with every other step, his megaphone slung over his back. As will be presented in more detail in the chapter on Okunchi (chapter 15), once the bearers of the *mikoshi* palanquins near the procession's destination, the custom is for them to come racing into the open area before the temporary shrine with a great yell. Naturally I wanted to be there, and after spotting Matsumoto-san at the end of the parade, I ran through the back alleys of Nagasaki's warren-like neighborhoods, reaching the waterfront only moments before the big drums from within the shrine began heralding the visiting Kami. Though I expected the golden palanquins to be first, I perhaps should have known that it would be none other than a sprinting Matsumoto-san, drum and megaphone flying, who, like some messenger of the Kami, paved the way for the uproar now following in his wake. What follows is a brief look into some of the energies and motivations that make him "run."

*　　*　　*

"I suppose you've heard about those mythical islands or places where there are only women? What's the name of that island in Greek mythology? Lesbon, no, . . . it's Lesbos, or something close to that. Well, the fishing village I'm from is a place like that because for centuries all the men have naturally been fishermen. When they leave to go fishing, sometimes staying away for months, it's the women who must carry on the business of the village—everything from administration to carrying the portable shrines through the streets at our shrine's festival. There is even a story, most likely true, about the women having sumo wrestling bouts! Now that's something I'd like to see.

"But that was before my time, of course. There is still a large fishing population, both on the factory ships and on locally owned vessels, but the majority of work is now done either in the terraced fields around the village, where the people grow rice or tangerines, or in Nagasaki. I suppose that makes me like everyone else, commuting forty minutes each way in my Honda, except that I'm trying to make the service for morning prayers instead of punching in at the time clock.

"We believe our family shrine to be about 1,200 years old, which puts it right up there with some of the oldest in the nation, like Ise and Izumo. Like many other shrines and temples in the Nagasaki area, it was burned by Christians in the late 1500s and all the detailed records were destroyed. But since it finally got rebuilt around 1650, someone has always taken care to write down dates and such, although I'll be the first to admit my own skepticism about that ancient founding date. There were people in the area that long ago, however, so it's maybe not as farfetched as it might seem. And this village does have a lovely harbor, so who knows? There must be some reason why the old ceiling murals in the lower shrine building depict scenes of Chinese and Korean ships landing here.

"What's always interested me about this village is the fact that even though 99 percent of the families in Tsuchimi would classify themselves as Buddhist, still, almost everyone participates whenever the shrine has one of its major festivals—either the spring or the fall—and, of course, everyone makes a visit at the New Year to pray for happiness and get a new amulet for the family altar.

"When I think about how I became a priest, it seems like a long time ago. My father, who was the Gūji of Tsuchimi Shrine, died soon after I was born, leaving my mother with one child: me. I don't remember him at all but she tells stories of his notoriety for drinking heavily and doing things that he shouldn't have, and probably that is what brought on his early death. At any rate, my mother took over the administration of the shrine and became its chief priestess. It was obvious that I was expected to follow suit eventually, and after high school, I went to attend Kokugakuin University in Tokyo. I probably would have just blindly drifted along doing my studies, but a couple of important things happened to me there.

"During my first year, one of my closest friends suddenly killed himself for what seemed like no reason at all. I met him at a recreation club where I'd been going to play around and socialize (I also met my wife there), but what he did really forced me to think deeply about a lot of things—in particular, death. As you know, this is not a topic that Shinto likes to even think about, but it does exist and I had to face it directly at that time. I became obsessed with trying to understand it and got the idea that I should talk with people who had some experience with it, you know, like surgeons and war veterans who'd been on the front lines.

"Well, I was really surprised. Out of a hundred veterans that I interviewed, I never heard even one of them say that he heard anyone cry out 'Long live the emperor! [*Tennōheika banzai!*]' at the moment of death. They said they heard 'Long life to Mother!' or

'Remember me, Papa!' but never anything about glory to the emperor, like some of the war movies would have you believe. This didn't help me understand my friend's death very much, but it was a revelation nonetheless—that all the mental conditioning the Japanese people suffered before and during the war, much of it through the misdirection of Shinto symbols and teaching at the hands of the militarists, was just a lot of empty words. It changed how I personally felt about the emperor as well, but I won't go into that. After all, he is officially the supreme head priest for all of Shinto [see Fisher 1987].

"Those interviews led me to pursue studies about the customs surrounding death in other cultures and I was determined to write my graduation thesis about all the research I was doing. You know, about the customs of people like the Zoroastrians and the Tibetans. But then I fell in love! Well, that changed a lot in my orientation to the world, and I went from being interested in death to being interested in children and things that my fiancée was interested in, like dance and the arts. I thought there was so much more to the world than being a priest in some remote fishing village's shrine, so that after graduation I didn't return immediately. For awhile I worked as a sales representative for a large publishing company, and even did a stint as a TV news announcer for the Asahi network. You don't believe me? It's true!

"But my mother frequently reminded me of my promise to her to return, plus her health wasn't good and the shrine needed tending, so I finally faced up to my responsibilities and decided to get married and come back to Tsuchimi. Of course, I couldn't support a family just on the small income from donations to this little shrine so I started serving at Suwa Shrine some twelve years ago. Just like the junior priests do now, I was initially in charge of the chores no one else of higher rank wanted to do. But one of those things was going to children's groups and talking about Shinto.

"As you can imagine, after the war Shinto wasn't very popular, and no one wanted to hear much about it, but by the time I came to Suwa Shrine people had become concerned about the loss of values that an industrialized society was causing. Especially students have no connection of any kind with a shrine, save for the Kami of learning, Tenmangū, whom they pray to before big tests, and the yearly New Year's visits. So it was one of my tasks to go talk to children and try to get them involved in a few shrine activities, like the Okunchi festival. The things they learn and experience from the festival are not something they appreciate at the time, but as they get older they realize that it was special and that Suwa Shrine played a part in shaping their life. That's what develops a relationship between the community and the shrine, I think. Kids might also hear about the shrine when their brother or uncle or aunt talks about their wedding ceremony, which was most likely performed here—and again, that deepens their awareness of the shrine as an important place where significant things happen.

"My current role as 'activities director' gives me the chance to try and help events move along, but it's really a lot of work. Still, I'm quite satisfied with shrine life, especially when I see one of my own ideas adopted and carried out. That's very rewarding. But I'm still young, in fact too young to have much weight in the overall say of things and that's frustrating. I wish I could get older quickly and advance in rank and start making policy instead of always being the guy who must carry it out no matter what he thinks about it. But I'll persevere.

"The thing I'm most concerned with now is not Suwa Shrine but the new road that the prefectural government is building along the coast right behind our shrine at Tsuchimi. We are being forced to move from our house because the highway would be one step in front of the entrance, but we can't find an empty house in the village to move into. Everyone thinks the new road will do wonders for the village economy and bring more tourists from the city out to our area, as well as cut down on the commuting time to the city for people like myself who drive there every day—but it will totally end our way of life. I'm sure my mother's mother, who is now eighty-eight and very frail, is going to have the hardest time, but it won't be easy for any of us really. The shrine will be okay, being up on top of the hill, but the entire environment will change when the cars and big trucks start roaring by. It's really a problem but I suppose there's nothing we can do about it.

"Somewhere in the future, I hope I get the chance to travel and observe the religions of other cultures. One of my great desires is to go to Tibet or India to see the Zoroastrian-type funeral customs, where the bodies are left for the birds, as well as see the big temples of Tibetan Buddhism and the little shrines of the older shamanistic beliefs. I'd also like to go to Korea and see the spirit mediums who are said to be able to communicate with the netherworlds—a tradition that predates Shinto, being connected with Taoism and Chinese folk religion. My interest still remains in the place where the vertical world of Heaven and the horizontal world of human beings intersects. To be a Shinto priest and to help others gain access to that place—well, though it might change in the future, right now there's really nothing else I'd rather be."

9

BACKSTAGE
AT THE
DOLLS' DAY
FESTIVAL

THE GŪJI AS PLAYWRITE

One of the aspects of shrine life that is even more veiled from the observer's eye than the rituals held in the inner Hall of Worship is the relationship between the "services" provided by the priests and the way in which they satisfy the "demands" of the public.[1] The terminology of business is appropriate here because Shinto shrines (as well as Buddhist temples and Christian churches) receive no assistance from the government (a separation put into legal effect by the Occupation forces after the war and then integrated into the national constitution)[2] and are thus wholly dependent upon the goodwill of their parishioners and visitors to supply the funds allowing the shrine to continue as a viable entity. The buildings must be maintained, reconstruction and remodeling loans must be paid on time, the priests' salaries must be met, membership fees in the various regional and national shrine organizations must be rendered each year—and then there are the emergencies, such as flood or typhoon relief efforts (Nagasaki suffered a disastrous downpour in 1982, resulting in landslides and flooding which killed 299 people), to which the shrine is expected to contribute or, one would assume, suffer a loss of face in the community.

But how does a shrine manage to "stay in the black" while at the same time maintaining the traditions so vital to its identity in the first place? Do shrines, like their counterparts in America, have bake sales or conduct "Monte Carlo nights" since there are no weekly services where a collection plate can be passed? In an age when the Japanese mass media hype anything from the latest personal computer or videophone to American rock or movie stars selling whiskey, ham, or fashion hot from Paris, it takes considerable skill to appeal to the necessary "support base" from which to operate. The leader of a large shrine must be not only an intermediary to the Kami and the conveyer of practical knowledge to the younger priests-in-training but also a skilled fund-raiser and organization man who knows how to use the local media to reach the populace in ways that his predecessors of even ten years ago could hardly have imagined.

This dynamic between what appears as "the sacred and the profane" was nowhere better witnessed than at Suwa Shrine during the 1980s. When I first visited the shrine in 1977, its buildings were everything I thought a shrine was supposed to be: deeply weathered wood, splotches of green moss growing on the rooftops, stone steps worn smooth by countless generations of worshippers, all encompassed by an atmosphere of calm, as if the twentieth century had yet to begin (in spite of the fact that the atomic age burst just on the other side of the mountain that shielded the shrine from destruction). Little did I know that the buildings were literally a hazard to be in, so weak had their roofs' support pillars become in the constant dampness of 130 or so years of service (both to the Kami and to sacrilegious termites). The old shrine had a very small staff consisting of an elderly head priest, who had been too sick to conduct services for nearly seven years; an assistant head priest, who, though he fulfilled his senior's obligations, lacked the proper status to be in constant communication with the Kami and therefore really shouldn't have been so busy; plus three or four assistant priests, who did everything from weddings to ground sanctifications to the poorly attended monthly rituals. The saving grace of that period was the annual Okunchi festival held on shrine grounds (as it had been since the early seventeenth century), whose high ticket prices temporarily filled shrine coffers.

Fortunately, a guiding light on the shrine's board of regents (for reasons of privacy his name will go unmentioned) had the foresight to see that the situation was deteriorating and it wouldn't be long before the shrine would be nearly nonexistent. The board therefore appealed to the Central Association of Shinto Shrines in Tokyo, the Jinja Honchō, asking them to recommend several candidates who would be interested in coming to Nagasaki as new head priest and in immediately undertaking a complete revival of the shrine's physical and financial well-being. As we read earlier from the interview with Head Priest Uesugi, he became their man and literally rebuilt the shrine from the foundation up: bonds were passed, renovations were financed, and, perhaps most importantly, the shrine began to assert its presence not only at Okunchi and New Year's but periodically on television news broadcasts and in the local newspaper, with the "Suwa Diary" column running weekly.

The citizens of Nagasaki suddenly noticed in the early 1980s that Suwa Shrine was the site for celebrations of a number of "old" and valued traditions. Demons were driven out by the casting of beans, children were encouraged to participate in the shrine's pre-Okunchi procession, and a Dolls' Day (*hina matsuri*) was celebrated, in which "live" dolls, all attractive twenty-year-old women, wearing the shrine's valuable formal kimonos, participated in a stately procession. As expected, people began to take notice and participate in the pageantry, with older individuals feeling a sense of continuity with the "good old days" and the younger generation enjoying the notoriety of perhaps getting on TV, since there were *always* TV cameras at a Suwa Shrine event. And it was fun as well, or at least more unusual than a shopping foray or new coffeeshop to tell one's friends about. Even if a majority of those in attendance couldn't directly relate to the slow pace of the stately rituals held inside the shrine, these public, dramatic expressions of reconstituted traditions and aesthetics served as entertainment as well as "good press" for the media when they needed to balance out the latest factory closing or budget debate by the municipal government.

As for Uesugi Gūji himself, after making the break with the past and boldly (some say audaciously) forging a new incarnation of the shrine, his reputation as a "mover and shaker" was enhanced with each success—winning him the admiration of some, the resentment of others, but the respect of all. A look at his style—variously the voice of authority and the voice of inner conscience—is afforded by his informal comments to the candidates for participation in the newly instigated Dolls' Day festival procession. The scene takes place in one of the shrine's large conference rooms. By 10:00 in the morning, almost all of the thirty-five chairs are filled with twenty-year-old women, who are wearing clothes meant to impress as well as what must be thirty-five different kinds of cologne. There is very little talk among the women as they nervously wait for the Gūji and his assistants to make their appearance and begin the process of selecting participants for the festival.

"Good morning everyone, and thank you so much for coming. It's a privilege to be in the same room with so many attractive young women all wanting to participate in a festival honoring the Kami of Suwa Shrine." Nervous laughter ripples through his audience, and he continues in a professorial tone, that of *sensei*, or teacher.

"First of all, I'd like to say a few words about the historical background concerning the Dolls' festival. It was officially recorded over a thousand years ago during the Heian period, but it's thought that it is actually much older, maybe as old as 1,600 years. It began because various impurities can accumulate unconsciously and the ancient people recognized that fact, especially at the beginning of the new year.

"When a new year begins, naturally you want to start it with a clean slate, so now we perhaps ring the bell at a temple, then go to worship at a shrine on New Year's Eve. This year probably two-thirds of you came to Suwa Shrine at night or in the morning, didn't you? Or a shrine in your neighborhood?" Many of the women shyly look down, as if remembering.

"But why does this custom of visiting a shrine and praying to the Kami exist? And what do you say on an occasion such as this?" He pauses for effect, studying the faces of the women looking up at him. "Well, as everyone knows, you say 'congratulations on the opening of the year [*akemashite omedeto gozaimasu*].' But what is it you are really congratulating each other about?" The pause after this question is even longer than the first.

"You might think it's because you have just come of age and become an adult and that it's your most lovely time of life. After five years you'll be twenty-five and closer to being a granny [laughter] but even then you'll say 'congratulations.' When you're thirty or even eighty, you still say 'congratulations' even though you grow closer and closer to death.

"The belief of we Japanese is that the new year is given to us from Toshi-gami-sama, or the Kami of years. Therefore, that fact alone makes it special and important, something that we can't waste. What comes from the realm of the Kami is inherently good, which is why we congratulate each other on having received such a precious gift as an entire new year to fill as we can. So, as we look out upon the possibilities of the new year, we want to purify our blunders and sins and cast off whatever evil influences we may have accumulated in the old year. This is really the belief of Japanese at the start of a new year, something I'm sure all of you shared in when you came to a shrine and prayed for a good beginning.

"But, what kind of festival is appropriate for such an occasion? At present, all you have to do is clean your hands and mouth at the water font at the gate of the shrine. In the olden days, however, people did something more formal. They went to a river or to the ocean and submerged themselves in water, thus purifying their hearts in the process.

"However, there was another way of purification, which was to make a small doll out of paper resembling the shape of a person's kimono—a custom called the *hitogata*, which is still around even today, used in the Oharae rituals of June and December. They would then rub this paper cutout upon their body [gesturing to his shoulder] so it could absorb a person's physical and spiritual impurities, then set it adrift in the ocean or river."

Adjusting his glasses, he says in a confidential tone, "But because we Japanese like to elaborate on an idea, gradually eyes and a nose were added to make the dolls more beautiful. But the custom changed so that instead of throwing the dolls in the water, they were placed upon a dresser from year to year. There is still a custom of setting the dolls adrift in a stream or, if you go to Izumo, of putting them into a boat made of rice stalks. This same custom can also be found at Suwa Shrine when you write your name and family on the paper doll and then bring it to the shrine, where it is purified and set adrift.

"Anyway, that was how the Dolls' festival got started. When you come here on March 3 and participate in the festival we're going to conduct, you have to think of yourselves as that type of doll—as an intermediary for others. So if you are acting in the role of the prince or princess doll, or the court noble, court lady, or gentleman or samurai archers, you'll put on the costume and leave yourself behind and try to become the person in that role.

"The order of activities is like this: first, you'll put on the kimono, then participate in a ritual, then ascend the stage, where people from the newspapers and television stations will be photographing your every move." With this bit of information, the women look incredulously at each other, some giggling, some wrinkling their noses, some putting their hands to their mouths as if in embarrassment. "You're all just twenty, very pretty, and at a splendid time in your life, so it's appropriate that you give thanks to the Kami, both for yourselves and the other people your age in all of Nagasaki, whom you'll represent, and for whom you're asking for happy lives.

"Naturally, it's not just one person who makes this festival work. Even though we have the difficult task of choosing only twelve out of this large group, please don't get disgusted or angry if you aren't selected. We would still like to ask for your participation in the festival. Also, if you aren't selected to be the empress, who wears the special twelve-layered silk kimono, we still want your wholehearted cooperation in whatever role you might be asked to fulfill. This is the real spirit of a festival—otherwise, the atmosphere isn't a real festival and the Kami will know it."

Suddenly the Gūji's tone changes, and he delivers his next lines with utmost seriousness. "So if you're a person who will only be satisfied by wearing the twelve-layered kimono, it might be best for you to leave now; otherwise we'll count on your good nature to make this festival a success. Whatever costume you'll be wearing, the important thing to remember is that you'll be worshipping before the Kami and will therefore have to wholeheartedly be who you are.

"When the festival is completed, you'll be presented with certificates of thanks and recognition for your participation, as well as a memorial photograph. So can I have your agreement that you'll be willing to be in any role? Otherwise you'll really give me a problem! You're doing this for the good and benefit of everyone else, and really, that is the key point to remember.

"Oh yes, there's one more important point." Looking at the floor, he audibly draws in his breath, a cultural signal to all that he is somewhat uncomfortable and apologetic about what he must say next. "You're going to have to sit on your knees for a rather long time, about forty minutes, so you'll need to practice a bit. We'll give the principals a low chair but everyone else will have to be on the tatami. But don't worry, we'll give you some pointers about sitting that way. However, if you really think you can't manage it, then it'll be a problem. I know this is a little tough but it's the way the festival is and we just can't change it."[3]

As his speech comes to a close, he is once again all smiles and warmth. "So after we decide today, please take care of your health so that, in case of a cold or sickness, you won't make a huge hole in our cast of dolls by your absence. You are rendering service to the

Kami and for that sole purpose, please look out for yourselves, and make every effort to be here in good health on the third. You can't cancel out, ok? Thank you very much for your understanding and cooperation on these points.

"Now, would the first person to be interviewed by our panel please come forth? The rest of you can get an idea of what the festival is by looking at the photograph albums that'll be circulating. That's right . . . [to the first candidate as she tentatively approaches the front desk, where two other men and myself sit], please don't be embarrassed . . . now what did you say your name was?"

EPILOGUE

Two weeks later, on March 3, the upstairs meeting room of the shrine's business office is transformed from a chaotic jumbling of modern fashion, hairbrushes, makeup, and purses into an imperial dressing room of the Heian period of over a thousand years ago as twelve excited women become the "dolls" of the festival. The most attention is focused on the prince and princess, who, with "his" swords and tall hat and her twelve layers of multicolored silk kimono weighing nearly fifty pounds, must be readied for the camera close-ups that will be shot along the procession's route to the shrine.

With three priest-musicians playing ancient court music in the lead, the prince and princess, their guards dressed in black kimonos, their maids-in-waiting dressed like the *miko*, and their other servants in various shades of green and ocher will pass under several huge torii, ascend three short flights of stairs, then laboriously climb the eighty-eight steps to the shrine's main courtyard, where they will face the final stairs leading to the Hall of Worship. Only then will the choreographed and elaborate preparations, actors, and costumes of the Dolls' Day festival assume their supporting roles as the Gūji rises from his mat and approaches the altar for his first solemn bow. That night on the evening news, the scene will fade as the camera pulls back from the shadows of the inner shrine, to the beams and graceful arches of the roof, then back further to show the entire three-tiered building flanked by very large camphor trees. Finally, as if on the back of a bird, the whole of the Suwa precinct comes into view, nestled in its greenery at the foot of a mountain nearly covered with tiny houses. From the splendid opening procession up the steps to the final somber bonfire where the broken bodies of un-wanted but once-cherished dolls are burned and their souls "sent to heaven," the viewing public will, for a short time, be reminded of some of their culture's foundations, leaving them with a carefully constructed impression that yes, there still are some things which time and the typhoon winds of modernization have not yet claimed.

Fig. 1. Aerial view of Suwa Shrine
(courtesy Mr. Nishida Yasunori, Nagasaki Photo Service)

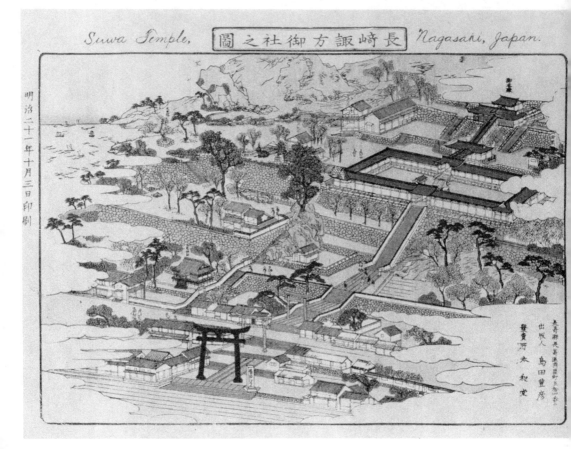

Fig. 2. Map of Suwa Shrine, 1889, property of Suwa Shrine
(courtesy Mr. Nishida Yasunori, Nagasaki Photo Service)

Fig. 3. Inner Sanctuary (*honden*) of Suwa Shrine
(courtesy Mr. Nishida Yasunori, Nagasaki Photo Service)

Fig. 4. A neighborhood visits the shrine

Fig. 5. Nigiwai machi commemorative pose, 1987

Fig. 6. Chief Priest Uesugi meets the press

Fig. 7. Inside the Hall of Worship (*haiden*)

Fig. 8. Blessing and protection via the *miko*s' bell-wands (*suzu*) following the ritual of Koya-iri for representatives from *machi* performing dances during the Okunchi festival. Note the leaf-sprig offerings (*tamagushi*) on the table ready to be distributed to the participants. (courtesy Mr. Nishida Yasunori, Nagasaki Photo Service)

Fig. 9. Senior Priest Matsumoto in front of the poles where visitors tie their paper fortunes (*omikuji*)

Fig. 10. Offerings (*shinsen*) include (*from back row, left to right*) turnips and Chinese cabbage, red snapper, rice, sake, radishes and carrots; (*front row, left to right*) water and salt, earth and seaweed, petitionary prayer, water vessel (the previous three trays are specific to this ritual), apples and oranges. In the background (*left to right*) are the wand of purification (*haraigushi*), the central altar with *gohei* wand, and the paper-wrapped front legs of a "stop lion" (see Appendix 2, no. 19).

Fig. 11. Senior Priest Takeshita performing the judgment by scalding water (*yutate-sai*)

Fig. 12. The descent of the portable shrines (*mikoshi*) from the main gate of Suwa Shrine in the rite *okudari*, the opening of Okunchi (courtesy Mr. Nishida Yasunori, Nagasaki Photo Service)

Fig. 13. The dragon dance (*jaodori*) of Okunchi (courtesy Mr. Nishida Yasunori, Nagasaki Photo Service)

Fig. 14. Beauty and the Beast

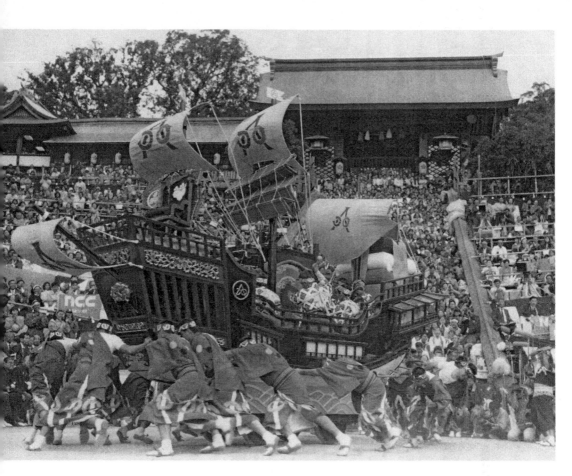

Fig. 15. The Macao boat (Goshuinsen) of Okunchi
(courtesy Mr. Nishida Yasunori, Nagasaki Photo Service)

Fig. 16. The *kokodesho* performance during Okunchi (courtesy Mr. Nishida Yasunori, Nagasaki Photo Service)

Fig. 17. Senior Priest Ureshino in the Okunchi procession

Fig. 18. (*Looking down from the shrine*) The performance of the lion dance during Okunchi

Fig. 19. The author in Heian period court attire and Chief Priest Uesugi
(courtesy Mr. Ureshino Noritaka)

10

JUDGMENT
BY SCALDING
WATER

Mention "cauldron" to a person from Europe
or North America and the word will likely evoke images of medi-
eval castle parapets from which cauldrons of boiling oil were poured
upon invaders. Or it will bring to mind the three witches of *Macbeth*
hovering around a blackened pot while making their fateful prophe-
cies. It is a word that has become associated with murky, magical,
or potentially sinister happenings. But it should also be remembered that a cauldron is an essential part of a traditional kitchen, in
which vegetables and meats are combined and then heated with the
magic of fire to produce savory soups, stews, and sauces. In traditional Japan, a kitchen without a cauldron would be like a carpenter's
workshop without a hammer—absolutely nothing of quality could
be made.

This same kind of cauldron, less deep than the "witches' pot" of
the Western imagination but equally blackened by the soot of countless fires, is what now sits in the middle of the purification enclosure adjacent to the shrine. The groundskeepers have cleared away a
portion of the stones to reveal an open hearth where a fire crackles
merrily under the blackened utensil. As steam rises in great clouds
into the February morning air, the bubbling water (drawn from the
shrine's sacred spring) looks perfect for parboiling shrimp, clams, or
perhaps a crab—but no cooking will be done. Instead, Senior Priest
Takeshita will prove his mettle by plunging his bare hand into the
water as the climax of a rite of exorcism and purification.[1]

In continuing to conduct this ritual, Suwa Shrine joins the ranks
of the few remaining sites in Japan where one can still see remnants
of the Edo era, a time when demonstrations of spiritual power were
part of the bread and butter of most institutions as well as of wandering holy men and women ascetics. These powers could be translated
into specific acts beneficial to the community, such as "opening"

a holy place for worship or conducting an exorcism, or they could be mere demonstrations of an individual's accomplishments in the magical arts. The sect known as Shugendō, blending the rituals and symbols of Shingōn and Tendai Buddhism with the more ancient belief in the sacredness of certain mountains, was and still is predominantly concerned with harnessing otherworldly powers for the benefit of others and for personal salvation.[2] The eleventh-century novel *The Tale of Genji* relates how mountain-dwelling ascetics (*yamabushi*) were summoned to quell the evil spirits blocking the efforts of Empress Akiko to give birth.

Carmen Blacker pointed out in her 1975 work on Japanese shamanism that most rites involving potentially harmful physical effects —such as the judgment by scalding water (*yutate-sai*) or the fire walking of the Shugendō sects—follow the same basic structure. First, the priest or devotee purifies himself or herself against evil influences and then either invokes or identifies with some kind of guardian spirit for protection during the ordeal. With this accomplished, the participant will be strong enough to withstand the mortification of flesh, especially if he or she also employs a loud and sharp magical cry, the *kiai*.

Though the magical elements of most shrine rituals have been toned down since the end of the war, the continued performance of the *yutate-sai* is evidence enough that, in Nagasaki at least, there is still a felt need for the kind of benefits the ritual is thought to bestow. But unlike the exorcisms of Shugendō, the *yutate-sai* is not concerned with spirit possession, hallucinations, or altered personalities. Instead, it can be thought of as focusing on the same impurities that are swept away at the start of a service before the main theme can be addressed—only this time, the pollutions themselves are the main theme at the center of the ritual. With their scale thus magnified, so are the methods with which the *yutate-sai* confronts them.

The ritual begins unlike any other described in this book. Instead of undergoing the initial purifications outside in the sacred enclosure adjacent to the shrine, the priests, *miko*, and guests have already individually performed the hand and mouth cleansing while waiting in front of the reception hall for the service to begin. Now, they come directly to the shrine, hardly looking at the boiling cauldron in the middle of the sacred enclosure.

Once inside, Ureshino-san intones the opening prayer and performs a self-purification with a small *haraigushi*, about the size of a whisk broom, which he taps upon his left, right, and then left shoulder. When he replaces it and takes up the larger wand, the priests and audience stir into positions of readiness. But he walks past everyone out of the Hall of Worship, down the steps, and, slipping on his black lacquered clogs, proceeds outside where the cauldron has been waiting all this time for its purification. Bowing very low and then waving the streamers of the wand dramatically, Ureshino-san's main task of ritually cleansing the water and its vessel is easily accomplished; the rest of the purifications, both for priests and for the assembled audience, are more standardized and businesslike. Matsumoto-san follows Ureshino-san, scattering drops with the single *sakaki* leaf dipped in a small cup of water.

The Gūji is absent today, summoned by the Central Association of Shinto Shrines to lead a tour group to China, and so, in his stead, Senior Priest Oka will read the *norito* prayer and Takeshita-san will plunge his hand into the cauldron. Most rituals follow the same basic steps: the Kami must be summoned, the food offerings must be placed on the altar, and the sacred words must be intoned in the right mind and spirit. But instead of the two *miko* dancing inside the shrine immediately after the *norito* is read, today they each take a bell-wand and a small scepter hung with two wide white paper strips (*gohei*) and, accompanied by the slow beat of a drum, go outside and stand on either side of the now mightily boiling cauldron. As the music begins from within the shrine, one of the young women faces east, the other west, with the cauldron's boiling water between their expectant faces like a third partner.

Their dance this time is not composed of the slow dreamy circles they weave before the altar in most rituals; the music (not to mention the loose stones underfoot) dictates a faster pace requiring more powerful movement. They bow and spin, rotating around the cauldron, then proceed to each of the four corners of the enclosure, their arms always straight in front, the bell-wands and *gohei*-wands serving as powerful charms against the multitude of evils and impurities thought to be lurking in the four corners of the world.

Though the *miko* are favorites of the Kami for their grace and beautiful dancing, they can only begin the war this festival wages against the evils of *kegare*, or pollution. Like their Shugendō predecessors during the Tokugawa period, they must join forces with a priest before the *yutate* ritual achieves its full expression. Before the *miko* reenter the shrine, a young priest dressed in a grayish-purple kimono-sleeved outfit emerges with a sword in his outstretched hands. He follows the route around the fire the *miko* established, but

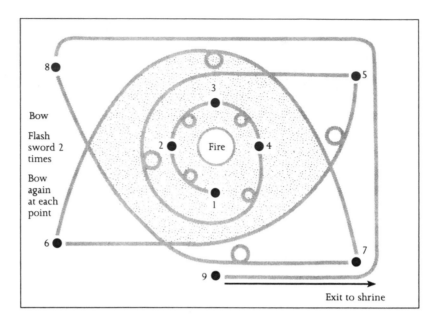

Bow

Flash
sword 2
times

Bow
again
at each
point

Exit to shrine

the sword is up, ready for use. His first circle completed, he bows
with the sword held in both hands, head lower than the blade (which
faces the cauldron), then positions the weapon and slashes twice into
the steam. After bowing again, he moves to the next position on the
route until, after four bows and eight forays into the steam and four
bows and eight cuts in the four directions (north, south, east, west),
he returns to the starting position and briefly drops to one knee as a
gesture of humility and closure before going back to the shrine.

The interpretation of what is happening here depends on the informant: each slash of the sword is a partial severing of the hold that
evil can have on people and places; or it is also a penetration into
the fabric of impurity which hangs like a curtain between ourselves
and our "divine" possibilities, obscuring a life closer to the way of
the Kami. We encountered earlier the power of water as a cleansing
agent in Shinto practice and it is to this climax the ritual has been
advancing. Takeshita-san, who tells me later it had been two years
since he last performed this role, uneasily takes his place facing the
cauldron and the west. Behind him stands one of the *miko* with a six-
foot-long bamboo pole adorned with *gohei* streamers. The raucous
drum and cymbals that accompanied the sword flashing are silent
now, poised for the moment the priest proves that he is sufficiently
pure to scatter the sacred water, boiling hot, from the cauldron into

the atmosphere, where it will magically disperse and further purify the world.

Several panels of the shrine's wooden wall have been removed to allow those inside a view of the proceedings. It seems as if everyone is holding his or her breath as the diminutive priest in his white kimono and tall black hat whispers a long prayer, then claps his hands twice and begins a succession of low, sustained bows. Three . . . four times he lowers his head so that his hat almost touches the stones; these bows are not mere ceremony but are deliberate and labored. The outcome of the entire ritual rides on the state of the priest's heart and mind, by means of which he attacks the impurities.

After the fourth bow is completed and he again stands upright, something about his eyes has changed; they now seem slightly glazed and unfocused. Almost mechanically he removes his right hand from the confines of the billowing kimono sleeve, takes one step forward, and without breaking his momentum shouts in a tremendous voice "Eh!!" while dashing his hand into the water (see fig. 11). A wave rises in the cauldron and then splashes upon the gray rocks below while from within the Hall of Worship the drum and cymbals erupt in a frenzy of clashing and pounding—all the better to frighten away the evil demons that just got drenched. Takeshita-san takes the bamboo pole from his *miko* assistant and begins stirring the remaining water, sloshing it upon the heated stones and coals below, which sends clouds of steam high into the air. Like a magician waving his wand over a magic hat, but with far more dignity and for greater benefits, the priest then passes the pole through the steam, one hand on his hip, legs spread far apart—a gesture he slowly repeats three times to varying crescendos of drum and cymbals. The process is not yet completed however because it is possible tenacious and clinging impurities still lurk here and there in the corners of the world.

And so the previous sword-bearer takes the priest's place before the half-empty cauldron and dips into the water the tips of bushy bamboo branches he has brought with him. This completed, he re-enters the Hall of Worship, where he allows the collected water to drip onto white porcelain plates before the main altar. Once these have been added to the offerings, he turns to the deeply bowing audience and shakes the branches twice, causing a shower of droplets to rain upon them. This is precisely what they have been waiting for. They respond by touching the place where a drop has fallen and then applying the potion to their weak knees, arthritic lower backs, or wherever else their bodies are afflicted.

The young priest bows, then strides back outside for another, lengthier dip of the branches in the purified water before heading to the north corner, where he bows once and sweeps the leaves upward, scattering the droplets into all regions of that corner of the universe, sousing any remaining impurities with a "million holy drops." He then approaches the cauldron for the final time as the drum, cymbals, and flute break forth in a spirited rhythm one usually hears in street festivals. The priest flings the branches high over his shoulders and somehow manages to retain his balance while maneuvering around the fire, dipping and waving the branches, scattering the droplets in choreographed precision. There is strength and determination here almost bordering on violence in these powerful last gestures, with water flying everywhere and vapor trailing in billowing clouds, as if this final step in the cycle of exorcism was the coup de grace to once and forever wipe the slate clean. When the vat is empty and the priest's own garments almost soaked, the branches are simply laid upon a table beside the shrine's side entrance. For many in the audience, the fact that these leaves have served such a worthy purpose makes them useful talismans to be stuffed in a purse or briefcase after the service and taken home to be placed on the family altar, hung over the front door, or positioned to ward off bad influences from the northeast "demon's gate."

The senior priests have resumed their seats in the center of the Hall of Worship to complete the service. Since the Kami is still considered to be present, having witnessed the efforts of the priests to dispel evil and thus increase the realm in which the Kami can interact with the world without impediments, a little entertainment is in order. And so the *miko* rise and, with their bell-wands, perform a short dance to traditional court melodies, after which the Kami is invited to depart. The offerings are carefully and reverently removed one by one, and the acting Gūji and the audience offer the sacred evergreen branches, the *tamagushi*.

It all comes to a close with the final, solo bow of the acting Gūji before the central altar. Everyone joins in, renewed and reassured that, not only has the world been transformed from a profane into a sacred and purified sphere, but they themselves, due to the efforts of the priests and *miko* on their behalf, have been cleansed and, in a sense, reborn. With their bamboo sprigs proudly in hand and the ceremonial sip of sake still sweet on their lips, a trusting, almost childlike innocence can be perceived on their faces as they descend the shrine steps and are absorbed by the city below.

II

FESTIVAL

FOR

FECUNDITY

At 6:45 A.M., the morning sun has just crested the range of mountains surrounding Nagasaki and now streams delicately through the high boughs of the camphor trees sheltering Suwa Shrine. After cleansing my hands and mouth at the *temizuya* font just inside the main gate and giving my regards to the Kami at the public altar, I am ready to enter the restricted area behind the open-air purification ground, sheltered from view by a tall grove of bamboo. I open a gate and pass by the little pond with its waterfall where the Great Purification rituals of June and December have their climax and join the already assembled crowd of priests as Matsumoto-san makes a last check of his fire-making tools. The generation of a sacred flame with which to cook rice offerings is the preliminary step for the important festival in honor of the Kami called Morisaki. Matsumoto-san glances around at his audience, signals he is ready, and bows twice.

He kneels on a grass mat spread upon the earthen floor of what one might first mistake for a tea-ceremony pavilion. The side facing the pond (and main shrine) is completely open, for ventilation I am told, so that the clay oven where the rice will cook can "breathe easily and thus assist the Kami of fire." Though some shrines' firemakers use flint when making their "pure flame" for cooking purposes, at Suwa Jinja tools of equal antiquity but greater sophistication are used. On the floor is a long board with a number of small holes, into one of which fits a dowel that Matsumoto-san rotates by the use of a rope coiled around it. To add leverage and weight, the bottom of the spinning pin is round like a ball, but it is difficult to balance and the first few attempts yield little but a few whiffs of smoke.

Advisors are in abundance. "You simply have to do it faster than that," the Gūji says. "Maybe if you tried getting above it more . . . you know, way up on your knees . . . ," Senior Priest Oka observes. "Why don't you move the dried pine needles closer to the base?" another priest adds. But Matsumoto-san, his jaw set in implacable concentration, ignores them all and keeps spinning the apparatus until he is rewarded with sparks. "I knew he'd get it eventually," the Gūji says to me. "After all, a tool like this is one of the oldest known to man." "From China?" I venture. "No, it's older than that, coming all the way from Egypt, maybe 4000 B.C." I make a mental note to check on the date and possibility he is right, but unfortunately that is all I do.

By now the fire has been transferred from the starting block to the pure white cedar shavings within the oven, filling the air with a rich, pleasing fragrance. The rice that is cooked here will be fashioned into circular cakes called *omochi* and presented to the Kami at 10:00. Matsumoto-san bows once more before the fire, and the group drifts away to their various tasks of cleaning, bookkeeping, and administration before the 9:40 robe changing begins. I give my congratulations to the fire builder as he leaves the little pavilion, to which he smiles and shakes his head; "I had my doubts there for a minute. Even though I'd practiced yesterday, I just couldn't find the rhythm of spinning the rod. Of course, everybody watching didn't help either—I'm soaked with sweat! I was really on the spot, you know."

The next time I see Matsumoto-san he looks relaxed and serene in his pure white silk robes (called *saifuku*), shiny black clogs, and a different, more formal kind of headgear called a *kanmuri*, distinctive because of its springy L-shaped tail that fairly dances as a priest moves. He leads the procession from the reception hall to the outside purification area, where the opening prayers and the cleansing rituals with the *haraigushi* paper streamers and *konusa* leaves are performed with a flawless and beautiful precision.

Just as I begin to anticipate entering into the Hall of Worship as during the Setsubun festival two weeks before, the Gūji turns away from the entrance and instead begins climbing an enclosed carpeted staircase to the upper sanctuaries. Situated on the side of a hill, Suwa Shrine is built in three tiers, with the Hall of Worship (*haiden*) on the lower level, the Hall of Offerings (*heiden*) twenty-one steps further up, and the Inner Sanctuary (*honden*) seventeen more steps up the side of the mountain—an increase of almost forty feet, all roofed in the most remarkable sweep of arches, peaked gables, and flowing lines.

The architecture of Suwa Shrine, perfectly adapted to its location on the side of a mountain, is a fitting example of the wide latitude a shrine's structure can take in meeting the requirements of the natural topography. As mentioned earlier, Shinto shrines are located at sacred sites (*iwasaka, kannabi*) which can be anything from a beautiful mountain like Mount Miwa in Nara Prefecture, a volcano like Mount Fuji or Mount Aso, a deep forest such as that behind Izumo Shrine, to special ponds, waterfalls, giant trees, strangely shaped rocks, or the confluence of two rivers. Because shrines are located in such varied settings, their arrangement follows whatever design is most aesthetically (or, in some cases, strategically) suited to their environment. For example, the well-known shrine of Itsukushima at Miyajima in Hiroshima Prefecture is completely surrounded by water at high tide. Tokugawa Ieyasu's shrine at Nikko is built in a succession of terraced courtyards on the side of a mountain—as is Suwa Shrine, though on a much smaller scale.

With the exception of those low-budget, ferroconcrete structures one is occasionally jolted by when traveling throughout Japan, all the basic styles of shrine buildings had developed by the Heian period. Those most free of Chinese influence resemble ancient granaries (Ise) or the houses of the nobility (Izumo Taisha). Of the other kinds developed during the Nara (710–94) and Heian periods (794–1192), the *nagare-zukuri* style, with its huge roofs sweeping forward and down, became the most common. And though some extant Buddhist temples date back to the eighth century, thus winning them the distinction of being the earth's oldest wooden structures, the oldest Shinto buildings date from the eleventh or twelfth century—but not because fire, earthquakes, or other natural or man-made calamities took a toll.

Since purity and renewal are such vitally important concepts in Shinto practice, and indeed are the central themes of the ritual to be conducted for Morisaki-no-Kami, it is only logical to find them extended to the very structures housing the Kami as well, resulting in the periodic dismantling and reconstruction of what an architect would consider perfectly sound edifices. Thus, not only were the materials of constructing the shrines themselves renewed but so was the original site. Though this practice ceased for the majority of shrines at the end of the Edo period (1868), it continues most noticeably at Ise Grand Shrine, where every twenty years the main shrine buildings are entirely rebuilt on an adjoining site.[1] This tradition of tearing down and rebuilding has actually been instrumental in ensuring a continuity of form and ancient construction techniques that would otherwise have been lost.

Beneath the almost feminine lines of Suwa Shrine's *nagare*-style roofs, the procession makes its way up the stairs. Though the wood is new and the construction sound, the hallway pops and creaks as eight priests, two *miko*, and ten guests make their slow ascent in a long, bobbing line. The low ceiling of the Hall of Worship and its atmosphere of intimacy are replaced by the high ceilings of the Hall of Offerings, from whose stout beams hang richly embroidered banners, gold-leaf calligraphy paintings, and sheaves of unhulled rice plants. Where the Hall of Worship is sunlit and open-air, the Hall of Offerings is shadowy and secretive. The wood here is older, some of it over a hundred years old, and has a more weathered glow than that of the fresh, almost bleached-looking whiteness of the recently remodeled lower hall. For some reason, the fragrance of the wood is twice as intense as in the hall below, which only adds to the sensual yet simple sumptuousness of the atmosphere. Everywhere I look is some treat for the eye—a wooden carving of a fish in rapids near the stairway, a gold-colored *gohei* streamer on the steps leading up to the inner sanctum, a beautifully painted gong-drum suspended from a lacquered bar—meeting and surpassing every expectation of what a shrine is supposed to be. And yet nothing seems ostentatious the way cathedrals in Europe sometimes are. The finery of design or fabric is balanced by the unadorned and aged wood. The hall's distance from and elevation above the ringing of the prayer bell and clapping of hands contribute to its atmosphere, charging it with solemnity and anticipation of imminent communion with the Kami.

After everyone is seated, with the Gūji, *miko*, and three musicians on one side of the slightly raised stage and the other priests opposite them in two rows, Matsumoto-san announces that the Gūji will now "open the way for the Kami" and asks that everyone bow. Slowly, as when a small child climbs steps that are too big for him, taking one at a time before moving on to the next, the Gūji ascends the two tiers of steps to the Inner Sanctuary. Then, as priests and audience alike bow deeply, the *keihitsu* begins a sacred call to the Kami to make itself manifest. It is a long, resonant single vowel which crescendos and fades three times as the Gūji raises a bamboo screen shielding the doors of the sanctuary. Adding to the effect of the call are the ethereal notes and chords sounded on the upper registers of the seventeen-chambered *shō* harmonium. Even before the final "ohhhh" fades away and we rise from our bows, one can sense a change in the chamber, a greater and deeper stillness, and, for the first-time observer, a tingling of the scalp.

Returning to his seat with the same graceful conservation of movement, the Gūji has performed the first of his two crucial tasks in any ritual. The Kami is now considered to be present in the upper sanctum behind the heavy doors and, like any formally invited guest, must be treated like an important visitor—food and drink must be served in an attitude of humility and gratitude for its presence.

Here in the Hall of Offerings, unlike the more accessible and more frequently used Hall of Worship, on the lower level (where, at this moment, some of the other priests are conducting a customized service for a family beginning a new business), it takes five priests to convey the *shinsen* offering feast from the little kitchen at the bottom of the stairs to the Inner Sanctuary's table just within its main door. Standing in the walkway surrounding the Inner Sanctuary, Oka-san, the most senior priest, is in charge of arranging the food on the table. The priest immediately below him in rank, Takeshita-san, brings the trays from the kitchen to the first of the bearers. The trays are then passed from priests lower in rank to those higher in rank at various points on the steps. Takeshita passes to Otaguro, who climbs the first nine steps and transfers the tray to Matsumoto, who climbs the next eight steps and passes it to Ureshino, who then simply turns and hands it to Oka, who shuffles in and out of the entry. Undoubtedly it is work, since several of the trays are piled high with fat white radishes, bamboo shoots, or the freshly cooked rice cakes from the pure flames outside. But the strength with which the priests hold high the trays, their nimble ascent and descent of the narrow steps, the wail of flute and flageolet, and the "*ton!*" of the drum turn the relay into a ballet of precise movement choreographed, some say, over a thousand years ago. As always, the final trays are the salt and water and sake vessels. One by one, from the kitchen upward, each priest who has completed his task goes down on his knees, leans forward so that both hands lightly rest upon the floor with thumbs pointing inward, and awaits the final arrangement of the trays within the Inner Sanctuary. The music continues even after they have all returned to their places in the Hall of Offerings.

Matsumoto-san now rises and glides over the empty space separating the two groups of participants and delivers to the Gūji the *norito* prayer that will directly address the Kami called Morisaki. The Gūji does not ascend all the way to the Inner Sanctuary but stops halfway up and seats himself upon a raised platform used only for the reading of the prayer. Like all invocational prayers, this one follows a basic structure, first thanking the Kami for its presence and beneficence, honoring its unique character with the type of offerings suitable only for it, and reverently requesting its continued blessings upon the community and shrine (see the representative *norito* in chapter 5). The archaic origins of Morisaki-no-Kami, the original Kami worshipped by the fishermen and hunters of Nagasaki long before the Portuguese arrived in 1543, and the fact that the deity may be a composite of a Christian saint and a Shinto Kami (see chapter 3) make it the most obscure of the three Kami at Suwa Shrine—though this is not to imply a lack of emotional involvement on the part of those individuals who feel its character provides the best point of access for managing forces impinging on their lives.

The final syllables of the *norito*, each one more distinctly enunciated and prolonged than the last, disperse like the closing chords of a symphony, filling the chamber with resonance and calm. More than the actual message of the prayer, it is this feeling of sublime closure that the participants will take with them back to their ordinary routines, believing in the "magic of words" to suffuse their lives with renewed equilibrium and hope.

As the Gūji descends and returns to his place, his movements are more relaxed, as are those of Matsumoto-san, who retrieves the prayer, returns it to the white paper sheath slung over his shoulder, and then reclaims his seat. Male members of the audience, mostly older men who have doubtlessly witnessed many such rituals, change from the formal sitting position on their heels to a cross-legged one almost as if on cue, though the women remain in the *seiza* position. With the petition presented, the ritual can now move into its next phase, beginning with the dance of the *miko*.

Each young woman is adorned with a garland of multicolored silk flowers in her hair. They rise from their places, arms outstretched holding large, opened fans instead of the *suzu* bells they usually dance with. Approaching center "stage" from the right, they position the fans in their left hands so as to symbolically shield their faces from the side of the stage closest to the outer world. They hold the variously colored tassles that flow from the fans in their right hands until they make their bows before the altar high above.

It is then the music begins, but surprisingly, there is neither flute nor harmonium, only a single drumbeat and the voices of the musicians in a dirgelike song. Minor upon minor tones, the music leads the *miko* around several circles with their fans held sometimes aloft, sometimes near the floor. At one point, they place them upon a table and take instead another version of the *suzu* bells, but with a type of short blade at its center.

As the *otome-mai* (which is hardly a "dance" in the Western sense of the term, so infrequent and subtle are the actual gestures) progresses, the slow rhythm of their circular movements, the poised and careful positioning of their arms and heads, and the periodic but perfectly timed shake of the bells elevate the dance, offered in humility for the pleasure of the Kami, far beyond the confines of the ceilings and walls into a realm of timelessness. It is a touching and emotional part of the ritual as these young women, who would most likely blush when saying hello to a man, here transcend their levels of maturity and personality to serve as vessels for the Muse of dance to work through. The spell they cast on the audience is broken only when they bow and spin toward their seats again, faces flushed from the exertion.[2]

The rest of the ritual proceeds rapidly after this. The Gūji offers the sacred *sakaki* branch with a white paper *gohei* streamer attached, and members from the audience follow suit at a lower table, each one bowing and presenting a branch, then bowing twice again, and clapping twice as they "lay their souls" upon the tendered sprig. Next, the food offerings must be removed (to leave them for any length of time beyond that deemed appropriate would allow spoilage and thus deposit impurity in the place that should be the cleanest), so the same process is repeated in the relays from the Inner Sanctuary to the preparation chamber. Once the food and sake have been taken away, there is no longer any reason for the Kami to be "on call," and so the Gūji makes his final trip up the stairs to close the screens (an act called *heihi*) with the accompanying solemn "ohhhhhh" that invites the Kami to depart.

Thinking that this festival is almost at a close, I become aware again of my aching knees and feet and am looking forward to being alone to digest what I have just seen when I glance up and see one of the attendant priests coming into the audience directly toward me. The Gūji and other priests are also looking in my direction and I think I have unknowingly violated some secret tabu when I hear the rustling of a grass mat being spread on the floor behind me and then realize they are only positioning themselves for the bow toward Ise, which the Gūji will lead from the eastern corner of the hall, where I just happen to be sitting. I need to move out of the way in the next five seconds but since my legs are asleep, all I can do is drag myself (in as dignified a manner as I can manage) to a neutral space at the side and join in the bows with priests all around me. Later I'll be roundly teased for having such long legs but will also be taught, for my "future deliverance," a way of discreetly restoring circulation during long services.[3]

In closing, the Gūji stands before the assembled guests and delivers what is not quite a sermon, not quite a soliloquy, though it has qualities of both. "Ladies and gentlemen, thank you for coming here today to partake in this festival honoring Morisaki-no-Kami. Spring is a time filled with new hopes and life, the very traits Morisaki embodies, so it is our privilege to perform this festival. The recent blossoming of the cherry trees, the proliferation of flowers in parks and gardens, the sprouting of rice seedlings, and of course the births of children to happy parents—all these are a part of the heart of Morisaki-no-Kami. Summer will soon be upon us, so let us use the blessings of Morisaki-no-Kami to make the most out of the new life given to us in the spring. It is really a joyful occasion that you could all be here today to be a part of celebrating this great Kami. Please follow us to the banquet hall for a small *naorai* feast that you are hereby cordially invited to attend. Thank you again for coming and take care."

SUMMER

12

BEING DIRTY,
GETTING CLEAN,
AND THE RITUAL
OF GREAT
PURIFICATION

Take a moment right now and look at your hands. More specifically, look at your fingernails. Are they nice and clean? Well-shaped or painted? Could your hands be the ones in a commercial on TV which clasp the cologne bottle in a close-up? Have they recently touched anything withered, dead, or afflicted with disease? And while we are on the subject of close-ups, how about the bottoms of your feet? Or the condition of your large intestine? Had intimate contact lately with any errors, sickness, or disaster? If the questioning above makes you uncomfortable or embarrassed, then it is likely you would qualify for a ritual purification—one of the central themes running through the core of Shinto practice. Any season or day of the year is suitable for purifications, but summer especially so, since it is a time fraught with danger from a wide number of sources. But more about this in a moment.

Purification of physical and psychological impediments to one's relationship with the divine is, in general, one of the great overarching themes shared by systems of ritual practice and belief throughout the world. As Mary Douglas observed, "Reflection on dirt involves reflection on the relation of order to disorder, being to non-being, form to formlessness, and life to death" (1970, 5). "Dirt" is perhaps putting it a little bluntly for the case of Shinto ritual practices, but certainly the notion of what constitutes order and disorder in early agricultural communities was intimately related and relevant to the survival of those communities and formed part of the foundation for Japanese social and cultural norms. In societies all over the world, rites of purification create numerous escape hatches from what is otherwise the sinking ship of our physical condition, afflicted as we are with periodic illnesses, emotional traumas, and inescapable structural degeneration. Via purification, however, healing and the expiation of afflictions can occur, even to the point of transcending the physical condition altogether. An individual or his or her religious community is not, however, the sole recipient of these benefits; purifications also restore a person to "spiritual" health and thus again render them useful to society.

To see how this relates to the cycle of rituals of Suwa Shrine, it is essential to first understand the importance to many Japanese, from priest to the poorest farmer, of beliefs about physical and spiritual purity. To do this, we have to go back to one of the earliest myths in one of the oldest books, the *Kojiki*, to the time when two important primordial Kami, Izanagi and Izanami, are busy creating the world.[1] Everything is proceeding apace until Izanami gives birth to the Kami of fire, thus burning her genitals and causing her to fall ill and eventually "die" and descend to the land of Yomi, the netherworld. Grief-stricken over his loss and her absence, Izanagi decides to make the journey to the netherworld to retrieve her, but because he breaks his promise to Izanami not to look at her corpse, he comes in contact not only with the putrescence of death but with various other kinds of defilement and pollution and barely escapes with his life. Being "seized with regret" and feeling that he "had brought on himself ill-luck" with these harrowing encounters, he proceeds to perform the "purification of his august body . . . from its pollutions and impurities" (*Kojiki*, 1, x).

He does this at the mouth of a river, where the water is neither very fast nor sluggish, and immediately numerous Kami spring newly born from his body, garments, and breath. What is important to realize here is that in spite of Izanagi's brush with all the impurities associated with death and the disasters of his journey, he is able to rectify his physical and spiritual well-being and return to the business he was originally about—creating the world. It is one of the beauties of Shinto mythology that allows Izanagi (and, through this precedent, ourselves) to continue in the process of growth and creativity even though he was temporarily waylaid. The fact that he could, by himself, rid his system of its evil contamination shows that Shinto holds basic human nature incapable of being permanently poisoned or distorted by what is known in the West as "sin."

A parallel with the Judeo-Christian tradition is unavoidable at this point: imagine what might have developed if Adam and Eve had been afforded the benefits of purification after acknowledging the wrong they had done. Would Eve have made a vow to henceforth stick to pears, or Adam to trust in God rather than the advice of his partner? Instead, accomplices in a "crime," they were driven out of their lush and idyllic garden by a quite unforgiving God. The myth of Izanagi, on the other hand, became part of the foundation for structuring a society that esteemed ritual purity an essential prerequisite for worshipping the Kami. Human beings, following the examples of the Kami, often make mistakes and betray the good impulses that are inherent in their being, but because Shinto maintains we are all born into the world in a state of harmony (however vaguely defined the notion is), those spiritual or physical imbalances we accrue can be rectified through purification rituals.

The most detailed prescription concerning ritual pollution and what to do about it, found in the *norito* invocation of the Oharae ritual, is also based on an incident in the *Kojiki*. We are into the next generation of Kami after Izanagi and Izanami, when the Sun Goddess's brother, a fairly wild rascal named Susa-no-o, commits a number of serious offenses, mostly agricultural in nature, that must be expiated. These actions (to be listed in the following pages) provide ample material for what is unconditionally not to be accepted as a natural state of existence and therefore requires a great cleansing if the world is to be resacralized and order restored.

Of course, there is more going on than meets the eye when one observes a purification ritual, not only in Shinto but in Buddhist, Hindu, Muslim, or numerous other religious systems. Primary importance is given to the actual event occurring within a sacred space and time that may (or may not) extend into the realm of myth, but there are also three other areas, fundamentally sociological and psychological in nature, that are also more than tangentially connected with these rites (Preston 1986, 98). Since a group instead of a solitary person is usually involved in public expressions of worship, a purification rite helps to reinforce the boundaries of this community, asking the "greater forces" to cleanse not every human being but a particular segment of humanity that is localized as the clan or tribe or village. If there are competing religious institutions, then it is possible that the boundaries of the community will extend no further than those adherents participating in the ritual at that time. Second, like other rites and festivals, those dealing specifically with purification help people cope individually with life crises. Once they are ritually cleansed, then perhaps a more direct channel of communication can be established between the Kami and the world of humans through which biological, sexual, or economic activities can be transformed and integrated into the "way of the Kami." Finally, there is the more practical aspect of human hygiene to consider as an element of purification rites. With all the emphasis on physical cleanliness that is made in Shinto—ranging from fingernails and toenails to the condition of the large intestine at the time of an important service—very basic principles of healthy conduct are reinforced for all who would participate. Traditionally, even the food that a person ate before attending worship had to be of the right kind, else its spicy or animal-based nature would disqualify whatever beneficial effect it might have for the body's role as the vehicle for religious expression.

In ancient times, the variety of defilements and pollutions were the same for Shinto as in many other cultures throughout the world. A long list would include (but not be restricted to) disease, blood associated with menstruation and childbirth, wounds, death, pestilence, earthquake, fire, leprosy, sores, boils, bunions, warts, incest, bestiality, excrement, flaying animals alive or backwards, injuring rice fields and irrigation canals, and witchcraft. This list should be modified with an important distinction separating those impurities that are deliberately created and those that are entirely accidental or physiological in nature. Even though these transgressions violate a "divine" state of harmony and are therefore loathed, they should not necessarily be thought of as "sins." To Western sensibilities, a "sin" directly affects the individual's soul like a kind of filthy cloak which only a priest of the church or the direct forgiveness of God intuited by prayer can remove via absolution. The defilements in the above list however, called *tsumi*, do not affect the "real" person but are thought of as temporary separations from the harmonious interaction of body, soul, and world. Western preoccupations with virtue do not apply to Shinto conceptions of impurity and purity, mainly because *tsumi* are not antithetical to virtue or harmony. They are simply a fact of existence afflicting all of us, Kami included, *but they can be completely obliterated*, with no lingering guilt complexes either, by rituals such as the one we will soon observe.

We have seen that ritual purification in Shinto is done as a part of the preparation preceding a ritual, sometimes outside in the sacred enclosure, other times within the shrine's Hall of Worship, and sometimes repeated within the Hall of Offerings. "Ideally, all purifications should be done outside on the stones, where the impurities can fall to the earth and be cleansed by rains or water sprinkled over the area once the ritual is over," observes Senior Priest Oka. "You would also have to say that one should not use the *haraigushi* [wand of white paper streamers waved over the objects or area or people being purified] more than once, since I always think of it as something that dispels the defilements and that, in doing so, is slightly contaminated. But shrine economics being what they are and the demand on our services so great, it simply can't be helped that we're somewhat pragmatic. They do the same thing at Ise you know."

Today's ritual, the Great Purification of the sixth month, is somewhat unique in its approach. Instead of focusing on a particular Kami, it emphasizes the *harae*, that part of a ritual usually performed in preparation for the main event. This old tale helps explain the underpinning legend:

> It was a hot day in summer during the rainy season and a traveler was passing the last two farmhouses before the trail led into the mountains. Being late, he stopped at the first and politely asked for a night's lodging but was rudely refused. At the second house, however, they kindly took him in and treated him well. As thanks the next morning, he revealed himself as a Kami and foretold of an epidemic soon to come. "But don't fear," he told the terrified farmer and his family, "if you make a ring out of the long-stemmed grasses growing near your house and put it above your door, you'll all be spared." And so it came to pass.

Although we moderns think of suntans, barbecues, air-conditioning, and vacations as a part of our "normal" summer experience, for Japanese farmers of both distant and recent times, summer is not a particularly enjoyable time. For one thing, the rainy season (lasting from late May to mid-July) could be as harmful as it was essential for the crop of rice—all that incredible humidity breeds insects that might devour the tender shoots. There might also be floods originating in the mountains, devastating typhoons, or epidemics spawned in the standing water of the paddy fields—any number of things to lie awake nights worrying about, wishing there were some way to petition the Kami to come to your assistance.

The ritual of Great Purification, while having its mythological roots in the cleansing of Izanagi after his descent into the land of Yomi, was performed at this time of year to answer just that pressing need of the community and its elite overseers. Almost everything bad that one can bring to mind is mentioned in the ritual as *tsumi*, or "defilements," of an original state of harmonious existence. Judging from what is considered terrible in the eyes of the Kami (and, by extension, the sociopolitical order they legitimated), one can posit that a state of harmony exists when rice grows in well-managed and maintained irrigated fields, when human beings cooperate in this endeavor and share the joys and sorrows of their lives within the embrace of the four seasons, the watchful mountains, and the bountiful seas, and when praise and gratitude to the Kami are a part of everyday household and communal administration.

*   *   *

On June 30 at 3:50 P.M., the drum from inside the shrine has started its slow acceleration of rhythm that signals the Gūji is about to appear and the procession to the outside sacred enclosure to begin. The rain of the past week and early morning has paused long enough for the ritual to be held as scheduled, but the air is tangible, like a moist, hot cloth pressed against one's skin. The priests, dressed in full ritual regalia with netlike outer robes instead of silk ones, remain placid and composed as they lead the procession of invited guests, *miko*, shrine staff, groundskeepers, and hangers-on like myself to either side of the enclosure. About thirty or forty people from the community at large are also clustered about, having read about the ritual in the morning paper's "Suwa Diary," and range from old Mrs. Yamagawa, bent nearly in half by arthritis from six decades in the rice fields, to young junior high school students in their summer uniforms. Everyone has a handkerchief at the ready to keep perspiration from rolling down their faces. Save for the crunch of rocks under foot as the assembly takes its place in rows within the sacred enclosure, the only sound to be heard is that of the small waterfall, just the other side of a bamboo grove. Senior Priest Ureshino, ever composed and soon to perform the central part of the ritual, looks down to see a green turtle lumbering over the stones toward center stage and gently putts it with his glistening black clog back to the shadows of the grove.

Once under way, the first movement of the ritual seems redundant: a purification before the purification. But, as Ureshino-san explains later, "to not have an initial *harae* would be like eating a Japanese meal without miso soup or rice—the sense of something missing would compromise the enjoyment of the entire meal. Besides, who knows what might have happened to the objects on the altar and the stacks of paper dolls and cars [*hitogata*] to be used in the ritual while they sat there unattended?" He laughs. "We don't like to take any unnecessary chances!"

Step by step, the wand of paper streamers and droplets of water sprinkled by the sacred *sakaki* leaf make their way from the altar to the Gūji, attendant priests, musicians, *miko*, and office staff, then to the guests and public, everyone bowing solemnly as his or her turn comes. Without any drumroll, speeches, prayers, or introduction of any kind, two of the younger priests go to the table adjacent to the altar and begin distributing white envelopes to all present. Opening it, one expects to find some written formula to recite but instead its contents are more tactile and interesting.

Suddenly, at the end of June, it is snowing—or at least so it appears when the envelopes' little white squares of paper and shreds of rice stalks are tossed high in the air to fall like confetti upon one's head. Magnets they are, magically drawing out the more easily removable *tsumi*. Some people are very serious, others are smiling and giggling with their friends—the atmosphere is relaxed and surprisingly informal as the next step in the purification begins. The *hito-gata* paper doll, mentioned earlier in connection with the Dolls' Day festival and cut into the shape of a kimono, is now removed from the envelope to begin a circuitous route over the body. Head, shoulders, aching elbow, abdomen—the older priests all bring the paper doll to their legs and knees, the first places that usually go wrong because of all the strenuous kneeling and rising in services. Before putting the doll back into the envelope, everyone exhales mightily upon it, allowing it to further absorb the impurities deep with the body's nether regions. Now filthy with contamination of all sorts, the envelopes are collected quickly by the younger priests and taken out of the enclosure to await their plunge into the pool.

As they are still arranging the envelopes, Takeshita-san, who performed the initial purification, strides forward and begins cleansing the four directions of the universe with *sakaki* branches waved in each corner of the enclosure. Their task is a mighty one and completely exhausts their sacred powers so that when finished, the branches are not only broken in half but tied with hemp fiber and cast to the stones under the altar like the trash they have become. No one will come forward to take these leaves home to their altar—they belong to the river, and to the Kami of purification who will claim them.

Without any words or accompanying music, Ureshino-san now approaches the altar and takes from it a long strand of hemp fiber pounded flat. Arms outstretched, he delicately positions the tips of his fingers and then, with a sweeping flourish of kimono sleeves, shreds it not once but eight times. As the *norito* prayer will inform us in a moment, the impurities must be symbolically shredded into eight divisions (but as to what the significance of the number eight might be, the priests can only sigh and shrug their shoulders!). A piece of white cloth, removed from a large envelope, is given the same treatment as the hemp fiber, then both are returned to the envelope and left upon the altar. The ancient prayer in the *Kojiki* tells us this is what must be done in order to enable the heavenly and earthly deities to "push open the heavenly rock door" and receive the "solemn ritual words" of the purification, but it provides not a hint as to why hemp and cloth are instrumental to the process. And no one seems to mind.

With a cordial gesture of his hand, Matsumoto-san, ever the facilitator, invites the assembly of priests, office workers, guests, and passersby to move to the pondside area immediately behind the sacred enclosure. It is a highly restricted area, used only four times a year, where recent remodeling has fashioned a small kidney-shaped pond out of which juts an octagonal island for the Gūji to stand upon during the Oharae festival. The water that surrounds him reveals mossy green depths and ripples a little from the waves caused by a small waterfall feeding into the pool. Once everyone is in place—the Gūji on his island, *miko* on the walkway holding a tray stacked high with *hitogata* dolls, the priests in a long straight line facing the pond, with the remaining *miko* and other shrine employees (janitors included) toward the rear, and the audience squeezing in wherever they can—the chanting of the long and essential *norito* begins. The voices are practiced and beautiful in their intonation of a poem said to be nearly 1,100 years old, and as the words flow forth, the Gūji begins to slowly cast the white paper dolls into the waters at his feet.

> Hear me, all of you assembled princes of the blood, princes,
>   court nobles, and all officials. Thus I speak.
> The various sins are to be exorcised, are to be purified
> In the great exorcism of the last day of the sixth month—
> Hear me, all of you.
> The eight myriad deities were convoked in a divine convocation,
> And spoke these words of entrusting:
>   "Our Sovereign Grandchild is to rule
>   The Land of the Plentiful Reed Plains,

of the Fresh Ears of Grain,
    Tranquilly as a peaceful land."
Having thus entrusted the land,
They inquired with a divine inquiry
Of the unruly deities in the land,
And expelled them with a divine expulsion;
They silenced to the last leaf
The rocks and the stumps of the trees,
    which had been able to speak,
And caused him to descend from the heavens,
    leaving the heavenly rock-seat,
    and pushing with an awesome pushing
    through the myriad layers of heavenly clouds—
Thus they entrusted the land to him . . .

The kimono-shaped figures flutter like leaves from the Gūji's fingers, some dropping immediately, others swirling back and forth as if reluctant to surrender the burden they carry to the embrace of the waters.

    The various sins perpetrated and committed
    By the heavenly ever-increasing people to come into existence
    In this land which he is to rule tranquilly as a peaceful land;
First, the heavenly sins:
    Breaking down the ridges, covering up the ditches,
    Releasing the irrigation sluices,
    Double planting, setting up stakes,
    Skinning alive, skinning backwards,
    Defecation—Many sins such as these
    are distinguished and called the heavenly sins.
The earthly sins:
    Cutting living flesh, cutting dead flesh,
    White leprosy, skin excrescences,
    The sin of violating one's own mother,
    The sin of violating one's own child,
    The sin of violating a mother and her child
    or a child and her mother,
    The sin of transgression with animals,
    Woes from creeping insects,
    Woes from the deities on high,

Woes from the birds on high,
Killing animals, the sin of witchcraft—

Many sins such as these shall appear.
When they thus appear, by the heavenly shrine usage,
Let the Great Nakatomi cut off the bottom and cut off the top
of heavenly pieces of wood,
And place them in abundance on a thousand tables;
Let him cut off the bottom and top of heavenly sedge reeds
And cut them into myriad strips;
And let him pronounce the heavenly ritual,
the solemn ritual words.
When he thus pronounces them,
The heavenly deities will push open the heavenly rock door,
And pushing with an awesome pushing
Through the myriad layers of heavenly clouds
Will hear and receive these words.
Then the earthly deities will climb up
To the summits of the high mountains and low mountains,
And pushing aside the mists of the high and low mountains,
Will hear and receive these words.
Then, beginning with the court of the Sovereign Grandchild,
In the lands of the four quarters under the heavens,
Each and every sin will be gone.
As a result of the exorcism and the purification,
There will be no sins left.
They will be taken into the great ocean
By the goddess called Se-ori-tu-hime,
Who dwells in the rapids of the rapid-running rivers
which fall surging perpendicular
from the summits of high and low mountains.
When she thus takes them,
They will be swallowed with a gulp
By the goddess called Haya-aki-tu-hime,
Who dwells in the wild brine, the myriad currents
of the brine,
When she thus swallows them with a gulp,
The deity called Haya-sasura-hime,
Who dwells in the land of Hades, the under-world,
Will wander off with them and lose them.
When she thus loses them,
Beginning with the many officials serving in the

Emperor's court,
In the four quarters under the heavens,
Beginning from today,
Each and every sin will be gone.
Oh diviners of the four lands,
Carry them out to the great river
And cast them away. Thus I speak. (Philippi 1959, 45-49)

Around the stone island upon which the Gūji and his attendant stand are now over a hundred little paper dolls floating upon the mirrorlike surface of the water, all of them on their way to the deity of the deep, who will wander off and lose them. As the last syllables of the long prayer fade into the sparkling sound of the waterfall, everyone bows twice, then claps twice, and, by bowing again, completes the ritual save for one last observance.

At the base of the stairs leading up to the Hall of Worship, a large seven-foot ring of sedge grass has been positioned, with a mask on either side to serve as guardians and scare away demons. The entire gathering descends the steps and forms a long line with the Gūji at the front and the other priests taking positions according to rank. Gruff and yet smiling, Oka-san shouts out the words to the song they will sing as they weave in a figure-eight pattern through the ring of purification, the same kind mentioned earlier that saved the peasant's household from the plague.

> All people who do the *harae* of the sixth month
> are said to lengthen their lives a thousandfold . . .
>
> (*Mina-zuki no nagoshi no harae suru hito wa
> sen yowai nobuto iu nari . . .*)

It is a beautiful sight as the priests, businessmen, grandmothers, *miko*, schoolchildren, toddlers, babies strapped on their mothers' backs, even a couple foreigners, all slowly proceed through the ring, each time "cleaner" than before, each time the song a little truer in their voices. No one acts embarrassed or as if they are a century too late to benefit from the magic of the rite—a quick glance at the faces reveals enjoyment and absorption in the moment.

And when the last old woman has waddled through for the final time, a number of shrine helpers appear with enough *odango* snacks (small rice balls on a skewer and covered with sauce) for everyone. It would be as if the staff of a major church served cookies and cake

to its congregation following an Easter or Thanksgiving service—
no one goes away spiritually or physically undernourished. The best
part of all, from the priests' point of view, is that not only is the
participant made anew within and without but the surrounding environment, community, and nation are purified as well. Perhaps the
taxi driver who takes you home or the snoring drunk beside you on
the streetcar is not aware of their altered state, but that does not stop
someone fresh from the purification ritual of the sixth month from
believing them transformed and cleansed. Such is the power of ritual
and the marvelous defenses it restores to the dedicated participant to
assist him or her in an ongoing alignment with the incomprehensible
and mysteriously varied world. The trip home is much more than
what it seems: thanks to the purification, it now becomes a sacred
voyage through the only safe passageway the dangerous summer will
ever yield.

13

There is something about the summer in Japan that drives one unaccustomed to its heat, humidity, and torpor into a kind of temporary madness. Perhaps it is the ferocity of the sun magnified by prisms of moisture, or the frequent calms that, in the absence of any breeze whatsoever, make one feel as if suffocating. Then again, it could be what happens after a warm rain provides momentary relief which then only thickens the atmosphere's wet, cloying density to the point that people create visible wakes when passing through it in a midday sun. But of course I exaggerate. The taxi drivers, fishermen, day laborers, and, yes, Shinto priests that man their stations throughout the stultifying months of July, August, and September would dismiss my lamentations as nothing more than the whimperings of a spoiled product of a temperate climate (Kansas!) accustomed to air-conditioning, central heating, and other spoils of war wrested from the environment.

But they are not the only ones linking climate to character. In fact, one of the most widely read books in prewar Japan was called *Climate and Culture*, in which Watsuji Tetsurō postulated the Japanese character to be based upon a peculiar version of the monsoon culture. Whereas those raised in a "desert" culture like the Mediterranean or in a "meadow" culture as found in Europe are capable of "gentle love" and "dry, abstract, contractual reasoning," the Japanese climate produces people that are "full of emotional vitality and sensitivity" (see van Wolferen 1989, 265). Carried a little further, the dichotomy progresses into the whole of Western civilization as it expanded out of Mesopotamia and the Mediterranean, where man is able to dominate nature because its flora and fauna are vulnerable to meddling. However, because of a variable, monsoon climate, which produces a rich fecundity that dominates all humanity does, the Japanese have nurtured "intimate, family-style relations" with the environment as the basis for social and political life.

Lest we get too carried away with this reasoning (it was, after all, used by ideologues stressing the "uniqueness" of the Japanese race to further justify the war effort), the fact remains that the Japanese summer is a powerful environmental force that has shaped centuries of human behavior. We have discussed some of this interaction in the preceding chapter on the Great Purification ritual of the sixth month, but for now the summer climate serves to contextualize the following comments, opinions, and confessions of many individuals at the shrine.

But here a problem emerges. When communication between individuals serves to expunge anger, frustration, or pain, it often acquires symbolic representations, as a few paltry words must stand for highly complex emotional states. The Catholic priest honors his confessional, the physician his patients' conditions, and the journalist protects her sources—but where does an ethnographer draw the line of confidentiality? What does a Japanese Shinto priest in southern Japan in the middle of a stifling summer mean when remarks are prefaced by, "I shouldn't be telling you this, but . . ."? Are these conventional words to be attributed to establishing good rapport, do they preface political maneuverings by the informant that will enhance his position in the shrine hierarchy, or is the exchange to be regarded as strictly confidential?

Perhaps, upon reading the following comments, the reader will understand why the chapter has the title it does (with the "I" referring to both myself and the priests). I am hoping, however, that by presenting these voices anonymously, they will open a world of discourse normally shielded from domestic, not to mention international, examination. But perhaps I am being overly cautious about protecting my informants' identities concerning a few off-the-cuff remarks. After all, no matter what the institution is—whether it be of a religious, economic, political, or academic nature—the face it projects to the outside is a composite of multiple voices from the inside, ones often of conflicting opinions and beliefs, which nevertheless manage to function within the organization's parameters and accomplish its objectives.[1] Therefore, it should not come as a surprise that a Shinto shrine, with its hierarchies of rank, seniority, and power, is any different from the model of a typical institution.

A shrine is not an autonomous entity guided by tradition and belief into a blissful harmonious functioning any more than the local
police station is. First and foremost, it is the people who, with their
various backgrounds, experiences, and personalities, determine how
the place is run and how it best meets the needs of those it is supposed to serve.

Still, a disclaimer is in order. Just as an evening of drinking with
Japanese colleagues will produce highly critical or acerbic comments
directed at specific individuals that are supposedly forgotten the next
day at the office, so too can many of the following remarks (collected
while everyone was sober) be contextualized by the languor of summer. They may indeed be representative of an individual's opinion,
but they may also be seen as venting steam to a disinterested yet sympathetic party. Although critical, our understanding of the "life" of
the shrine would be sorely compromised were these voices to remain
silent.

*   *   *

"You know, when it's hot like this—really hot and humid—that's
when I miss the old shrine the most. Yes, I appreciate the air-
conditioning within the Hall of Worship that we have now in the
remodeled shrine, and it certainly makes our official duties at weddings, dedications, and other rituals much more comfortable, but
when the shrine was remodeled we lost something of the old spirit
of Shinto. It's hard to explain what I mean.

"Perhaps you've seen old shrine buildings in other places that
protect the Hall of Worship with wooden shutters which are suspended from the roof over the veranda. If a typhoon or storm is
threatening, the priests unhook the shutters and they swing down
on hinges. But in the old shrine building here, we never used those
shutters because they were so old we were afraid they would break
apart. This resulted in a totally exposed Hall of Worship, at all
seasons of the year! Rain would come in and sometimes soak the
tatami on the floor, wind would knock over something on the altar,
sometimes with such precise timing in the course of a ritual that it
was uncanny. We really felt like the Kami were in attendance! And
in a way, with Shinto's traditional roots so deeply a part of nature,
it's right to have the Hall of Worship open to the elements.

"Originally in Shinto, there was no shrine building at all you
know—just four corner posts with sacred rope linking them, and a
single tall bamboo or tree at the center for the Kami to alight upon

after descending from the Heavenly Plain. Oh, I know, the old building was decaying and had a termite problem, and the way the roof leaked it would probably have fallen down on top of someone, causing a terrible legal and spiritual problem for the shrine, but I do miss it. This morning, for example, when we had a dedication ritual and closed the sliding glass doors around the veranda and turned up the air-conditioning, I felt like I was some kind of object on display in a museum, not a priest in a shrine. And you should see the electricity bills the shrine has to pay!"

*

"One of the things I'm sick of hearing is how out-of-date Shinto is with the times. People say that the *norito* should be updated to modern Japanese—just like the Catholics did with their mass—but it's not that easy. Even if it could be put into modern language, it's doubtful that people could understand it because most of its content is not about contemporary matters but mythical ones. Maybe I should clarify what I said. A common person *could* understand a *norito* in contemporary Japanese if they listened closely, provided they had some notion of what it was talking about; you know, the High Plain of Heaven, the Kami involved, and so on. Some say the mythical element should be condensed, but I think it helps locate the universe of the *norito* before turning to the contemporary concerns of asking for protection, offering gratitude, or acknowledging the Kami's gifts, such as the rice harvest or a new baby.

"A Buddhist prayer, on the other hand, is very hard to understand because the reality it is invoking is completely different. Does that sound like a contradiction? A *norito* is merely asking the Kami to give their attention to the matters of *this* reality, but a Buddhist prayer is asking for something apart from this world. Actually, I think it is in the Buddhist priests' interests to keep the prayers unintelligible, so they can retain their jobs. If it is a democratic religion like many sects claim, then *anyone* should be able to communicate their desires to the Buddhas—and if that's so, what's the need for a priest or temple?

"The fact is that people who come daily to the shrine are almost all concerned with real actuality. For example, the purifications we do for cars request of the Kami that the vehicle not be involved in accidents and not run into pedestrians. So in spite of the fact that all petitions are done in the *norito* style, with its distinct rhythm for these requests, the ultimate concerns are pragmatic. I just wish we could update the language a bit—but without the approval of the Central Association of Shinto Shrines, it'll never happen. I'm not even sure a small shrine in a rural area could get away with altering the orthodox style of delivery—although it'd be interesting to try and see what would happen! I wonder if anyone has ever tried it?"

*

(A debate)

PRIEST A: One of the things that I'm going to do when I become chief priest of a shrine is to change the way purifications are done before rituals. Here at Suwa Shrine we use the same *haraigushi* [purification wand] over and over, and that's just not right. You probably think that the *haraigushi* is only a symbol for the participants of a ritual to purify their own hearts, but it's my idea that it serves as a sponge and absorbs the defilements [*kegare* and *tsumi*] of each individual. It's only right, then, that it should be broken and put into a river where these defilements can be washed down to the sea like the story in the *Kojiki* prescribes.

PRIEST B: No, no, you've got it all wrong. The *haraigushi* separates the defilements from the individual's body and heart. When we do a *harae* outside, these impurities fall on the rocks and can be cleansed by rain or water. That's why we have those gray rocks and not white ones.

PRIEST A: Well, if that's true, then what happens when we do purifications *inside* the shrine? It especially bothers me to see the *haraigushi* used inside the shrine's Hall of Worship and then replaced right there on the altar.

PRIEST B: Right, I see what you're saying. What if the *tsumi* get scattered, according to my view, or if the *haraigushi* doesn't absorb them completely, according to yours? That means that the altar, the offerings, and the participants as well are all contaminated with the *tsumi* of each other—a state ten times worse than just one's own *tsumi!*

PRIEST A: That *would* be bad!

PRIEST B: It bothers me to even think about it. I'm sure most of the other priests never think about this but it really needs attention if Shinto is planning to systematize its procedures and develop some kind of theology. There's really so much to do . . .

PRIEST A: Say, where did you study to be a priest?

*

"The worst thing about August is the fact that schools are on vacation. No, I'm serious! That's because I can't go to the children's group that meets regularly as part of the shrine's preschool. This is the part of my work that I really enjoy—much more than participating in rituals where any little mistake is a major problem. The children ask so many questions, and when I can answer them and help them learn about Shinto, I really feel good. How are they going to learn about morality and ethics if they don't get it in school? Another thing about summer is that it's a time when house purifications aren't in demand, which is another of my many duties. It gives me a good feeling about being a priest, that I've unconditionally made the right decision to be one, when I perform these purifications and make a person's house more livable."

*

"Now I shouldn't be telling you this, but if you really want to understand how this shrine works, think of feudalism. There are fourteen people working at the shrine, including the chief priest, and for the younger people at the bottom, there's no doubt that we're going through some kind of feudalistically inspired training. We always try to do our best but when something is perceived as not being correct, then a reaction comes from the top and bounces down through the levels of hierarchy until it crashes on us here at the bottom! That way it has a chance to build up momentum and really lay us low. Part of the problem is my own thinking, because the top person's way of doing things is so different from my own ideal, and that my ideal is founded on that of Ise Shrine, where I went to college [at Kōgakkan] to become a priest. I'm sure that wherever I would go I'd find this or that shrine is just like Suwa and doesn't follow the Ise way—but if we could do just one or two things their way I'd be satisfied."

*

"You might think this newly remodeled shrine is normal, but let me tell you that we really suffered to get it built. I wish I could enjoy it but I always think of how the old shrine used to be and how the shrine's board of regents and moneyed supporters steamrolled their plans right over the protests and opinions of the priests—and it makes me mad. We had to raise over $650,000 from the community—which meant a lot of door-to-door begging for donations (of course, the shrine's women's group and lay members did much of this)—but each priest also had to donate anywhere from $2,000 to $4,000 out of his own pocket. We would have been shamed if it was a lesser amount. But once everybody got behind the idea of the '360-Year Commemorative Reconstruction,' how could it be stopped?

"I still think it was strange to rebuild the shrine for *our* comfort and convenience and not to have the Kami as the center of the plans. All one heard about during the planning stages was, 'let's make it comfortable,' and 'let's make it easy and convenient to do such and such a task,' as if the Kami wasn't involved at all. And that's frightening to me. We have a saying in Japanese about how you need troubles to form character: 'When you are young you need trials to get strong, even if you have to *pay* for them to come your way.'"

*

"You ask me if I'm glad to be a priest? What an interesting question! I work so hard from day to day that I don't really think about it. Actually, when I first started out from high school, I never thought that I would be involved in a shrine even though my father was a priest. All I wanted to do was get away from home and get a job and my own place—I guess I was a little rebellious. But when I was twenty I changed my mind. My grandmother was having these dream visitations from her ancestors and they were consistently pointing toward me as the one to take over the family shrine. How would you feel if your grandmother kept telling you her dreams like this over and over? It really troubled me! I had no idea of what to do. Also, the influences I was getting from my surroundings were of no help, since I was at that age when everything is difficult, but I thought that instead of simply taking over something like a shrine I should make my own way in the world. However, the more I thought about it, and the more my grandmother told her dreams, I began to think that perhaps my way was already made and her ancestors were desperately trying to help me realize this and save a lot of time and trouble later on. So my father and I consulted and now here I am in training, for better or worse I guess. I could leave Suwa Shrine at any time—maybe even tomorrow if I feel like it— but I know I still have plenty to learn."

*

"Sometimes I wonder what's going to happen to this country—
and of course to Shinto. Just the other day I heard from one of
my friends in Tokyo this story about Meiji Shrine, which is, as
you know, the biggest in Tokyo. It seems that, during the recent
hot spell, the shrine grounds were especially crowded with young
couples in the evening. This isn't surprising because Meiji Shrine is
so close to Roppongi, one of the real hot spots for young people in
Tokyo. Well, the caretakers found one couple actually . . . well, you
know . . . going at it in the bushes! Of course they yelled at them
and told them to leave immediately. While being escorted to the
exit, they were asked if they weren't ashamed for the offense they
caused against the Kami of the Meiji emperor. And the girl, a *Japanese*, asked, 'Meiji *who?*' Can you believe it? She didn't even know
who the shrine was for! Unbelievable! What kind of an education
did she have that she wouldn't know about Meiji Shrine? I tell you,
I'm worried about the future . . ."

*

"Now if *I* were chief priest of this shrine the first thing I would
do is to get rid of the stage leading up to the altar in the Hall of
Worship. That's something that our new Gūji added, and I think
it smacks of elitism. A Hall of Worship is supposed to place the
priests and parishioners on the same level, one below that of the
Kami altar. Now, with the addition of that stage, even though it's
only raised about five inches, the priests are above and therefore
seen as superior to the worshippers. It might seem like a simple
thing to you but I feel it upsets the balance of the ritual. Another
thing I'd do is to get rid of all the doors on the Hall of Worship,
because it should not be a place that can be closed off to the outside
world. If people want to come in during the middle of a service,
fine! Let them! It's their shrine after all. Now all they can do is
to peer through the glass and wonder what on earth is going on
in there.

"I know I shouldn't be telling you this, but the thing that bothers
me most is how the rebuilding of this shrine completely changed
the natural landscape, which is supposed to be what determines
how the shrine is constructed in the first place. There weren't any
hills or trees torn down—nothing like that—but we had a very nice
spring that came out of the side of the hill directly into a little font
where people could either use the water to purify themselves or
take it home to use for tea. Every morning, several of the city's res-

taurants would send an employee up here to fetch this good sweet water. The same font is here today but it's tap water that comes out now! What a shame. That spring water has a spirit that is not being looked after, and that worries me. I hate this kind of insensitivity. What is the future of Shinto going to be if things like this can happen at a shrine?"

14

A
WOMAN'S
PLACE
IS THE
SHRINE

In the wilting summer heat, visitors to the shrine at midday are few and far between. The front courtyard, with its off-white gravel bordering the gray limestone walkways and steps, shimmers and pulsates in the harsh light. And yet, faithfully on duty today at the shrine's amulet and information window (and without the benefit of sunglasses) is Suwa Shrine's single woman priestess, a pleasant and in many ways thoroughly modern young woman in her midtwenties. Listening to Ms. Mine describe her status as both a woman and a priestess gives us a chance to briefly examine the role women have played in the development of Shinto. For the sake of a little historical resonance, we will make a detour by way of her shamanic and priestly predecessors before hearing what Ms. Mine has to say about her place in the shrine.

The archeological and historical record points to evidence that the early cultures of the Japanese islands were very likely matrilineal in their social organization, with powerful women leading the hierarchy. A Chinese account from the third century mentions a queen, Pimiko or Himiko, who "occupied herself with magic and sorcery, bewitching the people" in the kingdom of Wa. Separated from the people of her clan, she was served by only her brother, who took care of her physical needs, acted as a spokesman for her communications, and managed state affairs.[1] Although Himiko was specific to only one clan, we can assume from this and other Chinese accounts that the practice was fairly widespread throughout the islands until the so-called Yamato began to centralize power and make changes based on precedents from the Korean and Chinese civilizations proven successful in maintaining hegemony.

After instituting a more male-oriented hierarchy, the Yamato
legitimized their clan's status through the written transcription of
old recitative poems and myths about the origins of the nation and
its early rulers. The *Kojiki* and *Nihon-shoki* both established the idea
of an Imperial family, descended from the great Heavenly Kami
themselves. But again, we can see in these early stories the importance of women, because it was to an Imperial princess that Sūjin,
one of the legendary emperors, turned when he became uneasy about
sharing his residence with Amaterasu, the Sun Goddess. As a temporary solution, the Kami was moved to a nearby village where a
princess was placed in charge of worship. It was not until the reign
of the next legendary emperor that another princess in charge of the
Sun Deity's shrine undertook a search to find a permanent location.
When at last she arrived in the province of Ise, Amaterasu revealed
in a dream that this was the site she wanted, and it is there this most
important and lovely shrine remains to this day, symbol of the Imperial family's continuing claim to an unbroken link with the Kami
responsible for founding the nation.

The infusion of Confucian and Buddhist values beginning in
the sixth century brought a decided shift toward a male-dominated
social structure for both secular and sacred affairs. However, the role
of "woman-as-shaman" continued as a part of many shrines, large
and small, as well as at the official Imperial level, where the highest rank in the ecclesiastical hierarchy is still held by a princess, the
saishu, or high priestess of the Grand Shrine at Ise. By and large,
however, the principal roles in conducting services for the Kami and
in managing the affairs of shrines were assigned to the male priests
of several important families.

Still, women had considerable influence in the shrines as spirit
mediums or performers of sacred dances, and some shrines had
full-fledged priestesses down to the end of the sixteenth century.
There were also spirit mediums not directly employed by shrines
who served as consultants to both the priests and the parishioners
and who operated on or near shrine precincts all through the Edo
period (see Smyers 1993). All this decisively ended with the advent of
the Meiji Reformation of 1868, when an edict intended to separate
Shinto from Buddhism (so the former could be better manipulated
as a rallying point for expansionistic goals) also turned out many
women who had been until that time legally employed at shrines and
denied them the option of recertification.[2]

The beginning of this period of refocusing the symbols and ideas of Shinto was especially restrictive regarding women. But as many smaller, local shrines were deprived of their priests when the militarists called more and more men to serve in the armed forces, an opportunity again arose for women. Since someone had to serve the local Kami, the parishioners, more often than not, pressed the head priest's wife into fulfilling the necessary obligations instead of someone from another region not familiar with the particulars of the community. Presumably, the earlier edict prohibiting women from being priests was pragmatically amended during the war years, because many women did gain the necessary education and certification required to serve as heads of shrines.

Shinto priests have always been free to marry and raise families, so, similarly, nothing prevents priestesses from choosing a spouse and having children. Unlike the monastic tendencies of Buddhism and some schools of Daoism, where to find personal enlightenment or salvation a devotee frequently must leave his family, renounce his social obligations, and endure an indefinite period of asceticism, Shinto is quite accepting of the human condition. After all, it is a natural urge of human beings to seek affection and then honor it by making a commitment to another person, thus gaining recognition as a full-fledged member of society.[3] In many ways this attitude (like many others) was strongly influenced by Confucian ideals, but it has remained a central part of the underlying "social" bond linking a community to their Kami (see De Vos and Sofue 1984).

About the only prohibition still in effect for women today comes not from a governmentally regulated source but from one of the earliest myths expressed in the *Kojiki*. It indirectly implies that because blood is thought to be a defiling impurity in the eyes of the Kami, menstruating women should not take part in ritual activities. Once the temporary state of impurity has passed and a priestess has been ritually purified just like any other priest, she can then resume her duties. It should be mentioned that all of this is merely an ideal requirement; whether priestesses or *miko* are actually this strict today about "following the rules" is rather unlikely.[4]

By far the most common role that women play at a contemporary shrine is that of the *miko*—a word that can be cross-culturally referenced (but not translated) as "unmarried female shrine attendant." In a tradition that goes back to the very heart of shamanic practices in Japan—where spirit possession by the Kami was an integral part of the services performed by *miko*—they are today relegated to a variety of important, yet subordinate, roles in relation to the predominantly male priests.[5] In their white kimonos and striking vermilion bloomers, these young women, usually just out of high school, perform a variety of tasks at the shrine during their tenure. In many shrines, their most important role is to perform the sacred *kagura* dance (called *otome-mai*) during all kinds of festivals and rituals. However, not all shrines have *otome-mai* as part of the worship service, in which case the *miko* are still *miko* but they will be found serving as secretaries in shrine offices, as waitresses when guests are treated to a meal in the *naorai* feast (coming immediately after a service), as musicians, messengers, or clerks at an information desk that provides details on how to arrange a private service or on which amulets are appropriate for which situation. The young women are usually recommended by some parishioner or recruited from local families of good repute and hence they generally do not live at the shrine. Though they receive a very modest salary, they are compensated in other ways by the respect they receive from parishioners as well as by the opportunities they have to learn proper etiquette, calligraphy, painting, cooking, and organizational skills—accomplishments that contribute to their eligibility as office employees or as potential wives when they eventually decide to get married.

In talking to Ms. Mine, one of the first things she points out is that she is most definitely *not* a *miko*. While not demeaning the role of these young women, her insistence on this point will be obvious from the following comments.

*　　*　　*

"I like the feeling of being able to walk down the street, looking just like any other woman my age, and to have this little secret that I'm a Shinto priestess. I guess everyone in Japan wants to have something that makes him or her unique—whether it's fashion, a hobby, or some special ability. I'm proud to be who I am, even though it is a bit unusual for a woman in this day and age.

"My family is a Shinto family and has been in charge of the village shrine at Aino for longer than anyone can remember. When I was in high school, I promised my grandfather to study Shinto when I got older, thinking at the time that it would be a good way to get to Tokyo from my little village down in Kyushu. I was like anyone else who watched TV and had their favorite singers and shows; I thought that Tokyo was where it was all happening, and to have the excuse to study at Kokugakuin University was just perfect. Strangely enough, my parents supported me all the way.

"But maybe I should say a little about my high school days first. I was very typical, commuting to Isahaya from Aino every day (about ten miles) so I could have the advantages of a larger school. The only time I felt a little different was when I'd have to take special holidays so I could return home to help with a festival or important ritual which my grandfather was in charge of. Then all my friends would tease me, 'Oh, poor Mine; the unfortunate child of a shrine!' However, I thought nothing of it, because there were students there from temple families, merchants' families, or who lived above their fathers' medical clinics who also had to help out from time to time—so it seemed normal. By the way, I should say that my father is a teacher and the only son of my grandfather. It's rather complicated why he didn't go into the shrine but it has something to do with the feeling people had for Shinto after the war. Since many people had grown up with the government forcing Shinto down their throats and since it was used as the justification for imperialism, it wasn't very popular following Japan's defeat. But that's another story however.

"The only time I really felt different from everyone else was when we finally went our separate ways after the senior year—some to nursing school, some to educational teacher-training junior colleges, others to become office girls in various companies in the area, and of course some to get married. But I went away to a university specializing in Shinto studies to become a priestess! That's when everyone started saying, 'What a strange thing you are!' It bothered me a little but when I got to Tokyo, all that was quickly forgotten.

"I know there's a stereotype of Kokugakuin University as being the place where the fanatics who caused so much trouble and got us into World War II went to be indoctrinated, and I was expecting to find something like this. However, it was pretty much a typical university, save that its specialty was Shinto studies, and I led a typical college student's life. I even played keyboards in a rock band— does that surprise you? To be honest, I was probably more interested in music, especially what was happening on the West Coast of America, than I was in learning about Shinto ethics or mythology, but eventually I matured and got serious about my studies.

"At one point during my university days, we had to undergo a training period. You know, the kind that is supposed to make you tough and pure and bright. We had to get up at 4:30 in the morning and thoroughly clean the shrine and gardens surrounding it, then study hard all day, even doing some meditation, and weren't allowed to sleep until 11:00 at night. The worst part was having to perform the *misogi* purification in the ocean while reciting the Oharae prayer about all the impurities and evils that we were washing away. Miyagi Prefecture is north of Tokyo, so that when we did it first in winter I was absolutely frozen to the bone. I remember thinking, 'Ah, so this is what they really mean!' There were only a few other women in my class but we all participated alongside the men. Other than that intense training session, it was all pretty much routine study.

"When I got out of school, I kept my promise to my grandfather and returned to Aino, and through his connections to Suwa Shrine, it was agreed that I come and further my studies. Now that I'm out in society, meeting a variety of people all the time, when they ask me what I do and I answer that I'm a priestess, their reaction is usually the same. 'Incredible!' they say. But this is my career and it seems very normal to me. I'm sure I'll have a relationship with a shrine all my life, even after marriage. If you ask what my career goals are I'd have to say that they're not easy to pinpoint in the way other young people talk about becoming the head of the department or making lots of money or marrying some up-and-coming young executive or doctor. No, for me, what I'd like to do is to make whatever shrine I'm involved with a place where people can come and feel like they are 'home' and want to linger.

"Maybe it's because I'm from a rural area where the shrine is old and there is a feeling of intimacy between the community members and the shrine, but I don't get that feeling from Suwa Shrine. Actually, I liked the old shrine buildings better before all the remodeling and rebuilding took place. Of course, it is really a splendid-looking place now and is growing and financially sound, yet I can't help feeling that people aren't as close to it as they used to be. Maybe because the Gūji spent so much time in Tokyo and his all-business manner gets things done so efficiently, and that his way of doing things is not a Nagasaki way, which is slower and probably more haphazard, but I do feel there is too much emphasis on nonspiritual matters. People need to be able to come to the shrine and feel, 'Ah, I'm glad I came,' and I don't know whether this feeling is as strong as it used to be. But on the other hand, I know very well that if the Gūji doesn't do what he's doing, I won't be able to have money to eat!

"I guess the biggest problem I face now is the old attitudes about women and what their role is supposed to be at a modern shrine such as this one. I don't have hard training or anything like that, other than the juvenile tasks I'm expected to perform because of my rank, which I suppose are similar to pouring tea or making copies in an office. It just seems that other priests, the men, who are licensed the same as me and of my rank do much more than I do. Maybe it's because people might be put off when they come to the shrine and see a woman officiating. They might say, 'Hey, there are men priests here—what's a woman doing at the ritual I'm paying for?' This is discrimination of course, and in a place like Nagasaki, which is still conservative and old-fashioned and where men are believed to be superior to women, I can't escape it, even here at the shrine.

"But you know, women have always had an important role in Shinto, right from the very beginning, whenever that was. The first priests were not men but women. Have you heard of Himiko? She was very powerful, not only as a priestess but also as one of the first rulers of Japan. Even today, at Ise Shrine, there is a woman priestess higher in rank than the chief priest. The problem is that most people outside the shrine don't know these facts, and that people within the shrine tend to be patriarchal because of their age and education.

"When I first came here I was participating in some of the rituals as a musician and attendant who places mats and helps with whatever the senior priests don't do, but recently I spend most of my time in the information office, selling amulets and writing requests for personalized rites. I'm not a *miko*, you know! But I can't do anything about it because the senior priest in charge of deciding who participates in what ritual is an older man. When it's a simple monthly service like that given for the women's club, well, maybe then I'll be allowed to play flute or the *shō*, but when a more important occasion comes along, I feel like I'm something outsiders shouldn't see. Car purifications, infant dedications, and maybe an occasional wedding, yes, but I really would like to participate more.

"So I've decided that since this is a big shrine and there are many priests, maybe I should just study other things until I return to my own shrine and learn about festivals from my grandfather. Which is something I'll have to do anyway: learn the way it is done at Aino and not the Suwa Shrine way, even though this is 'big-time' Shinto. Now, I can learn about the various amulets and answer questions concerning them and shrine activities, plus learn how to use a word processor and keep things organized in the business office — so I'm doing my best. But, to speak frankly, always being here at the information desk gets a little monotonous. I'd like to bring my Walkman and sit here listening to music but I'm afraid that wouldn't look too good.

"If I could change something about Shinto — whether it's the shrine at Aino or Nagasaki or wherever — I'd like to somehow restore the presence of the Kami to a more direct feeling or contact. It seems that people feel the Kami is something far away, that they have to go to a shrine or be at the family altar before they can share things with the deities. But for me, I think it's a fundamental part of Shinto to have a sense that the Kami is with you, so that if something happens or you need guidance, you can communicate with it immediately, wherever you are. This closeness to the Kami is something our modern civilization and society have completely lost.

"Though this might sound contradictory to you, I see myself as a thoroughly modern Japanese woman and not as some traditionalist. I mean, I like to go on shopping sprees, eat delicious food in fashionable restaurants, hope to get a driving license, or date the person I choose just like anyone else. That's normal, right? When I talk by phone to my friends who are still in Tokyo, I feel like I want to leave the next day and go to a place that will give me more freedom. But the feeling passes; I think because I know deep down that this place I'm in now is where I really belong. Eventually I'll go back to Aino and assume my place in the community after my grandfather retires, but it's still exciting to me to be here in Nagasaki, walking down the street just like anyone else, and to wear my mask which hides my role as a priestess. No one can guess!"

AUTUMN

15

OKUNCHI: A CITY'S HEART AND SOUL

If one were to challenge a long-time resident of Nagasaki — or of any other Japanese metropolis of the same size — to name one aspect of his or her city epitomizing the spirit, energy, and character of its inhabitants and history, my guess is that a majority would point not to the gleaming new buildings of the shopping district nor to the local delicacies nor even to those temples or historic sites for which the city might be nationally known. They would instead single out the *reisai*, the yearly festival of the city's principal shrine, as capturing the esprit de corps of what it means to live in this particular place. At no other time of year do the neighborhoods served by a shrine regain the cohesive intimacy characteristic of earlier periods. As their inhabitants come together to construct a float, to raise funds for repairing the pavilion housing the portable shrines, or to organize groups of dancers to perform throughout the city and in front of the main shrine's priests and Kami, we see how an observance that is "religious" at its core reaffirms social networks and promotes a sense of community in subtle yet tangible ways that more overt attempts of political or economic maneuvering do not.[1]

To most people, Japanese and foreigners alike, few events compare to the noisy, often raucous atmosphere of a stereotypical major festival, when the usually somber businessman or hard-working male student is transformed into a half-naked, semipossessed servant of the Kami, often roaring drunk and careening through the streets under the weight of the portable shrines. Many people have commented, in fact, on how roughly the venerated shrines have come to be treated, a "recent" innovation when compared with the historical record's account that the *matsuri* of centuries ago were stately, even solemn processions. A *matsuri* helps us remember that the original intent of this activity was in part to revitalize communal awareness of a reciprocal relationship with the Kami. Through its regenerating power, the *matsuri* ensured continued cooperation, upon which depended one's economic livelihood as fisherman, farmer, merchant, or even politician for that matter. Every time a ritual is held within the shrine, the Kami are called upon to invigorate the individual participants and, by extension, the community at large. But when the Kami's golden palanquin comes zigzagging through the streets of one's neighborhood or in front of one's own house, few can resist the feeling that *something* beneficial (the power of *riyaku*) has been transmitted through the sheer intimacy of the encounter.[2] And since the route varies slightly from year to year, eventually most parts of the central city receive this transformative magic, which, in theory at least, creates a fresh bonding between the people and their deities, easing the way for petitions and divine intercession.

While the regenerative aspect of the Kami's procession through what were once its formally recognized parishes is the oldest and most fundamental characteristic of a major festival, there are other possibilities as well. *Riyaku* is still involved, but its accrual is meant for a more restricted clientele. In Kyoto, for example, the Gion *matsuri* of July 17 commemorates the worship of an emperor who successfully petitioned the Kami in 869 to end a terrible plague and thus save the state from ruin. At Tōshōgū Shrine of Tokugawa Ieyasu at Nikko, twice yearly processions are held to commemorate the visits of Imperial messengers who formerly paid their respects to the recently deceased *shōgun* by worshipping at his shrine. Finally, there are also processions because the Kami want to "revisit" some particular place which has spiritual significance, such as a river or the site of a mythological incident, or they may leave the main shrine to serve as a "welcoming committee" for a "visiting" Kami.

In Nagasaki, the ideology animating the Okunchi procession is reflected in the progression of the festival's stages. In order to distribute the blessings of the three Kami of Suwa Shrine throughout the city they are removed from the Inner Sanctuary, placed into three portable shrines, then taken through the streets until they reach a temporary shrine (called an *otabisho*) which has been erected down by the waterfront.[3] There they stay two days and nights, during which time many different rituals are performed, a number of dignitaries pay their respects, and tens of thousands of townspeople come to worship and then enjoy the foods, souvenirs, and prizes found in hundreds of tent stalls of the gypsylike caravan of vendors who wander through Japan from festival to festival. On the third day, the portable shrines are carried back to Suwa Shrine, ending with an exciting and breakneck sprint up the steep flights of stone steps leading to the Hall of Worship.

But to say this is an adequate description of Okunchi would be like calling the Grand Canyon a hole in the ground. What gives the festival its true and distinctive character are the dances, costumes, and, most importantly, the floats upon which ride the identity and pride of those seven *machi* (neighborhoods) which are the "prime participants" out of the city's seventy-nine.[4] Though a *machi* may decline its turn to participate, the choice is usually to mobilize as many people and as much money as possible, with expenditures of thirty million yen (roughly $231,000) not uncommon in order that the float, costumes, and feasting be as splendid as possible. Needless to say, competition between different *machi* trying to outdo each other is fierce, but fortunately (or unfortunately, depending on one's penchant for exuberance often bordering on chaos) Okunchi is not a "violent" or "rough" *matsuri* of clashing floats or warring neighborhoods. Instead, its stately processions and sumptuous costumes follow the Gion style, with only sporadic outbursts of uncontrolled revelry (usually occurring at night) as the participants get carried away by too much sake or beer. During the days, starting on October 7, when the main procession leaves Suwa Shrine for the temporary shrine near the waterfront, a series of highly organized, by-ticket-only performances before seated audiences is held at the main shrine and repeated in front of the city's convention hall and then at the Ohato waterfront. But for those unable to obtain tickets, the various dances and floats can be seen throughout the city as the participants move on foot from one site to another, in what is an exhausting and exhaustive feasting on the traditions and history of the city.

ORIGINS AND HISTORY

Part of Okunchi's history as a festival predates the actual founding of Suwa Shrine. By the time Japan emerged from several hundred years of civil war and coalesced under the warlord Oda Nobunaga into something resembling a nation around 1570, Jesuit missionaries and Portuguese traders had already established bases in Kyushu. Nobunaga's curiosity and tolerance of these economic and proselytizing activities—based partly on his desire for trade and hard currency and partly on his fascination with things foreign—permitted Nagasaki to become a Christian stronghold. Inspired by the intolerant attitudes of the missionaries, new converts burned local temples and shrines, erecting churches in their places. The financial gains of the China-Macao-Nagasaki silk and munitions trade were so lucrative that these provocative gestures were temporarily overlooked by the government in far-off Kyoto. After Nobunaga was assassinated, his successors—the powerful Hideyoshi and strategically minded Ieyasu—gradually came to realize that Christian doctrines subverted the feudal code of loyalty to one's lord, and that the missions' links to the political and military interests of the Portuguese and Spanish Empires threatened not only the social order but also the integrity of the newly formed alliances between the central administration and its affiliated clans on the periphery. Christianity was periodically "outlawed" as early as Hideyoshi's somewhat ambivalent first decree of 1586, but it was not until Ieyasu's declaration of 1614 that missions actually began to close and the systematic "apostatize-or-suffer" policy was enacted.

Suwa Shrine, significantly enough, was founded in 1614 as a specific political gesture aimed at reestablishing Tokugawa influence in a city where Christian sympathizers were abundant. However, Nagasaki's importance as an international port had been recognized as early as 1570 and had lured many businessmen and entrepreneurs from major population centers such as Osaka and Hakata in northern Kyushu. Being the isolated backwater that it was, they brought not only their business skills but also some of their local traditions such as songs and dances, which were taught to the "entertainers" and geisha of the Maruyama district. The earlier fishing communities had long observed spring and summer festivals in honor of the local Morisaki and Sumiyoshi deities, but when the song-and-dance events of the 1570s gained popularity and a bit of refinement, they were organized into a loosely run annual rite of merrymaking and entertainment. The Christian missionaries may have frowned on these events and tried to discourage them, but they survived in one form or another until they gained the new military government's attention.

As a way to enhance the budding legitimacy of the shrine (and, perhaps just as importantly, the legitimacy of the Tokugawa administration), the locals' eclectic mishmash of dances and celebrations was still permitted, but they were appropriated by the shrine in 1634 as a part of its fall festival. Another dimension was added not long afterward, one that elevated considerably the status of the festival and thereby made it a showpiece of Japanese culture and aesthetics, not only for the local population but for the resident community of Dutch and Chinese as well. With the introduction of Noh drama, Tokugawa money flowed to the shrine. Thirty actors trained constantly, having at their disposal the tutelage of a respected teacher from Hakata as well as some of the finest kimonos and masks that money could buy. Whether this elaborate preparation and expense had the intended effect of awing the locals is not known, but certainly Okunchi was, for many years, intimately entwined with Noh. The connection lasted until the closing years of the Tokugawa dynasty when, in 1857, a fire, supposedly started by children playing nearby, destroyed the stage, props, many masks and kimonos, and seemingly the will of the performers as well. Funds were never allocated to rebuild due to the slow deterioration of the Tokugawa regime, but the absence of "high culture" finally allowed the people's dances and festival to come into their own.

In 1868, a blow to the festival's burgeoning development came at the hands of the new Meiji government's local administrator, who decreed the dances and preparations too costly and prohibited them entirely. Seven years later, after repeated petitioning, tentative permission was given the neighborhoods to again participate, and by 1883 the *matsuri* had not only regained all of its old characteristics but had gained new stature as well, bolstered by a surge in the city's population. A rich legacy of photographs attests to the grand performances and magnificent processions held until the final years of World War II, when the festival was again prohibited by the military leaders. But it was just one year after the end of the war and the horrendous bombing of northern Nagasaki that the festival was reinstated with the full approval of the Occupation forces as a way of lifting the people's spirits and fostering pride in their efforts to rebuild.

Today, according to local historian Etchū Tetsuya, in terms of scale, preparations, and media coverage, the Okunchi festival ranks as one of the top ten in all of Japan. To ensure that it stays this way is not primarily the task of Suwa Shrine but rather an organization called the Nagasaki Organization for the Promotion of Traditional Performing Arts (Nagasaki Dentō Geinō Shinkō-kai). According to Morita (1990), this organization was founded in 1929 as the Organization to Promote Kunchi (Kunchi Shinkō-kai), disbanded during the war, then started again in 1949 as a way to help poor neighborhoods bear the financial burdens of participating in the festival during difficult economic times. The group's current title dates from 1975 and reveals the original intent to organize businesses and companies, coordinate advertising, and implement policies aimed at promoting and preserving an event that is very good business for the city. In 1979, for example, they solicited and received from businesses a minimum contribution of ¥15,000 per establishment, creating an operating fund of ¥11,000,000.[5] The seven participating neighborhoods were then contracted to perform on the grounds of the municipal auditorium, for which seating was erected and admission tickets sold. About ¥5,800,000 was generated by this single performance, which, when added to a ¥35,800,000 contribution from the city government and a prefectural contribution of around ¥400,000, led to a tidy sum to be divided among the participating neighborhoods. During the economic boom years of the 1980s, we can safely assume that these totals increased. Significantly, the organization keeps up the appearance of having nothing to do with the Shinto rituals preceding the performances at the municipal auditorium. The succinctness of the organization's guiding principle in Japanese, shinji to wa "no-touch"; kankō ippon, is lost when rendered into English, but it roughly means "hands off the rituals; promote fully the touristic aspects [of Okunchi]." With this type of money and influence involved, one might care to speculate about the amount of influence the Dentō Geinō Shinkō-kai actually has on what happens at the shrine both before and after the Okunchi festival.

CHARACTERISTICS

One thing to keep in mind about Okunchi is that, despite its 360-year history, it can be thought of as relatively "new." Flooded as Nagasaki was by foreigners and the accoutrements of their cultures in its formative years as an international trading center, the participating neighborhoods had no inhibitions about trying innovative ideas in making their floats. And as competition for prizes and recognition increased, so did the daring. The guiding principle was "If it looks impressive, let's use it!" Thus we have today, as legacies from that upstart beginning, the "Hollander's" dance (satirizing the "barbarians" from Europe); the Kokodesho, or "let's do it here!" dance (taught to the locals by businessmen from Osaka); and the Jaodori, or dragon dance (reflecting the city's Chinese links in trade and custom); as well as some curious chants used by the bearers of the portable shrines instead of the typical "*wasshoi, wasshoi*" heard elsewhere in Japan. One neighborhood, fascinated with the logo of the East India Trading Company, decided to turn the symbol on its head and include it as part of the insignia for their *machi*.

In addition to the exotic nature of the performances, many first-time viewers are puzzled by another aspect of the festival: the *kasaboko*, or, to use a figurative, rather than literal, translation, "shrine-on-a-pole." At first, fancy *kasaboko* were never used in the solemn march from the *machi* to Suwa Shrine. The leading member of the community at the head of the procession was followed by someone holding a large parasol (*kasa*) with a small fringe along the rim to shield the neighborhood's dignitary from the sun. Eventually, the parasol at the head of the procession came to represent the neighborhood, becoming larger, heavier, and more decorative. Not only did the fringe nearly touch the ground, but other objects were attached to the parasol, among them a small pine tree or plant placed at the top. People thought the power of the Kami was absorbed by the plant and then later brought back to the *machi* for protection of its inhabitants throughout the year. These plants can be compared to the *mikoshi* palanquins in that both are temporary dwelling places for the Kami; however, the *kasaboko* bearers have to invite the Kami to enter, whereas it is believed the *mikoshi* already has the deity within. Since the Kami are known to favor high places and dancing, what better way to lure them than with a beautifully decorated abode, spinning some three to four meters in the air like a spiritual lightning rod?[6] The *kasaboko* grew to symbolize each *machi*, and its present form is thought to have started sometime around 1780. To modern eyes, accustomed to the pacing of television, *kasaboko* performances tend to be rather tedious since all these elaborate parasols can do is spin around. But we should remember that any bearer capable of dancing while holding a 50- to 70-kilogram weight deserves all the encouragement and appreciation the crowd can muster, and the performers are usually rewarded with calls (*Motte koi!* literally, "Bring it [back]!") for several encores.

Finally, although the event preceded its naming, the word *kunchi*, or *ku-nichi* (ninth day), has some interesting connotations. The ninth day of the ninth month in the old lunar calendar (what we now call October 9) was a highly auspicious day for festivals. A borrowing of Daoist number magic from China, this tradition ordered numbers into groups of yin (*in*), having negative significance, and yang (*yō*), with more positive, nurturing powers. Unlike the Western system of numbers developed by Pythagoras and others, the odd numbers have the positive yang, and the even numbers, the negative yin.[7] Thus, for a festival to begin on the seventh day and end on the ninth day of the ninth month places its numerical symmetry in harmony with the greater symmetry of the cosmos. This custom was not restricted to Nagasaki alone of course, and numerous *kunchi*, or "ninth day of the ninth lunar-calendar month," festivals can be found in other parts of Japan (particularly in north Kyushu, where Chinese influence has been strong). In other words, to say *kunchi* is to mean "festival." And to say *kunchi* in Nagasaki implies swirls of people, colors, spinning floats, dragon dances, gleaming palanquins, television cameras, and the azure sky of early autumn. It's time to plunge in and find out what *really* goes on.

SEAWATER CLEAN: OCTOBER I

The morning is overcast and balmy, and carries with it traces of Typhoon Fifteen's extraordinary clouds that dumped three inches of rain on southwestern Kyushu. Here on the backside of the ridge of mountains running down the Nagasaki peninsula, where a caravan of cars from Suwa Shrine has parked beside one of Ariake Bay's beaches, the farmers and fishermen take their clouds very seriously. Early-warning systems installed after the three disastrous typhoons of mid-August, in which fifteen fishermen drowned, prevented further loss of life and property in what has been a particularly turbulent year. This morning though, there is a rich texture to the mottled greens of the loquat and tangerine groves blanketing steep hillsides, and the sand of Miyazuri beach looks smooth and washed, as if a gardener had tended it all through the rainy night.

But typhoons and weather systems are the last things on the minds of a group of half-naked men who stand huddled together on the beach, awaiting the completion of an opening prayer. In just a moment these bearers of the festival's portable shrines (*mikoshi*) must be thoroughly purified in the most ancient, efficacious style—total immersion in saltwater—before they can even approach the Kamis' palanquins. Framed by the distant volcano of Unzen on the other side of the bay's gray waters and the long expanse of beach stretching away on either side, the men look fragile and insignificant in their white loincloths and headbands, not at all sure that going into

the sea is something human beings are supposed to do on the first of
October. Although being selected to carry the *mikoshi* is a once-in-a-
lifetime opportunity and honor, the lapping waves and great silence
behind them are more than enough to make this distinction appear
dubious. Most Japanese will tell you that swimming in the ocean is
simply *not possible* after August 15 because by then not only has the
typhoon season started in earnest, churning up the water and letting
the sea show its violent side, but also the jellyfish have found their
way into the warm currents, and leave nasty welts for those foolish
enough to go even wading. (Never mind that the jellyfish are gone
in two weeks, and that during all of September the water is mild
and warm.)

When the final bows are made before the portable altar loaded
with offering dishes, sake vessels, and *sakaki* branches, the priest picks
up the wand of purification and waves it above the bowed heads of the
group. Then, hesitantly, each man slowly wades into the water up to
his armpits, pauses an instant to silently recite the formula for purification while looking at the blue outline of the volcano of Mount
Unzen and, joining his palms together, suddenly disappears beneath
the waves. It is an eerie sight how completely they are "gone," for
there is no sign whatsoever that they ever existed at all. For that instant, the participant is no longer a human being but has become
the ancient deity Izanagi, who had no choice but to purify himself in
water after seeing the rotting corpse of his wife in the netherworld.
It was from this purification that numerous Kami were born from his
body, among them Amaterasu, the Supreme Sun Kami, who sprang
into the world from Izanagi's left eye. But it was also this ritual that
provided Shinto with one of its most fundamental and powerful orientations to the world: that of *misogi*, or purification by cold water.

In order to reap the full benefits of this purification, the bearers
should have abstained from drinking alcohol, coffee, and strong tea
since the night before, have taken a bath at home once already this
morning, and should ideally (according to some schools of Shinto
thought influenced by the austerities of Buddhism) have abstained
from sexual intercourse. Salt is thought to be particularly efficacious
in purifications, not only because it is mentioned in the ancient myths
but because of its preservative function in keeping impurity from
food. One can find several traditional extensions of seawater *misogi*
rites to everyday life, such as when salt is sprinkled before the gate of
the home in the morning and evening, or after an unwelcome visitor
has left. It is still quite common to see little white piles in front of

restaurants (stay away misfortune!) or for those who have attended a funeral to sprinkle salt on themselves before again entering their homes. Certainly, the most ceremonial and pervasive use of salt outside Shinto rituals is at the beginning of each bout of sumo, when the giant wrestlers cast handfuls of the stuff into the ring so that the match will be fair (see Cuyler 1979).

Once the bearers have emerged from the sea and dried off, the entire party of priests, attendants, *miko*, bearers, and assorted friends and parents drive back to the shrine for a change of clothes and a *naorai* feast of fish-paste cakes, sashimi (thin slices of marinated raw fish), pickles, and of course ample amounts of sake. The men will meet several times with shrine personnel to discuss techniques of carrying the *mikoshi* as well as the routes they are to take between Suwa and the temporary shrine at the waterfront, but their muscular services will not be needed until 5:00 A.M. on October 7, when the Kami's transfer to the *mikoshi* starts the breathing of the creature that is to become Okunchi.

SUPPLICATIONS AND CIRCUMAMBULATIONS: OCTOBER 3

This is the day Okunchi ends its yearlong hibernation and emerges in earnest from storage closets, sheds, and warehouses in the guise of kimonos, *kasaboko*, and neighborhood floats. Residents of those seven *machi* participating in this year's festival are invited to come to the shrine for a visit and purification (Yogoto-sai), an affair which sounds simple enough until, at 3:00 P.M. on this sweltering afternoon, one sees nearly a thousand people assembled behind the tall and flapping cloth standards of their neighborhoods, all decked out in their finest costumes and kimonos. It seems more like a scene from one of Kurosawa's period spectacles, such as the films *Ran* or *Kagemusha*. From the children in their multicolored *yukata* (thin cotton kimonos) to the old men musicians in their indigo *monpei* bloomers and *happi* coats, the scene is a historian's and photographer's paradise.

While everyone has been slowly gathering in the shrine's lower courtyard over the past hour, a ritual (called Kori-shinji) in honor of the shrine's three Kami (Suwa, Morisaki, and Sumiyoshi) helping them "prepare" for the rigors of the people's festival, is now winding down. A number of *machi* residents have been quietly watching from the veranda of the Hall of Offerings, and follow the priests as they conclude their in-house service and move to the little courtyard used for preritual purifications adjacent to the shrine. After everyone is lined up—on one side, the Gūji and two *miko*, with Senior Priests Oka, Ureshino, Matsumoto, and Otaguro on the other—several bows precede a final move behind the tall screen of shrubs shielding the Kami's pond from view. All the paper dolls tossed into this little pool during late June's ritual of Great Purification have been removed of course, so that now it seems like a green-surfaced mirror reflecting the trees and bamboo of the hillside. A small waterfall trickles down into it, sending ripples that set the reflections dancing. And in the stillness of those moments before the priests silently bow and clap their prayers to the Kami behind the pool's mirror, the thousand or so beneficiaries of this ritual in the courtyard below seem very far away. More than the place itself or the ritual under way, the music of the waterfall transports the pondside celebrants into an exquisite yet fleeting atmosphere of calm. Look no further than this intersection of time and space, one might be advised, for the poetics of Shinto in modern Japan.

Minutes later, a loudspeaker crackles to life: "Thank you very much for being patient. The circumambulation of the shrine will begin shortly. You can circle it up to three times if you wish but please be careful going up and down the stone steps. Some of them are covered with moss and are a little slippery. Women with small children should try to stay to the inside of the route, while those walking faster should be on the outside. Pendant- and standard-bearers, please take care not to snag your banners on the branches of trees. First we will have a *harae* for the whole group, and then you may begin. Let's have a wonderful Okunchi this year! Thank you all for coming."

Matsumoto-san strides to the top of the stairs in front of the Hall of Worship and, with a deep bow, begins the *haraigushi*'s three slow sweeps over the crowd. Left, the "alpha" of the Kami's beginnings, from which all creation issued forth. Right, the "omega" of the Kami's influence, which is nothing less than every particle of creation extending from those assembled here to the farthest reaches of the universe. Finally left again, symbolizing a return to the source of the Kami, which each ritual and *matsuri*—such as today's Kori-shinji and public procession around the shrine (Juretsu mizoroi)—is supposed to enact. Later I am shown a poem of this very moment:

The priest bows once again,
and the blossoming mass
of colors below him
begins to slowly ascend.

JOURNEY OF THE KAMI: OCTOBER 7, DAY ONE

At 4:30 A.M. it is very dark, very quiet on the grounds of Suwa Shrine. Above the range of mountains to the east, only the palest blue hint of morning is beginning to chase the stars from the sky. Inside, however, priests have been busy since 2:30 preparing the three portable shrines to receive the sacred essence (*go-shintai*; literally, "divine substance") of each Kami when it is transferred from the Inner Sanctuary to begin its ride through the city in the main procession of the afternoon. No one except the Gūji and most senior priest may see or handle the container holding the sacred essence, and even then they must have spent the night in seclusion within the shrine. They wear protective face masks to avoid breathing on the deities as well as special hand coverings of unrefined white silk. Repeating Jean Herbert's distinction mentioned earlier in this book, *go-shintai* can be either natural objects in which the Kami was discovered—such as a stone, shell, or, in ancient times, an entire mountain—or man-made objects into which the Kami descended upon invitation or command from higher deities (1967, 119). Those smaller objects are themselves concealed within layers of silk or several lacquered boxes which are in turn shielded when being transferred out of the Inner Sanctuary by a three-sided white silk screen (*sashiha*) supported by branches from the *sakaki* tree. This is not to repeat the misconception that these objects actually *are* the Kami; they are only the receptacles in which the numinous essences of the Kami are believed to temporarily reside.

The atmosphere of other early morning rituals—such as those of the pure-fire ritual or rice-harvest thanksgiving—could be best characterized by their air of calm and solemnity. The Senryō-sai (Kami installation) ritual of this morning, however, is singularly different in that a volatile tension fills the halls. Even though the ritual has yet to start, priests, *miko*, and attendants walk fast from place to place and have no time for chatting, for today marks the first moments of Okunchi's three days of great celebrations. If the festival is to have an auspicious beginning (which in turn implies that the city and its inhabitants will receive blessings), everything depends on a smooth transfer of the Kami's sacred essences from the Inner Sanctuary to the three *mikoshi* resting within the Hall of Worship like sleek carriages awaiting royalty.

At precisely 5:00 A.M., the charged silence is finally shattered with a beat of the drum. In what is still nearly total darkness, the ghostly white robes of the priests seem to float through the air to the pebbled court of purification beside the Hall of Worship. After a brief *harae* for the priests and gentlemen serving as central organizers of the procession, everyone enters the shrine and ascends to the upper level for a full ritual complete with offerings, *kagura* dances by the *miko* attendants, and musical accompaniment. The only sign that the ritual has retained its ancient function as a harvest *matsuri* comes in the variety of seasonal food offerings: rice (cooked, uncooked, and still in the husk) leads the dishes, followed by various seaweeds, an entire fish (sea bream), sprouted ginger, white radishes, cabbages, yams, carrots, apples, persimmons, and finally the deities' favorite drink, sake. It is a substantial feast and should fortify the Kami as they begin the nearly fifty hours they will be outside the Inner Sanctuary.

The ritual proceeds along familiar lines until the very end, when instead of final bows and a greeting from the Gūji, the guests are politely asked to leave. Even before the five of us have started down the steps, the priests begin tieing on the white silk filters that will cover their noses and mouths. Lingering behind for a moment, I see them pick up and light old kerosene lanterns of a Chinese design, then suddenly, without any warning, the lights abruptly go out and a tremendous explosion of noise erupts from all sides: the great drum of the Hall of Worship is being pounded as if to break, the *gagaku* musicians are blowing their flutes and reed-harmoniums (*shō*) at the top of their lungs, and as two priests handle the *go-shintai*, the impressive howling of the *keihitsu* both calls the Kami to be present and announces that it *is* present (Herbert 1967, 125). I try to hurry down the steps in the dark, excitedly thinking to see the *mikoshi* installment, but my groping progress is passed by a flurry of pounding feet and by eerie green glows within a concealed passageway I never knew existed beside the main stairs.

I see a dim white blur at the bottom of the steps and try to accelerate my descent only to find myself suddenly standing *outside* the Hall of Worship, shut out by the closure of all its sliding wooden shutters. For a moment I feel like a character in a detective novel almost on the verge of apprehending an elusive suspect, when poof! the suspect vanishes into thin air. The fearsome racket from within continues a few more seconds, then, just as abruptly as the whole thing began and before I even have time to think what I should do next, the shutters fly open and lights pop on, revealing the priests standing in front of the three gleaming *mikoshi* as if nothing had happened. The Gūji steps forth and leads everyone in a bow to the new home of the Kami, then turns, walks to the front of the Hall of Worship and conducts the group in another bow eastward, to a sky still showing stars. It will be a full hour before the sun peeks over the ridge. When it does it will find the Kami ready for their voyage into the community and the priests busily setting up the morning performances of Okunchi, which, if their just-completed magic act is any indication, should "happen" as effortlessly as a Kami descending to earth.

"Mrs. Takagi, where *are your children?"*

All the escorted trips to and from rehearsals, the hours of sewing costumes, and the drain on the family's savings have finally led to the first day of Okunchi for the Takagi family. Mr. Takagi cannot, of course, leave his job at Mitsubishi Heavy Industries to attend the festivities, but his wife will proudly be there. Their son, Hiroaki, and daughter, Satoko, ages twelve and ten, are among those lucky children selected from the households of the Nakagawa *machi* to ride on the float: a two-thirds size replica of a Chinese junk (on wheels) to be pushed by sturdy neighborhood men while eight children pound drums and cymbals in time to the men's chanting (see fig. 15). It is an exciting, once-in-a-lifetime opportunity, yet it is grueling work as well, both for the men who must push an unstable, cumbersome, three-quarter-ton wooden boat over miles of city streets, and for the children, who feel each jolt along the way while creating the same monotonous racket for their many performances during Okunchi's three days. It is also trying for the childrens' mothers as well, who hover nervously around the float (some in running shoes) at all times, scrutinizing their children to make sure they are doing what they should and to tend to those turning green with motion sickness or white from exhaustion before they embarrass their family and *machi*. With the eyes of the entire community upon them, as well as the cameras of three television networks, the "enjoyment" will come later when they watch the videotapes and laugh over the snapshots. But for now, the festival is single-minded, total devotion, "give-no-quarter" WORK.

Despite intensive preparations, things are not going according to plan for the Nakagawa *machi* contingent as they await their first appearance before the Gūji, festival judges, television cameras, and the large live audience assembled on the shrine's steps and portable platforms constructed for the festival. Certain important individuals, upon whom the whole performance depends, have yet to arrive, but perhaps it too soon for the float supervisor to fret. There are still a few minutes to wait. The boat must first make its slow way to the level performance area, pitching and lurching over the old cobbled streets. There, after taking center "stage" in what is usually a parking lot, the children will set out a rhythm with their drums and cymbals, and the men will spin the ship around and around in time as the audience howls for more (*"Motte koi!"*) and the photographers edge in for close-ups. The established custom is to pretend to ignore these calls and, when the performance is complete, start the float down the first of four flights of badly worn steps. The audience will not allow them to leave of course, and one designated "cheerleader" will spring from his seat on the shrine steps and sprint to the float, begging them for an encore while the crowd behind him calls out, *"Motte koi! Motte koi!"* It is ritualized spontaneity at its finest, because in spite of the show of hesitation and pleading, one can rest assured that the float will come back for *at least* two encores.

Then, beyond the eyes of the audience and cameras, the real test of skill begins as these heavy floats—ranging from boats to whales to portable dragons—are inched over the precipice of each step, creaking and groaning their way to the street below. The children riding these floats do not disembark during the frightening lurches of the descent, nor do the bearers enlist the help of passersby or assistants (though occasionally, if the vehicle's weight is more than thought, people will have to step in to prevent it from rolling over gawking bystanders). It is almost as if their just-completed performance was to please the Kami and thus enlist their aid in negotiating the terrible stairs, for no one I talked to ever remembered anything catastrophic happening in all the years they had attended.

Standing on a parked car to scan the tumult created by several thousand people together in a small place, the Nakagawa *machi* float supervisor—a burly bus driver in real life now costumed in red headband, green plaid bloomers, and a delicately flowered *happi* coat—is frantically searching the crowds for a sign of his two young musicians. They were to have met fifteen minutes ago at the shrine's office building with the rest of the group. "Where *are* those kids? Mrs. Takagi has been very regular about getting them to all the practices, so why should she not get them here now when we most need them? How can the float go on without her son as the lead drummer?"

A neighboring *machi* has exited from center stage, and with only one more *kasaboko* display before Nakagawa *machi*'s colorful Chinese boat, its red and green silken sails fluttering in the slight morning breeze, the float supervisor's frown becomes permanent. "Mrs. Suzuki!" he barks to one of the other musician's mothers.

"*Hai, kaichō!* What is it, chief?"

"Did you say Mrs. Takagi called you this morning and said she would *absolutely* be here?"

"Absolutely! She said she couldn't sleep all night because Hiro-kun was so nervous he kept throwing up. Poor kid . . ."

"What do you mean, 'poor kid'?!" he growls, still craning his neck to see over the parasols, bowler hats, and balloons around him. "You should be saying 'poor us' or 'poor Nakagawa *machi*' if those kids don't show up, especially Hiro-kun, and lead the drum chorus!"

Another mother steps forward and attempts to soothe the supervisor with the maternal demeanor most Japanese men expect from their wives and other members of the "subordinate" gender. "Now *kaichō*, I'm sure they'll be here," she coos reassuringly. "They probably are stuck in traffic—and anyway think how Mrs. Takagi must be feeling right now! I'm sure she's frantic! *She's* the one I feel sorry for!"

Motte koi! Motte koi! The calls for the first encore of the *machi* currently performing send a wave of terror through the supervisor. He has to face the fact that Hiro-kun will not arrive on time, and that the chorus will have to have a new leader—and this after two months of daily practice! "Hey you, Toki-kun! You're going to have to lead the drums today, because it looks like Hiroaki-kun isn't going to make it!"

"ME??" the boy exclaims in horror, clutching at his kimono. "In front of all these people and cameras?? *Dekinai yo!!* I can't!!"

"What do you mean you can't?" the supervisor retorts. "Who else besides you is old enough to do it? Where's your mother anyway? I'll get her to *make* you do it!!" *Motte koi! Motte koi!* The dreaded call comes again as the supervisor yanks off his headband and bellows, "MRS. SUZUKI!! COME AND TALK TO YOUR SON!!"

And at that moment, a smiling Mrs. Takagi, followed by her two children, suddenly emerges from the crowd milling around the wooden ship. "Good morning everyone!" she says sweetly. "I'm sorry we're a little late! Children, climb aboard the boat now! Good morning, *kaichō.* Everything going okay?" The supervisor is both overjoyed that his lead drummer has arrived and overwhelmed with anger at her calm demeanor. "Mrs. Takagi, *where-have-your-children-been?!!!?*" He enunciates each word separately, now quite red in the face. "Do you realize we are ready to go on at *any moment?!*"

"Ah, Mr. Float Supervisor, I'm afraid it's all my fault," says a debonairly attired man with three large cameras slung over his shoulders and a fine white silk scarf around his tanned neck. "I saw Mrs. Takagi's cute children in their lovely outfits and just couldn't resist a few photographs for our magazine." Before the supervisor knows it, he has the man's business card in his hands and is now looking in astonishment at the name of one of Japan's most popular weekly photo magazines. "It wouldn't have been the same after the performance, you see, because then the look of apprehension, excitement, and awe would have been replaced by something else, satisfaction or gleeful relaxation perhaps. It just wouldn't have been the same. Now, if I could get a picture of you standing beside that marvelous looking boat of yours . . ."

Suddenly the supervisor is all smiles, bowing in thanks to the photographer who nearly ruined his drum chorus and nearly caused him to have a stroke in the morning sun here on the grounds of Suwa Shrine. "Just think," he says to himself, smoothing his pepper-gray hair and refitting his red headband as the photographer clicks away, "a picture of me or perhaps Mrs. Takagi's kids in the *Asahi Weekly*, with 'resident of Nakagawa *machi*' below the photos. That'll be *very* nice indeed . . . wait'll the people at the bus company see that!! I wonder if he would send me a copy to frame?" But before he can ask, the loudspeaker has begun their introduction and he twirls around, all business with his charges. "All right, now remember . . . we've practiced this a hundred times . . . it's '*chong, chong, chokka-chokka, chong, chokka-chong*' . . . and you men, let's give it your all! Make Nakagawa *machi*'s Chinese boat something these people won't forget!!"

Jaodori and the Kami's Departure

If there is a climax to the morning of performances before the portable shrines embark for their temporary home at Ohato pier, it would have to be the Jaodori (dragon dance; see fig. 13). Perhaps it is the strong Chinese influence on the costumes, music, and long green beast; or perhaps the dragon's sinewy movements are in such contrast to the muscular spinning of the bulky *kasaboko* and neighborhood floats as to render it ethereal and "alive." But for sheer drama coupled with aesthetic enjoyment, harking back to the long history of cultural and economic exchange with China, the smoothly co-ordinated writhing of the dragon/serpent as it chases a golden moon around the courtyard is surely in the realm of the finest performing art.

An early myth from the *Kojiki* informs us that the sacred sword — which figures as one of the three Imperial treasures (along with the *magatama* [jewel] and a mirror) — was found by the Sun Kami's brother in the tail of a dragon, but the Jaodori does not correspond to that story. Instead, the myths animating the dance come from ancient China and have two possible interpretations. Both begin with the fact that dragons are notoriously irascible creatures, with this particular serpent intent on devouring the moon and thus upsetting the smooth flow of the seasons. (It is not clear why this would be in the dragon's interest, but never mind that for now. Rational questioning only impedes the power of myth.) Naturally, the moon does everything it can to elude the hungry beast and leads it on a wild chase through the cosmos, twisting and turning to the accompaniment of gongs, drums, and the shrill peals of elongated trumpets before the creature is slain. The other possibility holds that the dance is actually a rainmaking ritual. If the dragon can swallow the golden moon, clouds will appear and rain will fall, preserving the life-giving crops and thus saving the people.

First performed in the sixteenth century by the Chinese residents of Nagasaki, the Jaodori was later held yearly on January 15 in the Chinese settlement as part of their New Year celebration. The tradition took root as a part of Nagasaki's Okunchi when the residents of Kago *machi* imitated their Chinese neighbors and likewise strung together the straw baskets used for unloading cargo from visiting ships and created the body of a serpent. Candles were then placed inside the baskets and the whole thing painted to look like a dragon. According to local scholar Brian Burke-Gaffney, the dragon is a traditional symbol of the human spirit, with its cries carried by the eerie wails of the trumpets. "In this sense," he says, "the dance portrays the eternal struggle after truth. Like the human mind striving after peace and truth amid the noise and hardships of the world, the cries of the dragon reach above the clamor of drums, gongs, and firecrackers — its white fangs, bristly mane, and bloodshot eyes lurch through the air, furiously chasing the ever-receding golden ball" (Burke-Gaffney 1987, 7).

For audiences viewing the Jaodori throughout Nagasaki —

whether in front of Suwa Shrine, at the floodlit city center performance, or by chance in the main shopping arcade—the philosophical overtones are absorbed in the power of the dragon's presence. Suddenly, the dragon is *there* among the members of the audience; all eyes are focused on it, not on its eight skilled "handlers." At the shrine, its entrance is heralded by Chinese-style trumpets as it moves slowly down the main steps where half of the audience sits, its fearful head twisting left and right, searching, ready to pounce. And since it enters from a totally opposite direction as the other performances— all of which begin with bows to the Kami first and to the seated dignitaries and the Gūji second—one might very well wonder if the beast came from *within* the shrine or somehow has the sanction of the Kami, since its dipping undulations and fierce countenance appear to be animated by a divine presence. But after all, what other reason *is* there for dancing before the deities if not to become possessed?

After three and a half hours of performances by the seven neighborhoods' *kasaboko*, floats, singers, and dancers, the Kami are considered well entertained and ready to begin their journey to the Ohato pier. To say the morning's activities have been solely for the benefit of the three Kami would be accurate in a strict religious and historical sense but would show a lack of appreciation for the social dimensions of the performances. Okunchi is an opportunity par excellence for seven communities—through the dedication, financial outlays, and skills of their members—to gain prestige and recognition by offering performances for the pleasure of the Kami as well as of their fellow citizens. To repeat a theme mentioned earlier, sacred *and* secular worlds are addressed and merged in a *matsuri* like Okunchi. Their juxtaposition, in what is often an intense experience shared by many people, gives these festival events a resonance extending far beyond the actual performances, into social networks and culturally consensual expectations about cooperation, reciprocity, and communal identity.

The principal performers have moved on to other locations to repeat their dances before larger audiences. Now, however, their relatives and neighbors have a chance to get into the act. Just as Americans are said to love a parade, a majority of the people of Nagasaki enjoy the slow-moving procession that accompanies the Kami on their journey through the community to the temporary shrine by the harbor.

Of course, it all begins at the shrine. Matsumoto-san, among others, has been planning this event for months and now directs whole blocks of gaily attired mothers and children, amateur dancing groups, squads of mascots, attendants, and even horse riders to stay in formation while the portable shrines are readied for departure. When the three heavy palanquins are finally brought down the steps and into the streets (see fig. 12), it is exactly two o'clock. At the very front of the procession is a sacred mirror and *sakaki* branch bedecked with white paper streamers atop a small cart, clearing a path for the Kami through the profane world of the city. Carried behind these rolling purification amulets are two long stalks of thick green bamboo, which are simply, and rather unceremoniously, dragged along the ground as if to scratch an actual line of separation to further delineate sacred from secular space.

No marching bands of flute players or drum corps from local high schools precede the *mikoshi*—only the three musicians from the shrine who play the same eerie *gagaku* melodies they do in most rituals. And as the three shining shrines are smoothly borne along by the squads of young men earlier rendered seawater-clean, a first-time observer suddenly realizes why this is a procession and not a parade— *it's too quiet*. It was noted earlier in this book that festivals can assume a raucous and wild demeanor or a dignified and solemn one, but to actually hear how muted the sounds are is somewhat unsettling. Aren't these people happy, one might wonder? Why don't they show their true emotions about accompanying the Kami through the city and thereby revitalizing the whole community? Even the children walk calmly alongside their mothers, their kimonos as brilliantly beautiful as an array of garden flowers but their wearers just as silent. The only voices one hears belong to the crowds as they comment on the noble-looking horse the Gūji rides or on the beauty of the row of *miko* in their white tops and striking red bloomers. The actual sounds of the procession, in addition to the soft wail of *gagaku* music and the dull scraping of the bamboo, are a distant drum at the procession's end and the shuffling of feet along the asphalt thoroughfare. Is anyone actually *there*—or have they all been subsumed within the august aura of the deities?

Only when the temporary shrine at Ohato comes into view does the mesmerizing pace of the procession change. Suddenly, Matsumoto-san is running at full speed ahead of the *mikoshi* bearers, madly banging his drum while his megaphone bounces against his side (see chapter 8). Then, with a single loud yell, the bearers also break into flight, somehow managing to balance the heavy shrines' weight on their shoulders and sprint at the same time. The people in the grandstands, who moments ago were sleepily waiting for the Kami to arrive, now burst into applause and shouts of encouragement—*Wasshoi!* You can do it! *Ganbatte yo!*—as the bearers storm into the metal building that is to be the temporary shrine and set down their burdens on a raised tatami stage.

The priests arrive momentarily and with them come the procession's five hundred or so participants as well as seemingly every other person along the route. The entire area is now swarming with people trying to get close to the shrine, some joining their hands and offering a prayer from where they stand and others heaving coins into the netting that has just risen at the building's front. With little or no delay (and, interestingly, no hand and mouth water purification) Uesugi Gūji and four senior priests launch into a welcoming ritual by waving a huge wand of purification first over the three inert *mikoshi* and then over themselves. Oka-san places the *haraigushi* on a central altar, predominantly displayed, where it remains like some kind of shield between the Kami and the mobs of people pressing to pay homage at the front of the building.

Babies cry, coins clatter against the tin paneling of the building before sliding down into the nets above the coffers, and the Gūji struggles with feedback as his portable microphone squeals during the *norito* prayer. Decibel upon piercing decibel feeds a widening maw of noise until the whole scene crescendos into an ear-splitting yowl as loudspeakers carry the violent death of the central fuse box shorting out. Only then does the prayer assume its true dimensions: one weak human voice representing the many, obviously inadequate (from a human perspective) yet believed sincere enough to reach the distant "ears" of the Kami, microphone or not. "You had a long hard trip but now we welcome you here to your new home among the people of this community. We will bring you offerings and rice wine, and ensure your comfort during the three days you are here. We humbly beseech your indulgence of our efforts, and praise your powers in awe and dread."

Eventually the crowds will subside and busy themselves with the goods and foods sold in the numerous rows of stalls on the streets around the temporary shrine. And while everything appears to be "normal" and well controlled by various chairpersons and attendants, one must not lose sight of two important facts. First, Okunchi, or any festival for that matter, is a time when the routine of daily life is interrupted by the sublime of dances, costumes, and heightened sensory stimulation. Second, because the festival occurs in a kind of timeless liminal period which exists between its "normal" beginning and the final return of its participants to a state of revitalized regularity, the Kami are thought to be in a similar state of slightly uneasy arousal. Therefore, to keep them from manifesting their "rough spirit" (*aramitama*) they are indulged in a most solicitous manner by those tending them, as if they were bad-tempered children ready to fly into a tantrum. After rites of "consolement" on each of the two nights the Kami rest at Ohato pier, the lights over the *mikoshi* burn around the clock and a priest is always nearby in an adjacent chamber. The Kami start the day with "wake-up" rituals at 6 A.M., followed by an exorcism by scalding water (see chapter 10) and presentation of silks and other official gifts from a representative of the Central Association of Shinto Shrines in Tokyo. In the afternoon, little snacks of tea and sweet cakes are elegantly presented by the shrine's women's groups. But this is in addition to a steady stream of privately arranged rituals for families or companies, who pretend they are the sole beneficiaries while all the time thousands of citizens and visitors come and go, dropping a few coins in the offering box and paying their respects on the other side of the net.

SWEAT BEGETS THE BEAUTY OF COMPLETION: OCTOBER 9, DAY THREE

By the third day of Okunchi, October 9, the Ohato area is beginning to resemble New York City during a sanitation workers' strike. Try as they might, the local sanitation workers cannot keep pace with the tremendous amount of debris generated by carefree (and careless) festivalgoers. The cotton candy wrappers, the skewers for roasted squid or braised corn, the popped balloons, paper containers, drained juice cans, and generic litter all unite and conquer.[8] Though many of the vendors are still selling their products, a large number have already departed, en route to the next festival of October in northern Kyushu, which will begin in two days. The area around the temporary shrine has a low fence around it, preventing the smaller pieces of trash from blowing inside the immediate grounds, but it has taken several of the younger priests considerable time to prepare the front of the shrine for the exiting ritual of the *mikoshi*. Today, the last day, they will begin their trip home, but not before the seven neighborhoods repeat their performances in front of the temporary shrine and the two facing grandstands. If only formal appearances before paying audiences are counted, this marks the seventh performance for each of the *kasaboko* and floats and their entourages of bearers and entertainers. If one includes those performances held in the various shopping arcades, on major streets, and in the neighborhoods of the *machi* itself, that figure could easily be tripled. It will, after all, be seven years until the chance to participate again rolls around, so that each performance is a way of etching the *machi*'s name and particular style in the annals of Okunchi. From 7 until 10 A.M., the people have center stage, performing first at Ohato and then trekking across town to make their final appearance at Suwa Shrine, where everything began two long days ago.

By one o'clock, the day has turned still and stifling. There are no longer any crowds to see the palanquin bearers (dressed once again in their black tops, white shorts and leggings, and straw sandals) assemble at the temporary shrine and undergo a brief cleansing by the wand of purification. The Gūji and senior priests are likewise cleansed before taking their respective places behind the little cart with the mirror and *sakaki* branch, a positioning they will yield after the bearers come out of the tin building with the three black *mikoshi* on their shoulders. Once in the sun, the gold fixtures atop the portable shrines glisten with a fierce intensity and are so bright that one cannot manage any kind of sustained gaze. When I comment later to Ureshino-san on how bright the *mikoshi* seemed to have become, he smiles and says cryptically: "It's like that every year. But are you sure it's only the sun?"

In those festivals before the war, the same neighborhoods that walked the deities to the temporary shrine would accompany them back to Suwa Shrine. But in recent decades, this practice has been abbreviated so as to render the return procession quite small. One could speculate that the people have received what they wanted from the Kami and are now content and secure in their rejuvenated worlds and need not bother with closing the ritual circle since the priests are there to fulfill that very purpose. It is more likely, however, that individuals have already returned to the demanding pace of modern life—their schools, offices, factories, and homes—which can only temporarily accommodate a return to older rhythms. One should also not rule out sheer physical and mental exhaustion. From my standpoint as only a casual observer of each ritual held at the temporary shrine, I can fully attest to the draining effect that heat, excitement, and the logistics of human interaction have on even the most enthusiastic participant.

The first great procession on October 7 saw the police department close down one of Nagasaki's main arteries so that the Kami and their minions might pass smoothly through the city's streets. Today, however, a single police car at the front and one at the back accompany the return journey with their flashing red lights, an odd juxtaposition of temporal authority commanding far greater respect from taxi and truck drivers than the three *mikoshi* ever could. Office workers and shoppers still appear at windows along the route or stop, shielding their eyes from the sun, to stare at the procession, but, if anything, it proceeds even more quietly than the first time. Everyone involved seems to be straining to reach the shrine, plodding heavily along the asphalt as the sun bears down, turning the faces of the priests in their silken robes and the bearers in their cotton garments a uniform beet red. I wonder how they will ever manage to make it up the many flights of steep steps without collapsing.

But as the procession nears the huge torii at the entrance to the shrine precincts, I notice a large group of people awaiting the arrival of the three *mikoshi*. Suddenly, as a warm breeze starts to blow, the pace of the bearers picks up. They pause at the foot of the pathway leading directly to the main shrine buildings, gain fresh handholds on their *mikoshi*'s supporting beams, and at *exactly* 1:30, transform themselves from sullen, listless young men into frenzied, even fearful demigods bursting with sacred energy. With a single loud shout, they are off—attacking the flights of stone steps with a singularly powerful focusing of intent, as if by running with the Kami on their shoulders they could burst into divine flight. Crowds of people cheer them on all the way to the top. When the dust settles and exhortations subside, the *mikoshi* are again inside the Hall of Worship, though now they face inward to their sanctuary instead of outward to the community. Having completed their sacred duty and thoroughly soaked with sweat, the bearers collapse on the steps.

It takes the priests much longer to make the ascent, but once they do, and have undergone a brief purification of hands and mouths before entering the building, the younger priests and their attendants move into action. The sliding shutters are again closed, sealing off the building from the outside world, and the silk masks and white gloves again protect the Kami from profanation by the world of men and women as they are transferred back up the secret passageway and into their separate sanctums within the uppermost hall. The clamor of the temporary shrine and the street sounds of the procession have been left behind, and the drum rolls, *gagaku* music, and fragile-sounding "ohhhh's" emanating from within the sequestered Hall of Worship are soothing and familiar.

During the ensuing ritual of welcome and appreciation held in the Hall of Worship, everyone seems to be brimming with relief.
All the bearers—dirty, exhausted, and sweaty as they are—participate in the ritual after a cleansing by the *haraigushi* wand, which does nothing to alleviate the "locker-room" air they exude. Offerings are presented, the *norito* prayer is read by the Gūji, and the little branches are taken before the altar first by the Gūji and then by the members of the audience. The only difference that separates this ritual from any other is that the *miko* do not dance. "The Kami have had plenty of dancing and entertainment in the last three days and are tired and want to rest," I am told without asking. Ever attuned to the human world, the ritual ends quickly with no fanfare or final bows to the Grand Shrine of Ise (it was a local event, after all) nor is there a *naorai* afterward where the priests and their guests partake of sacred sake. The bearers do get sips from the *miko* as they leave the building, but basically, everyone is simply too spent and hot. "I smell like a horse!" Matsumoto-san says as he leaves the shrine en route to the dressing chambers, his face still flushed from the sprint up the stairs. "I can't wait to get out of these robes. You know, I haven't even seen my wife and kids for three days. I need a long hot bath and a cold beer—*and* about three days of sleep."

With the completion of this "ritual of welcome," or, as it is splendidly called in Japanese, *honsha onchaku sengyō-sai*, Okunchi is history for another year. The sumptuous floats and *kasaboko*, now covered with the glory of multiple encores and a media-instilled notoriety, will first be lovingly repaired by each participating *machi* and then go into storage for seven years. At the same time, those neighborhoods due to perform in next year's Okunchi will in a matter of weeks choose their coordinating committees and begin the initial planning, centered primarily on fundraising. Construction crews will dismantle the Ohato temporary-shrine structure and the grandstands at three locations, the sanitation squads will sweep, rake, and hose down the main festival sites, and the shrine's dry-cleaning service will do a booming business in robes, outer vests, and bloomers. Usually the weather cooperates to change the city as well, with cooling breezes and fluffy clouds enlivening the atmosphere. Okunchi marks the end of the sweltering heat of what seems an unnecessarily prolonged summer.

Matsumoto-san and the other hardworking priests are soon to be awarded a brief respite from their duties at the shrine, but there is one final ritual intimately connected with Okunchi that cannot be neglected: the transitional *naorai*, held on October 13. Its purpose, as we have seen earlier, is to end the condition of "festival" liminality and return all the coordinators, as well as the members of those communities they represent, back to the secular world. Not only is it important to ritualistically observe an end to the "tension engendered by contact with the Kami" (Ross 1965, 69), it is the shrine's way of expressing its gratitude for the cooperation of all involved, *and* of soothing egos that might have been bruised during the actual proceedings, especially those administrative ones fundamental to next year's festival.

In terms of sheer logistics, the city of Nagasaki's police, sanitation, transportation, and fire departments are all crucial to the ebb and flow of Okunchi's tidal wave of people and participants, and so a representative from each group attends the ritual.[9] However, the real "heroes" of the festival are those individual chairmen and chairwomen, supervisors, and organizers from each *machi* responsible for coordinating the various parts of the festival and then oiling its gears with either money, promises of future favors, or (never to be left out) voluminous amounts of beer and sake. There are the dance supervisors, the fundraising supervisors, and the portable-shrine, refreshments, and float supervisors. Everyone is dressed in their formal kimonos and looks quite satisfied and relaxed as they take their places in the Hall of Worship, but none more so than Nakagawa *machi*'s float supervisor, who still seems to be basking in the prestige that awaits him once those photos of himself and Mrs. Takagi's children standing in front of the Chinese boat are published.

Traditionally, the *naorai kai shinji* ritual was part of all main *matsuri* in that the principal participants and priests would gather to partake of the consecrated sake as well as the food offerings. Although most shrines no longer observe the formal "after-ritual feast"—substituting a simple sip of *o-miki* served by the female attendants—Suwa Shrine periodically follows the old form when guests and circumstances merit. Without a doubt, the dignitaries and functionaries invited to the *naorai kai shinji* warrant as sumptuous a "snack" as its 2 P.M. time can accommodate. During the actual ritual in the Hall of Worship I am curious as to why only a bare minimum of priests attend. Surely the doubling up of certain roles—such as the priest who conducted the opening purification and who now presents the script of the *norito* prayer to the Gūji, or the musician now serving as the first link in the human chain conveying offerings to the upper sanctuary—is an affront to the guests.

My puzzlement ends when the simple rite is concluded and all retire to the shrine's banquet hall, where several of the younger priests and a full contingent of *miko* and members from the shrine's women's group have been setting three rows of tables for a feast. Full plates of sashimi, ready to be dipped in sauce, are flanked by diced white radish, fish-paste cakes, orange slices, pickled plums, vegetables, rice, and tea—and there is a sake container for every two place settings, as well as dripping bottles of ice-cold Kirin and Sapporo beer. The guests settle down on their cushions and listen to a brief speech by the Guji, who thanks them again for all their work and diligence and implores them to enjoy the food and drink. He leads the toast— *Kanpai!!*—and then begins to circulate, stopping before the tables of important donors or organizers to pour them sips of sake or beer. By doing so, he is both gracious host and humble servant, subtly imparting his gratitude on behalf of the shrine while making the guest feel obliged for the feast.

But then, this is the same comportment he adopts in each ritual addressed to the Kami—thanking them for all they have done while, through the means of offerings and entertainment, requesting a continuing relationship of reciprocity. In this sense, the filling of a cup of sake, the enactment of a ritual within the shrine, or the massive outpouring of communal energies that go into the Okunchi festival, all can be seen as part and parcel of a cultural belonging which encompasses and promotes religious, artistic, and politico-economic aspects of Japanese society. While it is true that rural areas are suffering a degeneration of committed activity needed to maintain local festivals, shrines in major cities show increased levels of participation in their yearly *matsuri*.[10] As more and more young people discover the contagious enthusiasm and communal pride created through festivals such as Okunchi, they often encounter as well a sense of heritage that comes to resonate emotionally with notions of cultural identity, a spiritual homeland, and their places in the modern world.

16

CHILDREN
AND SILK

Like the sheen of sunlight on black silk, the
child's hair glistens in the fine light of an autumn morning. Her
eyes dart restlessly from the face of her mother, who is concentrat-
ing on smoothing the pleats of her daughter's first kimono, to the
noisy five-year-old boys punching each other near the stone lions,
to the dimly lit interior of the shrine which she and the other children will soon enter. She has seen and done a considerable amount
in her three years, and by now knows how to brush her pearly whites
in the morning, say thank you to adults, charm her father into getting her way, and, one might also point out, bow before the Kami of
Suwa Shrine (thanks to the family's New Year's visits) or the Buddha that sits under a little canopy near her grandmother's house. All
these skills are important to a three-year-old getting on in the world.
However, rather than try to develop and add to her repertoire on her
own or with her parents', grandparents', and teachers' assistance, she
is here at the shrine to enlist the aid of the Kami, so that she might
someday, at age seven, look and act as stately as the seven-year-old
girls that she sees clustered nearby. "Mama," she says sweetly, "when
I'm seven and we come here again, will you buy me a kimono that
has 'Hello Kitty' on it instead of these cranes?"

Rendering the name of this dedicatory festival (*shichi-go-san*) into
English (seven-five-three) evokes none of the unstated emotional
associations that tend to resonate for an average Japanese when hearing the name. While they may not remember their own participation
as children, they will in all probability have a few photographs of a
day in mid-November when their own parents bundled them up in
a kimono or new Western-style outfit and brought them to a shrine.
Whether this was done out of belief in the Kami or simply because
it was just one of those socially expected activities a person *does* with
one's children seems to matter very little. Swirls of brilliant colors,
voices variously loud and hushed, the boom of the shrine's drum as

busy priests come and go, all serve as backgrounds for that moment when the young girl (aged three or seven) or boy (aged five) stood or knelt before the shrine's deities and, for the briefest of moments, turned solemn and wide-eyed as hands joined together in supplication for a healthy, happy life.

For many of these children milling around the main hall of Suwa Shrine, this is not the first time they have been on the receiving end of the Kami's goodwill. The *hatsumiyamairi*, or "first shrine visit," is customarily held when a newborn is at least thirty days old and past that initial transition into the world when a child's soul was thought to be easily "recalled" by the Kami (or Buddha) if conditions were not right.[1] Japan has one of the lowest infant mortality rates, and yet a large percentage of parents still spend the time and money to have a short ritual performed to enlist the Kami's protection and blessing.

In the past, however, there was far less choice about the matter, especially during the heavy-handed promulgation of Shinto as a "national faith" from the 1890s to 1945. Designed to make *every* Japanese a patriotic pawn in the hands of the militarists, the requirement that each individual register as a parishioner (*ujiko*) of a shrine drew upon practices that had been around for at least a thousand years in Japanese society. As mentioned in chapters 1 and 2, both rural and urban settlements in Japan have traditionally venerated a deity (*ujigami* or *hitogami*) associated with either the specific place or with the dominant clan's legitimacy to exert power and control resources. Thus, not only did a household's relationship to a local shrine foster a sense of communal and regional identity for its members, but there were also "ethnic themes" of Shinto practice (Reader 1991, 60), which, when emphasized via certain rituals (such as the Great Purification or the Harvest festival, to be encountered in the next chapter), integrated the local community within the "nation" as a whole, however imprecisely the concept was rendered by the political realities of the day. While most visitors to a shrine in contemporary Japan are unaware that this chain of relationships exists (individual-shrine-community-nation), the view from "inside" most shrines remains surprisingly traditional, as priest after priest told me there is no more important way to foster both communal and national identity in children than for them to participate in the rituals of *hatsumiyamairi* and *shichi-go-san*. According to Uesugi Gūji, who always seems to state matters succinctly, "These rites instill respect for the Kami as well as the feeling that the Kami is intimately involved in that child's development, much as a kindly relative is."

Returning then to one of the opening themes of this book, these very public events in an individual's life are two of the many ways that culture gets practiced via a Shinto-inspired orientation to the seasons and cycles one encounters in progressing through social and physical worlds.[2]

Today, with the massive migrations from rural to urban and urban to urban areas brought about by modernization, job transfers, and improved transportation systems, times have changed since those days when (even as recently as twenty years ago) the household to which a child belonged was considered to be automatically affiliated with a local shrine. However, as the growing popularity of *hatsu-miyamairi* and *shichi-go-san* seems to demonstrate, a local sense of belonging guides the choice of the shrine in which one's descendants will be dedicated. I met one family from as far away as sixty kilometers and another from forty kilometers who told me they felt some loyalty to Suwa Shrine since they and their grandparents had been brought before the Kami here; therefore, why not their children as well, especially since the family fortunes had suffered no strange or calamitous twists of fate. Far more common were people from the other side of the city whose parents had moved there after the war and could have gone to the local Sumiyoshi Shrine but chose instead to come back to Suwa. When asked why, their responses ranged from "Well, it's kind of a family tradition," to "Suwa Shrine is the main shrine of Nagasaki, so its Kami are the most powerful. This is the place for our child to come." One little old woman admonished her son and his wife, "As long as I'm around," she says with a menacing tone, as if she would come back from the dead to make sure, "this family's shrine worship will be conducted at Suwa-san."

So much for the adults, who, after all, are supposed to be in the background for this festival, taking pictures, videos, and generally fawning over their precious children. By 10:15, a group of about fifty or so families has gathered by the Hall of Worship's lower steps, and now follows a young priest to a recently constructed hall situated above the garage used for car purifications. (My own family is included, qualified to participate by having a four-year-old son. When I admitted earlier that he was not the correct age, Matsumoto-san said with a nonchalant smile, "Yes but he's *close* to age five!") Upon entering the main room, we find neither priest nor *miko* attendants but men belonging to two television crews, several of whom are smoking and looking quite relaxed on the tatami floor, waiting for their chance to conduct interviews with the "specially invited children," who will be participating in a ritual within the shrine. As the only obvious foreigner in the room, the cameramen are already looking at me and despite basic instincts urging me to grab my son and partner and flee, I meekly find a spot and await the microphones and blinking red camera lights that signal "RECORDING."

"Uh, Nelson-san, could you and your son come here for a moment?" asks Matsumoto-san from the doorway, providing a means of temporary escape. "Although Junet looks very nice, the Gūji thought that it would be more appropriate if he wears these robes from the shrine's collection. Would you mind?" The question is directed at me rather than my son, who, mounting little resistance, easily slips into a powder blue quilted upper silk kimono and royal blue *hakama*-style bloomers with the shrine's white crest flowering like peonies here and there. "This is similar to what children at court wore during the Heian period," Matsumoto-san kindly informs us. "I did this with my own kids too, and though it's somewhat uncomfortable for the children, the Gūji is sure you'll all enjoy the photographs later." A little gold headpiece is supposed to crown the costume, but a finicky strap and too-smooth hair render it more trouble than it's worth. And speaking of trouble . . .

"Uh, Mr. Nelson? Glad to meet you. We are from TV Nagasaki and would like to ask you why you are participating in this Shinto festival today." RECORDING. Gulp. I managed to say something about the importance of maintaining traditions in modern Japan, and that we wanted our son to participate in these traditions as well as receive blessings from the Suwa Kami.[3] RECORDING. "And you, Joonay—is that how you say it? Junet? My, what an interesting name. Tell me, do you like your kimono?" I hold my breath and wait for his reply, which will surely embarrass us far less than my own comment, but he diplomatically answers that it's fine, even *kawaii* (cute). With this excellent answer, the camera's appetite is temporarily satisfied, and it turns away, already having located another unsuspecting subject—a little girl of three playing quietly with her braids.

They have only a few seconds before the drum booms forth notice that the ritual will soon start. Purses, combs, comics, socks, toys, handheld computer games, and still and video cameras are all gathered up as parents gently guide their children into shoes or slippers for the short walk over to the Hall of Worship. There, everyone again removes their footwear and, following the gestures of

Matsumoto-san, takes their places, with adults in the rear and children in the front, although even closer to the altar (off to the side) are the two TV crews, who film the entourage, gliding from face to cherubic face. The excited chattering of the children comes to an abrupt and startled halt as again the drum signals the first movement of priests to the altar for the *haraigushi* purification. Younger children look to the older girls for cues and somehow each and every child manages to have his or her head lowered as the wand slowly passes over. It is a dramatic moment, but not a single parent dares rise from their own bow to capture it on film. They are, after all, in the presence of the Kami, as well as the TV cameras, though it is perhaps the coercive power of the latter and the chance that, caught by the camera, a parent would have to answer to her or his neighbors for appearing disrespectful during the opening purification. The event is, after all (in what must be one of the rallying cries for any number of noble, self-sacrificing acts throughout Japanese history), *for the sake of the children.*

It is likewise for the children's benefit, as well as their short attention span, that the ritual has been much abbreviated compared with those of earlier periods. After the camera crews are "invited" to leave and the priests take their places on the raised dais, I notice that the fruit and vegetable offerings are already in place upon the altar, thus dispensing with the slow and stately movement whereby each tray of food is conveyed from priest to priest. The *norito* petitionary prayer, without which a ritual isn't a ritual, is also considerably shorter than those delivered in other contexts, yet asks for the same seminal blessings—those of health, happiness, and fulfillment—that are of foremost concern in the lives of the Japanese.

After the Gūji has returned to his round-woven hemp-fiber mat on the floor, Matsumoto-san walks to the altar itself at the very back of the hall and, much to my surprise, removes the sacred *gohei* (also called *heihaku*) from its stand. Imagine a stout wooden pole, coated with beautifully gleaming black lacquer and inlaid with mother-of-pearl filigree, from the top of which two gold-leaf streamers in the shape of lightning bolts descend.[4] Coming directly from the altar immediately after the *norito* prayer, it not only is one of the most sacred objects in the whole shrine at the moment but is, like its earlier archetypes, thought to be charged with the numinous presence and power of the Kami. For all intents and purposes, the *gohei is* the Kami, and Matsumoto-san handles it as if it might explode. Turning in place, with this powerful device gripped by one hand and cradled by the other, he approaches the innocently upturned faces of the children!

I am totally unprepared for what happens next. Expecting that he will only gently wave the *gohei* over their heads as he did with the *haraigushi* wand for the opening purification, he begins at one end of the line and then slowly, taking care to make sure no child is missed, allows the streamers to brush against each child's head. The children seem to know that this is not play and make no attempt to reach out and touch the wide golden streamers that hover over, then softly touch their heads. From the largest seven-year-old girl to the rowdiest five-year-old boy to the cutest little three-year-old angel that ever wore a kimono, the children are charmed, bearing silent witness to an exquisite suspension of both themselves and their ordinary worlds. All that matters is the approach, touch, and receding wake of the *gohei's* protective breath.

The moment stays with me as we file out of the shrine after hearing the Gūji's short speech on the predictable themes of becoming citizens, participating in community and national affairs, and growing up with the Kami as a companion. I continue to see the *gohei* hovering over the children as my son collects his shopping bag filled with Suwa logo-inscribed toys, headbands, a few traditional sweets, and a talisman, as we walk down the many flights of stone steps out of the shrine grounds and back to the noisy streetcar stop—even as we soak in the steaming water of the bath that evening. *Something happened* is the basic theme of my thoughts, something that I now hesitate to force into words but that is central to the potential and power of ritual activity worldwide. That this "something" may not happen each time a ritual takes place, or that it may have happened for only me and no one else, in no way diminishes the altered inner state that prescribed, highly focused, and intense actions can bring about in human beings. Shinto rituals in particular offer no explanations and no resolutions and promise no results in ways that other religious activities do.[5] And yet they do provide a vehicle whereby the individual, however small and insignificant he or she may be, can become a temporarily sanctified participant in a divine order.[6] For children in particular, these early encounters with the Kami—framed by the efforts of their parents and grandparents and captured on film for posterity—provide points of reference about the possibility of forces beyond their comprehension that they must acknowledge and harmonize with if the challenges, hardships, and goals of their own endeavors are to be successfully resolved. As part of growing up

"Japanese," a trip to the shrine may not be as consciously valued in later years as, say, visiting Tokyo Disneyland or a grade report with high marks. But it is one of the few occasions when an excursion in one's best clothes can become an encounter with cosmologies essential to how a Japanese orients himself or herself to the world.

17

THANKSGIVING
FOR NEW RICE

In the early morning hours of November 23, two men, roughly the same age but of very different backgrounds, awake at about the same time: 5 A.M. Some five hours later, their social and occupational roles will complement each other in the service of the sacred, yet the two men will remain strangers to each other. One rises slowly out of habit, his arms and back still aching from the strenuous work of lifting full sacks of rice during the harvest of last weekend, sacks that had to be heaved from the threshing machine to the back of the family truck before being hauled to the local grain cooperative. His daughter says he is too old for this kind of work and should stick to running the hulling machine or harvester, but when a full sack of rice is ready to be loaded, "It's not going to jump up there by itself!" he says. As he stands by the window, looking out across stubbled fields that not long ago shimmered in the morning sun with the golden hues of ripe grain, he remembers that his workclothes, rubber boots, and headband are to be replaced today by his best (and only) black suit. An invitation card, propped up against the family's Buddhist altar, announces that he is soon to be the guest of Suwa Shrine; an honor that will, to his delight, cause his neighbors much envy and his family great pride. Suddenly, his back and shoulders feel much better, and a smile crosses his deeply lined face.

The other man also rises slowly, his slightly arthritic knees reminding him of the amount of time spent kneeling in silent meditation the night before. He too has made preparations for this morning by isolating himself for one day in a special room within the shrine, where neither work (except that urgent for the festival itself), visitors, nor amusements of any kind should be allowed to enter, for this is the period of abstinence that is essential to the process of priestly purification before the festival of New Rice. Before entering the shrine, he had his hair trimmed, cut his fingernails and toenails, and shaved at home. Immediately upon beginning the abstinence period, he changed clothes, bathed, engaged in contemplation, bathed again around midnight, and, after a few hours' sleep, will bathe once more before joining the other priests for a brief ritual at sunrise. Since the most important thing in this preparatory *saikai* is to establish "calm, peace, emotive stability, and receptivity to the Kami," all his activities of the morning should be carefully regulated, because it is the outward manifestation of his state of mind reached during *saikai* that becomes the "mental thanksgiving" of the *matsuri*. As he thinks about his fellow priests all over Japan—including the emperor, who, in his role as chief priest of the Imperial household, is also preparing this morning to perform the same ritual—he is warmed by a sense of continuity and community, the very message he hopes the service will impart to the invited guests.

The Japanese myths recounted in the *Kojiki* and *Nihon-shoki* relate that rice was a gift from the Sun Kami, Amaterasu, to the people of this world. This meant that rice was grown even in the High Plain of Heaven, with Amaterasu herself performing the harvest rituals. When her grandson, Ninigi, descended from heaven to rule the earth, the responsibility for the harvest festival was passed on to his wife, Adatsu-hime, presumably because of women's closer proximity and accessibility to the Kami (remember that many served as shamans) as well as to natural cycles and growth. This rite, which acquired a later interpretation designating the emperor as rice cultivator, became one of the legitimating factors of the Yamato clan as it increased its political control over the "Land of Luxurious Rice Ears on the Bountiful Plain of Reeds" (Toyoashihara no Mizuho no Kuni). Because the emperors' role in rice cultivation was probably mostly ceremonial (though the current emperor does get his hands dirty by transplanting a few seedlings in the palace rice paddies), the task was delegated to the farmers in a way that made them feel the work was done as much for the service of the Kami as for their own livelihood.

According to Ishikawa Takashi (1987, 46), this concept of delegation (*yosashi*) is important to the early Shinto myths and to the Japanese idea of "labor" in general. In classical Japanese, "labor" is either *tsutome* or *hataraki*, with the first word derived from *tsutoni*, "early morning," and the second meaning "to be active." Another reading of *tsutome*'s characters results in a meaning of "duty" or "mission," which combines into a concept of work that is a "duty to be performed diligently from early morning." At the foundation of this way of thinking, following Ishikawa, was the farmers' idea that labor was a sacred activity, delegated from the Kami (by way of the emperor) to them. And if this sounds oddly familiar, remember that it was this same logic that led the Japanese people to accept the ideologies of their military rulers that they were "delegated" to establish an empire abroad because of their ancestral ties to the emperor and his to the Kami.

It is because of these mythic links that the festival of New Rice, with its emphasis on gratitude for a successful harvest, is deemed the most important in the whole cycle of Shinto rites. But there are other, equally significant dimensions to this ritual as well. With rice as the primary staple of early communities, it was of paramount importance that the food supply be protected by maintaining a harmonious relationship with the forces of fertility and fecundity. Following Hori Ichiro's description, it is to agriculture that humanity owes its self-consciousness of limitation and finitude—as well as its idea of life and cosmology as cyclical—because of the stationary (as opposed to nomadic) life agriculture requires. And although we might be skeptical that "the discovery of the seed as the source of continuity of plant life increased awareness of tradition and the importance of ancestors" (Hori 1968, 26), we can agree with his conclusion that certain feelings of dependence, even fatalism, were basic to the formation of magic and rituals among agrarian peoples. Japan is not alone among the societies of the world which, at one time or other, have held farm products as sacred in themselves, as the gifts of deities, and as requiring various magico-religious or magico-artistic rituals (often of sexual and orgiastic excess) in order to ensure gestation, ripening, and harvest of the wheat or rice plant. Not only were there rites for harvest and seeding, there were also those for transplanting, for stopping storms or long rains or droughts, for frightening away predatory birds and devastating pestilence, and for regenerating divine power.

This last category is at the heart of much of contemporary Shinto practice, as we saw earlier in the Okunchi festival when the three Kami of Suwa Shrine were carried through the streets of Nagasaki. But it also applies to the regeneration of both community and nation when rites are performed to ensure the succession of divine ancestry from one emperor to the next. This has traditionally been accomplished by the partaking of food in general and newly harvested rice in particular, because in many societies in Asia (as well as elsewhere in the world), the idea of eating together is equated with becoming an intimate member of a group.

The Daijōsai is that rare event whereby a new emperor fully assumes the sacred qualities of his title. Thus, it is one of the most elaborate of all Imperial household rites as plate after plate of food, as well as refined and unrefined sake, is brought before the specially constructed altar, where it is shared only by the emperor (on behalf of the Japanese people) and the Kami in attendance (thought to be Amaterasu, who in turn partakes on behalf of the rest of the heavenly deities). The new rice, constituting the core of the sacred meal, has been carefully grown by prosperous and healthy local families in fields chosen according to standards established by the National Department of Agriculture. But, with some minor variations, the same practices are applied to those special rice fields selected by regional and local shrines in the production of rice used for their own in-house rituals of thanksgiving, which grew out of the Imperial one. Instructive in their blending of ancient traditions and principles of modern plant husbandry, the regulations tell us a good deal about the process involved (see Ross 1965, 85).

1. The land must be cultivated as one piece and be about one-fourth of an acre in size.
2. The land must be near a river so that rituals of purification can be carried out easily.
3. Drainage and irrigation must be good, and the land should be in an area protected from the dangers of floods and storms.
4. The district where the land is located must be advanced in agricultural knowledge and techniques, as well as having a reputation for good manners and benevolence.
5. Areas having recently suffered epidemics must be avoided, as is the practice of using manure fertilizer on the fields.
6. The men and women farmers who nurture the rice must wear clean clothes.
7. The fields must be protected by bamboo mats erected on all sides as well as by high fences of interwoven bamboo.
8. All tools and implements used in the rice's cultivation must be purified by Shinto rituals, conducted in front of a small shrine built in the corner of each field.

Perhaps by this time one is convinced that the Niiname-sai (festival of New Rice) held in every shrine in Japan on November 23 deserves the importance ascribed to it. Preparations begin in April when the fields are selected and continue through the year until the new rice is finally brought to the shrine (or Imperial palace in the case of the emperor) and arranged as the foremost part of the *shinsen* offerings presented to the Kami.

At Suwa Shrine, the opening phase of the *matsuri* begins in the Hall of Worship, on the lowest of the shrine's three levels. But this is not quite accurate, because below the hall is a rather large, tastefully decorated meeting hall, with framed calligraphy on the walls and deep purple carpeting on the floor, where the invited guests have been assembling over the past hour. Upon arrival, each farm couple (some bent almost in half by arthritis produced by years of stooping over rice paddies) would have come into the shrine grounds, washed their hands and mouths at the water fonts (*temizuya*), and performed their own brief hand-clapping prayers before the dangling bell-ropes and offering coffers of the main shrine building. Thus purified, they now unknowingly begin the affirmation of community at the heart of this festival by renewing acquaintances, making new ones, drinking tea served by the pretty *miko* attendants, and generally enjoying the pleasurable hospitality of the shrine.

Their relaxed and jovial demeanor quickly changes when a junior priest comes to announce the seating arrangement according to their status and seniority. He leads them back outside, where they must slip on their shoes to walk the flight of steps up to the entrance of the Hall of Worship and then slip them off again. After some minutes of quiet chatter and anticipation, the invited guests are all in place within the hall. At precisely ten o'clock, preceded by an explosive drumroll, the priests enter, led by the Gūji. All wear white kimonos with black outer vests except for Senior Priest Oka, whose crimson vest signifies his coming role in arranging the offerings within the uppermost sanctuary of the Kami. The farmers sit in rapt attention, most attending a formal ritual like this for only the second or third time in their lives, but by and large there are only minor variations to distinguish the outer form of this ritual for New Rice from any other shrine festival. The four basic movements of a shrine ritual—purification, presentation, petition, and participation, all mentioned earlier in this book—are still central to the arrangement of the event.

The red-vested priest rises to deliver the opening prayer of purification in front of the lower altar. Then, another stands, flourishing the wand of purification over the heads of Gūji, senior and junior priests, *miko* attendants, musicians, and assembled guests, followed by droplets of water flicked from a single sprig of *sakaki* leaves along the same route. Once he has returned to his place, the Gūji rises and leads first the priests, then the musicians, and finally the slightly bewildered looking farmers (who are whispering things like "Isn't this incredible?" "Father, stop clearing your throat!" and "What's happening next? Where're we going?") out of the hall, up a steep flight of stairs behind a sliding panel that no one noticed until now, and into the fragrant, shadowy embrace of the Hall of Offerings.

Here we see for the first time the new sheaves of rice tied to each pillar supporting the ceiling, as if their placement on these immense tree trunks shows how it is rice that bolsters the protective structure of Japanese society. Elevated and further removed from the noisy clanging of the "attention-getting Kami-bell," which worshippers ring outside the Hall of Worship at all hours, the atmosphere is scented with the smell of the rice mixed with the sweet aroma of the chamber's mellowing cypress wood. One of the musicians raises his *shō* and blows a series of single notes while the Gūji slowly ascends to the uppermost sanctuary of the Kami and everyone bows low. The long vowels said to usher in the deities from the High Plain of Heaven are intoned five times, and when everyone looks up from their completed bow the bamboo screen over the entrance to the Inner Sanctuary has been raised, revealing weathered wood, deep shadows, and the presence of an awesome "emptiness" wherein *anything* can happen.

The Gūji then ascends a dais at the foot of the eleven steps leading up to the Inner Sanctuary, and after a cue from the priest closest to the audience, everyone joins in a single profound bow to the recently arrived Kami. The presentation of offerings comes next. Eight different trays are passed along a human chain from the little kitchen at the bottom of the steps to the uppermost sanctuary, where the red-vested Oka-san moves quickly, in and out of the shadows, arranging the foods in the proper order. Coming first is the new rice of course, followed by many of the same dishes mentioned earlier — raw fruits and vegetables, seaweed, water, fish-paste cakes, sake, and so on — each new tray the subject of whispered comments from several of the farmers' wives, all nicely concealed by the flute, harmonium, and drum of *gagaku* music.

Now that the Kami, through this meal they symbolically feed upon, have "accepted" the shrine's hospitality and become intimate members of the group, they may be presumed upon to hear the petition of the *norito* invocational prayer, delivered with great solemnity by the Gūji from his dais as, again, the assembled worshippers bow. He thanks the Kami for their aid in this year's harvest, praises their life-giving powers, beseeches a continuance of their protection and assistance for the coming year, asks their blessing for the nation, and finally thanks all the farmers who have taken great pains to grow this elegant and lovely rice as tribute to the Kami.

As soon as he is finished, one of the older men in the front of the audience, who acts as if he has been to a hundred rituals, shifts from the formal sitting style (on knees) to a cross-legged position. Like a group of adolescents who have to check what their peers are doing before joining in, the back rows of men look from side to side to see if everyone else is following suit before they too assume the more comfortable cross-legged style — and breathe a sigh of relief. The women, however, are not afforded this luxury, although some elderly matrons do sit with their legs to the side and not directly underneath. All this shifting around is appropriate at this point in the ritual because after the delivery of the *norito* prayer, even the Gūji seems more relaxed as the *miko* glide to the center of the chamber, posing before the Kami as the music begins.

The farmers perk up even more when the *miko* begin their slow processions of dreamy, intertwined circles, frequently shaking ornate bell-wands from which colored streamers trail, colors representing the eight directions. For such a joyful occasion, the minor key of the single accompanying flute seems, to Western ears, especially mournful and austere, but to judge from the faces of the young women performing this entertainment for the Kami, there is no such emotion. I even notice a couple of the women nodding in time to the steps of the *miko*, as if they too know the motions of *kagura* or have perhaps studied traditional Japanese dance.

Again taking a cue from the old man in the front row, everyone sits up straight again as the two young women finish their dance with a final bow and return to their places beside the chief priest. When the music ends, the Gūji is presented with a small branch of the *sakaki* tree (*tamagushi*) and places it on a special table just below his dais. Soon, the front row of farmers all have *sakaki* sprigs, which, after two bows, two claps, and one final bow, they must offer to the Kami while remembering to reverse the sprig so its stem points to the Inner Sanctuary as a symbol of connectedness. After nearly twenty-five minutes of inactivity (a rare situation for these agricultural folk), they rise unsteadily and stagger in choppy little steps across what seems like an immense distance of grass mats to the eight-legged table that will hold their offerings. The subsequent rows of women and men follow until everyone has made their offerings, bows, and claps — some forgetting to reverse the sprig, others forgetting to clap twice, others needing assistance before they are able to rise from the floor—but it is here the ritual regains its human dimension. There is no feeling of censure or impatience by the rows of priests that watch these presentations, as if the little lapses of protocol are a natural part of the way humans are—forgetful, embarrassed, sometimes bumbling, but sincerely well-intentioned and thus dignified nonetheless. Having completed their offerings and returned to their seats on the floor, many turn to their partners and giggle about their gaffes or shake their heads as if to say, "I didn't know I was going to have to do *that!*"

The rest of the ritual moves quickly to its conclusion as the offerings are removed from the Inner Sanctuary along the same line of priests as before, the chief priest closes the sanctuary screen accompanied by the eerie calls, and everyone bows, feeling like this is the finale. Some even rise to their knees when the priests all stand, but they quickly drop back to a formal posture and then hurry out of the way when the Gūji leads his attendants to the east corner of the audience's floorspace so that a final bow may be offered in the direction of the Grand Shrine of Ise, home to the Kami of the sun, who bestowed rice on the emperor all those ages ago.

Finally, the Gūji addresses the guests with a short speech thanking them for coming and then praises the natural bounty of the Kami and of the land that allows rice (and other agricultural products, such as oranges, tangerines, and loquats) to be grown in this area. It is then the farmers hear what they have been waiting for: an invitation to join with the priests in a "small repast," the *naorai*, where they will partake of some of these wonderful foods and gradually reenter the secular world after their encounter with the sacred. All follow the priests and *miko* back down the stairs and outdoors, where the shoe dance begins again: slipped on for the minute it takes to walk across a small courtyard leading to the banquet hall, then slipped off before entering. Inside are five rows of low tables, cushions for the fifty guests, and an impressive assembly of white porcelain dishes (at least seven for each place) containing slices of raw sea bream, fish-paste cakes, seaweed, fruit, rice cakes, pickled plums, and radishes that were offered to the Kami not thirty minutes earlier. The same two *miko* who danced so beautifully moments ago are now, with the help of about ten other young women and several of the younger priests, pouring sake in everyone's little cups, preparing for the formal toast that will kick off an hour of feasting and drinking. The food is tasty, the raw fish superb, and the sake is second to none—*kanpai!!*—and if you imagine farmers are happiest when the harvest is completed and the grain is in the storehouses, then you haven't seen them at a *naorai*. They know better than city folk how fleeting the warm autumn sun is and how soon the cold winds will be howling down from Siberia, across the Korean Peninsula, and rattling the shutters on the windows. It is then, perhaps, on a cold day hovering around the stove or sipping tea while sitting at the *kotatsu* foot-warming table, they will think back to the festival of New Rice, remembering the honor of sharing a feast with the Kami of Suwa Shrine.

WINTER

18

ON SPIRIT, GEOMANCY, AND SAKE

It is a common experience for most of us to be able to name only one or two teachers who have made a positive impact on our sense of personal development during the long years of institutional socialization we conveniently call "education." Though we in Western countries restrict the title of "teacher" to those individuals associated with schools, the Chinese and Japanese have a long tradition of seeing their teachers—called *sensei* in Japanese—in all walks of life. The word itself is composed of two characters—the first being *sen* (先), or "previous," and the second *sei* (生), "life"—which nicely embody the many nuances and manifestations of the title. A teacher is one who has "previously lived" or "gone before" others and is therefore held in high esteem by virtue of his or her experience with a body of knowledge, craft, or skill. Schoolteachers, from kindergarten to the university, are all *sensei*, but so are doctors, lawyers, calligraphy instructors, master artisans, Buddhist and Shinto priests, and even experienced makers of tofu, car mechanics, or anyone teaching his or her trade to an apprentice.

One of the characteristics of a *sensei* is an acceptance of a hierarchical relationship between himself or herself and a "disciple" hungry for the knowledge or skill the teacher can impart. In Itami Juzo's film *Tanpopo*, this relationship was humorously satirized as the struggling owner of an unsuccessful "ramen" noodle restaurant sought out the holy grail of a new soup stock that would transform her mundane fare into something unique and special. Turning from the instructions of one *sensei* after another, she eventually found the secret ingredient by which she attained financial deliverance and the perfect bowl of ramen. Lest the reader think this is straying too far from the topic at hand, there are many whose spiritual hunger has likewise driven them to teacher after teacher, with one's version of a profound "truth" yielding to the next's most recent revelations.

Partially because of shrine Shinto's continuing veneration of traditional ritual practices emphasizing the needs of the group and not the individual, millions of Japanese have found the "new religions" such as Tenrikyō, Sōka Gakkai, Mahikari, and Kurozumikyō (to name a very few) more responsive to their spiritual needs. In these new religions, according to Reader, individuals encounter a syncretic blending of Shinto and Buddhist symbols, themes, and ritual practices addressing everything from ancestors and malevolent spirits of the dead to "concepts of spiritual causation, the emphasis on *genze riyaku* (or this-worldly benefits), and on the goal of finding meaning and ultimate happiness in this life."[1] The techniques of healing, exorcism, or purification employed often seem radical and fresh, but what is often overlooked in the new religions is how these apparently "new" ritual approaches are reworkings of precedents and established practices in more traditional Shinto and Buddhist institutions.

To answer the challenges posed by the loss of parishioners to the new religions as well as to modern-day anomie, the academic elite of shrine Shinto are once again slowly attempting to formulate a systematic theology. However, little in the orientation of traditional Shinto is amenable to reinterpretations highlighting the individual, nor is this reformulation particularly encouraged by the more senior leaders of the Central Association of Shinto Shrines in Tokyo.[2]

Nonetheless, there can be found those rare individuals in contemporary institutions of shrine Shinto who cannot wait for official doctrine to be handed down and are ready and willing to share what they know with the curious, confused, or indifferent. In every sense of the word, the Gūji serves a traditional role of *sensei* to the parishioners of the shrine. But, depending on the personality and learning of each individual chief priest, his role can be either passive and limited only to ritual occasions or, if possessed with confidence, charisma, or chutzpah, he can have considerable influence on the perspectives, loyalties, and beliefs of the local community.[3] The reader may have discerned by now that Uesugi Gūji is of the latter type.

The following conversation took place on a blustery day in early December at one of Nagasaki's choice Russian restaurants. Coming shortly after the festival of New Rice and before the business of New Year preparations, Mr. Uesugi was relaxed and well rested, looking quite distinguished in an olive suit and paisley silk tie and carrying a briefcase of fine English leather purchased the last time he was in London. I have left our discussion in the question-and-answer format to give the reader a sense of the dynamics of his thought processes—flowing, organic in causal patterns, and rich with examples.

Q: One of the many things that has puzzled me is why, at the end of certain rituals, you go into the easternmost corner of the Hall of Worship and lead all the priests and guests in a series of bows. Certain American Indian tribes buried their dead so that they would be able to rise up facing the east and have their reborn spirit looking toward what they thought was the direction of Paradise. Does Shinto hold a similar belief regarding the direction east, or other directions for that matter?

A: At the end of the Sumiyoshi festival and others as well, it's by chance that we bow to the east. That kind of observance is done because from where we are in the far west of Japan, that's the direction of the Grand Shrine at Ise (which is dedicated to the Sun Goddess, Amaterasu). If you were in Hokkaido (in the far north) you'd have to bow toward Ise to the south. So actually, there is no connection at all to the sunrise or directions or Paradise! [laughing] But don't look so disappointed, because there is a similarity between us and the Indians. The Japanese do believe that the east is holy, but it's for a different reason than the one you suggested. Our way of thinking is that Amaterasu Ōmikami is the Kami of the sun, and that it is correct to bow to the sun in the morning and offer prayers. But when Buddhism came into Japan and started to merge with Shinto practices, then things changed. The Buddha was born in India, which is to the west, and therefore that became the direction of Paradise. Now, when you die, you go to the "Western Paradise" . . . which is kind of a holy land for the Buddhists. Those following the Kumano and the Jōdō beliefs are among the many that have this view, but even the Nachi Shrine (located beside a huge waterfall near Kumano) has a Kami of the west. Also, when a person dies there is the Buddhist and folk custom of the "western pillow," where you place the person's head to the west so the soul will fly in that direction when it exits the body from the top of the head. But you should never do this in a house while everyone is still alive. Any normal house won't arrange their bedrooms so as to have the family members pointing to the west. This is a Buddhist principle, but since the sun rises in the east and sets in the west, and since the sun has traditionally been associated by Japanese with life itself, the belief really sticks. A parallel in the Western world would be the ancient Egyptians and their belief in the gods of night and day, riding their boats in the appropriate directions. Because death is hated, Japanese want to face to the east and south in spite of the west being associated with the concept of "Paradise."

But a pillow that faces north is also bad, because of the idea of *kimon* or *oni no mon:* the "demon's gate." North is the direction of demons[4] because of a very strong belief during the Heian period which associated the Tohoku region in the north with the land of demons. Most likely these were the Ainu people, who were fighting against the expansionist policies of the military government. So when you build a house, you have to put the toilet or the bathing area, anywhere impurities are released, in the northern part of the house. The "Tohoku" direction doesn't get any sunlight of course, and where there is no sunlight sickness and bad influences breed. If you put a bedroom in this part of the house, you are guaranteed to have sickness and troubles among the family members. All of this is part of a tradition called *ie no so* or *kaso,* which is a way of learning about the physiognomy of a house in order to avoid bad influences. If there is some problem in the orientation of a house to its good and bad directions, we say, "*kaso ga warui,*" or the "influences are bad." At a shrine, we always put a smaller subshrine dedicated to Inari in the northeast corner of the grounds because that direction needs careful consideration and attention. At home, this is where you can put your *kamidana* [Kami altar] so that it will dispel the lingering bad effects from being far from the sun. This is the wisdom for old societies but it's also a very practical belief with a lot of science behind it.

Q: In looking back at the calendar, I noticed last week's Jichinsai [Earth Sanctification ritual] fell on a day that was designated as "good" but not "great." Why didn't the participants wait for a day that would have been wholly auspicious?

A: Perhaps you looked at a typical calendar that every gasoline station or insurance company gives out, one cataloging the days into "bad," "so-so," "good," and "auspicious" days. These are based mostly on Buddhist calendars and lack an essential component of the directions associated with the days of the month, which is only found on calendars we use at shrines to determine what days are good for Jichinsai rites. This is all based on ancient methods of divination that find the good or bad direction for an individual on any given day. Say, for example, you want to visit me here at the shrine, which is north from where you live, and you learn that today, north is a bad direction for you to go in. You can't contact me because for some reason I'm not available, so what do you do? Well, you approach the shrine in a series of angles that offset the "bad" direction by balancing it with "good" or neutral directions.

Now, since directions can change in their daily influences, this gets interesting when you have a house. A rich person with a fantastic house isn't going to tear it down and rebuild just because their house isn't properly aligned with the shifting patterns of the directions. What they do is to entrust the care for these influences to the Kami by coming to the shrine and performing a ritual called the *hō ii yoke*. They might say, "My house faces east, but this year east is a bad direction for me," and we'll conduct a purification that asks the Kami to take care of the bad direction by offsetting its influences. The most famous place to have this done is at Samukawa Shrine in Kanagawa Prefecture, but people come to us as well as to other shrines all over Japan. I might add that offsetting or neutralizing inauspicious influences for individuals, families, or even companies, a practice called *yaku yoke*, is one of the most important services we perform at Suwa Jinja. A person might come to us at a certain age regarded as unlucky (especially at thirty-three for women, and forty-two for men) and we'll perform a short ritual to protect that person as well as make them less anxious about this time in their lives. This whole tradition, I think, began in China with ancestral spirits and how they interacted with the many directions of the universe.

Q: That sounds very practical. Japanese religious culture seems full of pragmatic ways of dealing with issues like these.

A: Well, this is a little different, but to continue talking about directions, this same kind of practical approach can also apply to the day when you move from one residence to another. Say that you've scheduled a day for the movers to come and to start packing their van when you discover that the day you've chosen is not a good one at all for something as important as moving. What we advise in that situation is for the family to do a symbolic move—that is, to choose a good day before the movers come and take the family to the new house or apartment and spend a little time there, have lunch, drink some sake, and let the kids play around, which becomes, symbolically at least, the move itself. Then you can actually relocate at your convenience, even though the calendar may not be totally on your side.

I guess the point is that you don't simply give up even though it seems bad influences are working against you. You ask the Kami to correct the imbalance. This is something you can do at a [Buddhist] temple as well of course, but on the whole, most people come to a shrine to have it done.

Q: It's interesting you mentioned having a little sake at the new residence. I know it's an important part of shrine rituals and festivals, but is there any practice or belief in either folk or shrine Shinto that treats sake as a kind of drug or sacred medium for gaining access to the Kami? I guess I'm thinking of how other peoples all over the world frequently resort to some kind of stimulant to enhance their contact with the deities.

A: You can see something of this in the influences from China, where many kinds of drugs were used for shamanistic or Taoist practices. Look at the old way of writing the word "sake," for example: the *sa* means "to hurry," or to speed up like a drug does, and the *ke* means "energy." Put them together and you have "to hurry up the energy." But there is another word which needs to be considered when talking about sake, and that is the word for rice in a field: *ine*. This is the source of sake, and its basic component, the *i*, equals "living" and is the same character in *iki*, or "breath." Farmers sometimes talk about the roots of the rice plant, *ne*, as having "breath" (*ne no iki*), which is a pretty interesting concept. Rice is alive, it's breathing out there in the field, and because of its life-giving properties to those early communities, it was considered divine, with a Kami dwelling within it. After it was harvested, some was always put into a small bale and offered to the family shrine [*kamidana*] before the rest of the work proceeded. From this you can see that sake was originally something used only at religious observances, where it was first offered to the Kami and then, being practical people, it was enjoyed by all the participants. In fact, the consumption of sake after a festival was sometimes a license for all kinds of carrying on, but this didn't happen on the grounds of a shrine.

Q: Isn't this sacred aspect of rice still very much a part of the Imperial household's duties? I'm not so clear about the relationship but I know the emperor himself plants rice on the palace grounds.

A: The relationship between emperor, rice, and sake is very important. You could even say that it is fundamental to his authority.
If, for example, I become emperor and say in a proclamation
that I will now rule Japan, there is no difference between this
and the power plays in many other countries. The emperor's
authority depends on the Daijōsai festival, when he announces
to the Kami that he will be the emperor and asks for their help.
This was especially important during the period of the civil
war, when history records a number of half-emperors who made
themselves emperor by law but did not have the divine ancestry
and connections to ask the Kami for assistance. I won't go into
all the details of the ritual, which is a very interesting one,[5] but
what basically happens is for the new emperor to make offerings
of sake to the Kami and then drink with them in specially constructed rooms, thus sealing an agreement and having them join
into his body.

This is not so different from the marriage ceremony when
you look at its function of joining individuals together. Even
though the law says you are married just by going to the city hall
and registering as a couple, many people, myself included, feel
the new couple are not really united until they ritually exchange
the cups of *o-miki* [consecrated sake]. If I'm officiating at a wedding, I say something like this: "Today we are together in front
of the Kami of Suwa Shrine to join the blood of this man and
woman." The way we do it, of course, is through the sake. Even
the *yakuza* [gangsters] have a custom of joining like this, where
if they really want to trust each other they'll exchange a vow
over an exchange of sake cups. All this goes back to the sanctity of sake, which should be thought of like medicine, like holy
medicine. If you don't exchange the cups at a wedding, I don't
consider the couple to have much chance of making it since the
Kami is not involved. Likewise, if you don't partake of the *o-miki*
after a ritual, you really haven't paid your respects to the Kami,
because that is the occasion where they come into your body.
We always have the *miko* attendants serving people after rituals,
and of course there is always a ready supply of *o-miki* available
just outside the shrine for whoever comes to worship at whatever
hour of the day—but you'd be surprised how many people think
this isn't important.
Q: When I think about sake as "sacred medicine" I extend the association to the head priest as a kind of "medicine man." Among

the North American Indian tribes, the medicine man, or shaman, was closest to the deities and therefore the ceremonial

leader of the tribe. Was the role of the *gūji* [chief priest] similar
in old Japan?

A: Yes, that's true. And why do we know? Because the *ujigami* [from
uji, "clan," and *kami*, "deity"] was originally only the Kami for
one clan—for example, those deities that were the ancestral
founders of the Uesugi clan. The person chosen to perform
rites was the highest in rank because the job was extremely important: asking the ancestral Kami for protection and blessings
in growing rice. Gradually the clans grew into communities,
and depending on who was most powerful, a place to worship
one principal Kami for all clans was established, although the
subordinate Kami were also included.

After a festival honoring these Kami, they would hold a
naorai, which not only is an interesting practice but is an interesting word as well. As you know, in the old days priests and
worshippers had to live in seclusion, apart from their wives and
families in order to be pure for a festival. But when the period
of worship and formal celebration was over, the *naorai* marked
the transition back into a free or normal lifestyle. Which makes
sense of course, because if you are a high-ranking official in the
clan whose periodic function is to worship the Kami, you have
to be pure and holy, but if you are pure and holy all the time,
how can you sleep with your wife and make children who will
further the life of the clan? *Naorai*, which comes from the verb
naore, means "to relax" the prohibitions, but it's not a period
of wanton excess. No, it's still controlled as a banquet of sorts
within the shrine grounds after a service, where again the consecrated sake was enjoyed but in a more relaxed atmosphere. The
officals in charge of the ritual could now return to their normal
roles, being priests only for the duration of the festival. The
same thing applies to the emperor when he serves in his role of
chief priest for the Imperial household's shrines. After the ritual,
he goes back to only being the emperor and nothing more. If
you study history a bit, you'll find that his most important job is
to conduct these observances—something called *matsurigoto*, or
the blending of ritual and politics. In ancient times, *matsurigoto*
was politics, because the traditional meaning is for the Kami to
be the foundation for all political affairs, which were to be con-

ducted in harmony with the feelings of our ancestors. Of course, the mayor or neighborhood leader was also supposed to be in line with this way of thinking, which is very different these days, of course! A leader should have the same feelings for politics as he does for a *matsuri*.

Q: Since the *gūji* is the closest member of the community to the Kami, in times past as well as now, why doesn't he perform the purification at the beginning of every ritual? This would seem an important aspect of how he demonstrates his power.

A: The purification [*harae*] is only preparation for the main ritual. You have to be pure and have defilements [*tsumi*] cast off before you can read the invocational prayer [the *norito*], but the purification is the job of subordinates. There are a couple festivals in June and December where I have the job of purification, but those rituals are exceptions. Usually, the opening purification, the offerings, and even the *kagura* [sacred dances] of the *miko* are all done for the sake of the invocational prayer—that is the most important part of any rite. No matter what the occasion is, whether there are five or six or ten other priests in attendance, they are all doing their tasks for the *gūji* so that he may concentrate all his energies on the main prayer.

Sometime I'll explain to you all the movements of a ritual, which are all set and regulated. The speed of all the actions—from the purification, to the presentation of offerings, to the *norito* prayer—are all supposed to follow a certain form. My speed, those of the other priests and the *miko*, the person using the wand of purification, the messenger carrying the *norito* prayer, they're all supposed to be different. All the rest of the priests are like shadows, but they too are regulated in their movements. They can move very quickly, but the main celebrants must be slow to give the ritual its stately and dramatic atmosphere. For example, until the *norito* is read, one speed is followed—and when it is completed, we go into another mode. If you can see this far into a ritual, a *matsuri*, then it's a lot of fun at a level of aesthetic appreciation.

Q: As a final question, I wonder if you could help me understand what the word "spirit" means in a Shinto context. In your opinion, how does it differ from what the Buddhists say about it?

A: Have you heard of the phrase *yamato-damashii?* Even though your dictionary would probably say that *tamashii* is a "soul" or "spirit," it's more like what you mean in your question about "spirit." When life passes away, it's what's left over, but this is different from the idea of *seimei* [existence] because that is what physically dies. We have another word, *reikon*, which again means "soul" or "spirit" in English, but it's not the same as *tamashii*. When a person or thing is still alive, you would not describe its essence as being *reikon*, but the living thing does have what you call a "soul," right? You can also say that a person's beliefs have *tamashii*, or that his true feelings are there.

Q: So, to return to the American Indians once again, is this the same as their belief that people or clouds or living things in general all had a kind of *tamashii* which linked them together in a circle of life?

A: Well, in a way it is the same—in that the idea of "God" is equated with life, which is true for the Christian conception of the "Holy Spirit" as well—but there's an important difference too. In Shinto, life is full of the presence of the spirit of the Kami, but this closeness is not linked to omnipotent deities. Actually, this idea was shared all over the world in the old days— in Germany, France, Greece—all had the same belief about the proximity of the spirit of the Kami in the world. When you look at Greek mythology, you see this idea in the power of the spirits of animals, or, in Europe, in the custom of the Christmas tree as a place where the Kami is invited to dwell awhile, or in beliefs about propitious directions and orientations to the earth based on the presence of Kami.

Q: But why do you think this idea became subordinate to Christianity?

A: My idea is that it all centers on the place where Christianity got started, out there in the desert. It was a place where only the sky could be seen. All else was just the surface of a rather uninteresting and dry land, so obviously God had to be in the heavens. But when you get into Europe, you have a place where there is more than just sky; you have forests, water, or places where the spirit of life, the *seimei*, is. So you can say *seimei* for this in Japanese, but I think the English word "spirit" is not strong enough to really catch and express the full range of this idea.[6] The idea of an omnipotent God, when you compare it with all the complexity of life, is a rather weak idea. The Indians, as well as Shinto, believe that there is something stronger which has its source in the mountains, rivers, and lakes from which our life is given. A tree has a spirit and you know there's something alive in there, that can come out. But really, it's the mountains that we think our life is drawn from and that, when we die, it's the mountains to which we return. It's that kind of belief.

19

SANCTIFYING
THE EARTH

In most countries in the Western world, all one needs before starting construction on a house or building is the appropriate financing, skilled laborers and carpenters, and, of course, a location. But in many parts of East Asia and especially in modern Japan, in addition to the above prerequisites one frequently has an important ritual performed at the site itself before a single shovel of dirt can be turned. Dating back to some of the earliest communities of the Asian continent, the recognition that the very earth underfoot is charged with a sacred presence was an accepted and very basic orientation to the cosmos. The process of choosing one particular location, perhaps because of its beauty or strategic alignment, and making it the center for rituals and divinations is fundamental to how communities situated themselves not only to the land but to their conceptions of the supernatural as well. By designating one place as sacred, often through techniques such as divination, spirit possession, and ecstatic revelation, these early cultures gave their world and societies a spinal column around which everything else could be structured.

In Japan, possibly as far back as 10,000 years, this same practice was well established in pre-Yamato, even pre-Ainu, cultures.[1] As villages became more fixed and nomadic cultures gave way to more closely knit agricultural communities, the Kami of a particular clan eventually acquired names, personalities, and specific spheres of influence, much like any member of the village. With the success of the Yamato clan in exerting a dominant hegemony of myth and symbols, a clan's local land deity was incorporated into the Yamato framework as being a local manifestation of a more generic land deity called O-kuni-nushi—the Kami upon whose "face" a structure would stand. Naturally, something had to be done as a way of propitiating this important spirit.

In its most widely accepted manifestation, the Jichinsai (Earth Sanctification ritual) is arranged by a private individual or construction company and seeks to fulfill three very pragmatic purposes corresponding to its three principal categories of participants: priest, owner, and worker. First, and most obvious for all involved, the Jichinsai asks for safety during the construction and a harmonious, trouble-free existence for individuals committed to the project. While not everyone in attendance would agree what the Jichinsai means, nor is there any preaching to these ends during the actual event, it is generally considered de rigueur and the socially consensual "right" thing to do before beginning construction.[2] Second, to the priests involved, the ritual is a vehicle to placate the local Kami as well as O-kuni-nushi, the Kami of the entire land. Although the particular sacred energy that is thought unique to a place is not named, this site-specific Kami is both an independently functioning entity requiring its own ritual and offerings and also a part of the more encompassing body of O-kuni-nushi. The Jichinsai's final purpose (after the calming and acknowledging) is to exorcise the place of both known and unknown impurities that might still be lingering from the battles, fires, and earthquakes of ages past. Were the existence of these impurities to be disregarded, they would eventually exact a devastating toll on the lives of those coming in contact with the structure or the activities it shelters. A story is told in Nagasaki of how carpenters hired by missionaries to construct a Baptist church were prohibited from holding a "pagan" Jichinsai rite, but rather than take the risk of offending the Kami and suffering possible injuries on the job, they went ahead with a secret service in the middle of the night!

Though there are minor variations from one end of the country to the other, the Jichinsai is always initiated by a call to the shrine giving the date, place, and particulars of the construction—whether it will be a family dwelling, an office building, an apartment, a place of business, and so on. (Though I have not seen it personally, I am positive that all segments of society, regardless of their "legitimacy" in the eyes of the law—from the so-called soapland brothels to pinball gambling parlors [pachinko]—would request the services of a shrine to conduct a sanctification ritual. Their already substantial risks would only increase without one!)

At least an hour before the ritual, a representative of the family or construction company will come to the shrine to pick up whichever priest (usually a younger one) is in charge of the ritual, as well as the numerous metal lockers containing his or her "tools of the trade." Not only must these be loaded, there is also the priest's hat, robe, shoes, purification wand, and the seven different kinds of food and drink offerings to be presented upon an altar that, like everything else, is portable. Somehow everything fits into the trunk (or into a taxi called especially for hauling), and the driver delivers his august load to the site. Prior to the priest's arrival, a rental company specializing in portable pavilions will have erected a canopy tent whose walls are a distinctive "celebratory red" (from the Chinese) and "cloud white" stripe, creating a three-sided enclosure with peaked roof. For smaller structures and incomes, this luxury may be dispensed with altogether, but it's generally agreed that it is not only desirable but that the color red, thought to be synonymous with good fortune, adds to the auspiciousness of the general scene. The path leading into the soon-to-be sacred area is usually of damp sand or fine gravel, carefully raked into a smooth surface that, theoretically at least, should be first "visited" by the feet of the priest.

At the far end of the area inside the tent will be at least one and usually two large branches from the *sakaki* evergreen tree, signifying one of the earliest practices of Shinto, that a tall place is needed for the Kami to alight upon after its descent from the celestial fields of heaven. Indeed, for the very first shrines, this is all there was: a single tree standing in an area designated as sacred. For the modern Jichinsai, the *sakaki* is accompanied by the leafy branches of young bamboo, which serves as a symbol of strength and flexibility, essential ingredients for all life not to mention a permanent structure in a land frequented by earthquakes, typhoons, and floods.

When the priest arrives, everyone is at his service, although he personally arranges the offerings upon their little stands on the portable altar. It is interesting to contrast the "in-house" rituals at the shrine with what happens at a Jichinsai because unless it is a particularly important sanctification, the priest must do all the work himself. It would take much too long to present each little stand individually during the services and so he prepares and arranges them beforehand: the white radishes, sake, hulled rice, and fish in the back row, with oranges and apples, tomatoes and peppers, and the important and ever-present tray containing salt and water vessels in the front. Before the offerings, on its own eight-legged table, is the purification wand of white paper streamers, the "featured attraction" of the ritual. As we have seen elsewhere, it is through the symbols of the ritual that the participants construe their interaction with the Kami and it is the *haraigushi* wand which snaps the ritual to full life.

Again unlike at the shrine, there is no drum calling everyone present to be aware the service is starting, only an "announcer," who has received from the priest beforehand the sequence of events that compose the ritual. Although everyone has rinsed their hands and mouths upon entering the pavilion, just as they would were they at Suwa Shrine, they rise again for the opening purification prayer and remain standing as first the offerings are purified, then the table upon which sits the scroll of the *norito* prayer, then the audience in attendance. The swish of the white paper streamers above the bowed heads of those assembled — left, right, left — temporarily leaves a great silence in its wake, a somewhat uncanny moment considering the busy location of the site in the center of the city.

With the place, offerings, and people thus prepared, the priest almost silently murmurs a prayer of invitation to the Kami, not even loud enough for those in the first row of seats to hear him. It ends with a more audible call for the Kami to invest the *sakaki* tree with its presence, a request which, when made inside the shrine, is eerie and dramatic. Here, in the middle of a neighborhood, as cars, buses, and other noises intrude, the sustained "Ohhh!" is fragile and otherworldly, as if someone were to suddenly pull from his pocket an exquisitely crafted porcelain figurine while crossing a congested street. One is not quite sure this is the right time or place for such a sound but there it is all the same — a single long vowel, followed by two claps, which brings the presence of the sacred fully into the proceedings. But which Kami, although invisible, is it that has manifested itself? When I ask the question later, I am met with a look of perplexed curiosity that overwhelms my own a hundred times. It obviously matters little to the priest or those in attendance. Perhaps the Kami is like the priest in that whoever was on call that day is the one now present.

Like any guest, the Kami must be treated well, and so the lids of the sake flasks are lifted so that it can wash down the feast of "offering essences" it has just enjoyed. And besides, who would expect anyone to listen to words of praise and supplication on an empty stomach? The *norito* is quite long, since it must not only cover the heavenly realm, with its compliments and humble requests for safety and good fortune for all who come in contact with this place, but also name the family who owns the land, the construction firm, and anyone else, like a bank or rich uncle, who is instrumental to the building process.

. . . protect this structure from the wrath of heavy rains, strong winds, fire, pestilence, earthquakes, and thieves, and make all who dwell or work here prosperous . . .

With the Kami thus acknowledged and duly praised, it is assumed that it is fully attentive to the proceedings. Now is the crucial moment of actually confronting the specific character of the land itself. With everyone and everything previously cleansed by the *haraigushi* at the beginning of the service, a different method is employed for the forces of energy coiled beneath the raked sand. In each of the four directions, beginning with the east, small white squares of hemp fiber are scattered like confetti into the air. Recalling the *norito* of the Great Purifications of June and December, the act evokes Izanagi's return to the upper world after his descent into the land of Yomi to find his departed wife, Izanami, and the various purifications he enacted to rid himself of contamination. As the priest makes his journeys to each of the four corners of the cosmos, no chant, prayer, or song is uttered—only the quiet of ritual activity echoing a great, primordial stillness in which this spot of earth was once utterly unspoiled.

The final movement of the priest brings him to the main altar, where the little squares are showered upon the offerings and tables. Senior Priest Ureshino says to think of this purification as a rain of magnets which draw out and absorb the negative or impeding barriers between the Kami and the land. Whether they be of a human source, such as a death or sickness in a house three centuries ago upon the same spot, or of animal or vegetable origins occurring in some ancient forest of immense camphor trees that once blanketed the hills around the bay of Nagasaki (did a predator bloodily devour its victim here?), in the words of the prayer, "every defilement is now gone."

The completion of the purification ritual opens the door to participation by the audience, but it is not the usual offering of the sacred evergreen branches at this point. Until now, little attention has been paid to a three-foot-high cone of carefully smoothed sand at the left and front of the central altar. Images of pyramids and possible influences from Egypt would come rapidly to mind were it not for the delicate wisps of long-bladed grasses which shoot forth from its top, as if a fountain were issuing from a volcano.

A man approaches it with a vicious-looking curved scythe, grasps the plumes with his left hand and, using the power of a ritual magic spell called the *kiai,* shouts "Oi! Oi! Oi!" while administering three cuts to the grass, severing it completely. He sits down, and immediately two different men, the construction company president and a subordinate, walk unceremoniously to the cone with a wooden mallet and stake of white cedar. The mallet-wielding president yells "Ai! Ai! Ai!" with each blow he directs upon the stake as it plunges into the right side of the sand mountain. In five seconds the action is finished, leaving the cone violated, as if a spear had been thrown into its side.

However, all that happened was a nonverbal, symbolic communiqué given to the Kami of the place. The land's owner acknowledged the original fauna and flora by the grass protruding from the summit of the cone and that some of it might have to be altered for the structure to be built. The construction company representatives then showed the Kami that the very earth itself, the sanctuary holy to us all, will be gouged and broken in the grounding of the building to the spot. This demonstration of intentions, and the propitiatory offerings and prayers presented, allow O-kuni-nushi to vanquish whatever feelings of ill will it might harbor against these puny humans as they impose their designs on this fraction of its sacred form. A potentially disastrous situation—that of a Kami angry with a human—has been averted and the ritual's principal function thus completed.[3] Everyone is once again seated and the hardworking priest makes his offering of the sacred *sakaki* branch upon the altar, bowing and clapping twice as he would do in the shrine. Various important people in the audience are also invited to make their offerings, with perhaps a company president coming forward to make the actual presentation as the five or more people who accompanied him stand at their seats and follow along with his bows. By this time, the Kami should be pleased and have finished bestowing its blessings upon the ritual and place, so that the priest can now cover the sake bottles and water container vessels and murmur another silent prayer inviting the Kami to ride the powerful trajectory of the long vowel "Ohhh!" back to the heavens.

All that remains is for the entire party to reassemble at another part of the site (or later at a restaurant) for a partaking of the rather generous amount of gifts of sake offered on separate tables beside the altar. Of course, food and catering services or sushi restaurants are frequently called in to make the transition back to the normal world more memorable, but the *naorai* will still leave enough sake for the carpenters and other builders to periodically wet their whistles during afternoon break for some weeks to come.

And the cost for all this? In our case study here, it is paid by the construction company, of course, though the word "donation" might be more appropriate since Suwa Shrine does not dictate a price for its services. It might be ten thousand or a hundred thousand yen ($90–$900), depending on the size of the project, but whatever amount is offered, it is done discreetly, directly to the shrine. A priest may be permitted to take an honorarium for a particularly well done service. On the whole, the costs are worth it for all involved; the land is purified, the Kami is pacified, the construction process is blessed with safety and care, and the individuals either using or dwelling within the cosmos of this spot are assured that no hindrance to their fulfillment has been inadvertently overlooked. Life, and construction, can now proceed. There is nothing left but to bring on the bulldozers.

*   *   *

I would feel somewhat irresponsible if I let the matter of Jichinsai remain in downtown Nagasaki. It should also be pointed out that the ritual has become a political bridge from local to regional and national concerns, although the controversy surrounding this relationship has by and large died down. As the reader may have already surmised, not only private individuals and construction companies contract a shrine's services for a Jichinsai. In the early 1970s, the matter became very complicated when the city of Tsu was taken to court on grounds that the 1946 constitution's law "strictly" separating church and state funding, support, and interests was being compromised. A citizens' group charged that the Jichinsai the city government had arranged for a new municipal gymnasium amounted to sponsorship of a "religious" act and therefore should not be paid for by public funds. Significantly, this case went all the way to the Supreme Court, which rendered a decision in 1977 that ground purification rites were performed so routinely they had become secularized and thus could no longer be said to be religious. The court also indicated that not all religious activity was prohibited to the state—only that which gave support and patronage (or which hindered and did harm) to a particular religious institution.[4]

Thus, one now finds Jichinsai quite freely conducted wherever there are intersections between Japanese corporate and governmental interests, such as at the Tanegashima space center, the new Osaka International Airport, and the Tsukuba Science Exposition, to mention but a very few. Uniting these diverse examples of national significance with Mr. Sato's empty front yard to be used for a new garage is what Terrence Turner calls a "transcendental ground" that remains central to their significance and continuation and, despite smokescreens generated by the Japanese Supreme Court, to the basic insecurities many Japanese feel about the world. The Jichinsai asserts a dual message that the cosmos is first of all a manifestation of powerful forces held in tenuous balance (any Japanese farmer, fisherman, or politician would agree to this) and that the ritual itself is a way to temporarily manage the ultimately uncontrollable nature of the cosmos and thus index the rate of change affecting the endeavors of human beings. Its "logics of operation" evoke earlier conceptions of the universe and dictate an ongoing relationship between fragmentation (what happens to the face of the land Kami when it is broken by construction) and reconstitution (what the ritual does to avert the chaos of disrupting forces) (Handelman 1990, 63).

One of the crucial elements permitting such flexibility for the Jichinsai in particular and Shinto rituals in general is a minimum of spoken commentary during the event itself. There is neither doctrine to be imparted nor textual message for the participants to ponder; instead, a performance is perceived and one prayer intoned, both framed by an abundance of symbolic objects in shifting interplay. Thus, depending upon who sponsors a Jichinsai and in what context it is held, the ritual occasion frequently becomes an ideological exercise underpinned by strategies to legitimate the power of the rite's sponsors and keep conflicting or opposing forces at bay. Similarly, though a particular ritual held at a shrine may be centuries old—such as a fall harvest celebration or the ritual of Great Purification—the multivocality of its symbols and actions can be directed toward any number of themes should a head priest follow the ritual with a speech that advances, to those assembled, the interests of a particular group, advocate, or cause. I have attended rituals at a variety of shrines which became vehicles for espousing concerns as varied (and contentious) as respect for the emperor and flag, the need to honor the founding myths of the nation, and, most recently, an espousal of trade restrictions so as not to compromise the "spiritual" contribution of "Japanese" rice to the national character of "we Japanese." Though I wish it were otherwise, I am reminded by Benedict Anderson that nationalism is most often aligned not with "self-consciously held political ideologies but with the large cultural systems that preceded it" (1983, 19). The current manifestation of shrine Shinto under the direction of many chief priests educated before or during the war, and the type of nationalism mentioned above, are often formed in each other's image.

One of the frequent criticisms against Shinto is precisely its situational flexibility, that it can accommodate any circumstance (even death rituals if it has to) and fulfill any sponsor's intent. Scholars ranging from Robert Bellah (1957, 1970) to Kato Genichi (1973) to Kuroda Toshio (1981) all find in Shinto a singular lack of transcendental principles that would better guide its ethical and moral activities and make it less of a pawn for those seeking to use its symbols to legitimate their authority and power. One need only follow the activities of the Central Association of Shinto Shrines for a short while to see that a substantial campaign is under way to promote veneration of the "national" shrines at Ise and thus, by extension, veneration of the emperor and Imperial family. A simple Jichinsai ritual may seem an innocent and useful tool for an individual to harness anxieties about a substantial investment of money and material, but given the right time, circumstance, and motives, its symbols and cosmic evocations can be easily used to feed a resurgent nationalism that again seems quite ready to reappropriate Shinto rites. One can only hope those priests, both young and old, who see beyond these opportunistic manipulations can maneuver the future of Shinto practice into directions that promote understanding and personal fulfillment instead of a state-based ideology.

20

THREE

RITES

FOR

ENDING

AND

BEGINNING

THE

YEAR

It takes a considerable amount of ill luck and cynicism before an individual in Japan will regard the ending of the old year and the beginning of the new as being without hope and fresh possibilities. The cultural messages about the chance to make a clean beginning come via advertising, the news media's coverage of year-end celebrations and customs, and even the educational system's urging of serious students to rededicate themselves to their lessons. For religious institutions throughout Japan, Buddhist, Shinto, and Christian alike, any number of significant rituals are conducted on behalf of the faithful, but perhaps nowhere is the New Year so crucially important as at a shrine. A survey conducted by the Yomiuri Shimbun news agency in 1992 showed a steady number of visitors to shrines during the New Year; about 70 percent of the Japanese people (83.6 million) visited a shrine during the 1991 New Year holiday. This would seem to translate most obviously into an increased interest of the general population in shrine visitations (*hatsumōde*) as part of the holiday festivities (which may or may not have religious import for these visitors), but the phenomenon provides an important source of income to shrines, with many institutions basing their salary, maintenance, and rebuilding budgets on projections gleaned from attendance figures in January. I will go into more detail about the Japanese New Year in the second section of this chapter but will frame that discussion by beginning and ending with two of Suwa Shrine's "classical" in-house celebrations.

SUSU HARAE: DECEMBER 29

The ritual of Great Purification for the end of the year is still two days away, but today the priests, attendants, and groundskeepers turn their attention to the physical as well as spiritual tasks of cleaning the shrine.[1] For millions of traditionally minded Japanese, the last three days of the year are appropriate for removing the dust and grime, or *susu* (soot), from the household, a carryover from those days when heating and cooking were done by poorly ventilated wood fires inside the house and *susu* collected on all interior surfaces. Especially in the rural areas, not only will a good sweeping and dusting of every nook and cranny of the house be undertaken but the tatami, which are the floor itself, will be removed and, weather permitting, placed in the sun's sanitizing rays. The shrine no longer is quite so thorough (if it ever was), but it is logical to think that, with Shinto attitudes about purity and defilements being what they are, this custom has its roots in creating a suitably clean place for the Kami to inhabit. And if it is appropriate for the Kami, should not human beings follow suit?

But more than physical dirt receives attention in this Susu Harae; there are invisible impurities as well to be dislodged from their hiding places by means of long bamboo poles with a few leafy branches remaining at the end. When I ask what kind of impurities might possibly be lurking in the shadowy corners of the upper rafters, I am told that since the priests are human and since many guests and worshippers have passed through in the course of a year, the harmful, selfish, or lustful thoughts toward others, the physical and mental illnesses, and the mistakes and sufferings and frailties might all have left a little "something" behind here in the shrine. And that is why, at the end of the year, it doesn't hurt to physically dislodge them. "But if you're going to knock them out of their corners," I ask, "what happens then? Aren't you worried that they will fall on you?" Senior Priest Ureshino just smiles. "That is why I have this hat on! And even if they do, we have the ritual of Great Purification two days later to take care of EVERYTHING." As the Japanese are fond of saying, *Naru hodo!* (Oh, so that's the way it is!).

The morning's activities begin with a brief ritual which seems to be performed almost entirely for the benefit of the television cameras from all three local stations. It is almost a given that the media would be in attendance, because an event such as the Susu Harae makes excellent footage to round off the evening's newscast and to strengthen the public's perception of the media as an institution involved in perpetuating the old traditions at the heart and soul of the nation. For the shrine, however, it is great PR that costs nothing, having become an essential part of Suwa Shrine's self-presentation to a public that would otherwise have little opportunity to keep track of shrine events. And so the camera crews and news photographers are tolerated as they talk during prayers, fail to bow when ritual audiences are supposed to, and probably bypassed the water font where hands and mouths are supposed to be cleansed before entering the building. While they frequently film events in the courtyard or in the Hall of Worship, today is the *only* time of year they are allowed upstairs into the Hall of Offerings.

I have been so distracted by the preparations, gestures, and positionings of the media that the opening ritual has reached the *norito* prayer before I realize I am the only one in attendance who is not either a priest or a member of a news crew. Does that mean I will be the only one presenting the offering to the Kami on behalf of the people of Nagasaki? Or would that be too ludicrous for the worship of the Kami: a foreigner raised in a different culture and religion standing alone as representative of the entire body of the shrine's parishioners? Everything has been slightly abbreviated about this opening ritual—with very short prayers, no *miko* dance, and only three plates of offerings put on the altar. But not until Matsumoto-san beckons me to come forward and presents me with a *tamagushi* branch do I realize just how pressed they are for time and how much work there is to do, and how tactfully they have solved the questions I was asking myself. The Gūji is standing and waiting for me to take a place by his side, and together we kneel in front of the offering table, reverse our branches' stems to point to the altar, and do a pretty fair job of delivering the bows and claps in a synchronous harmony. *This* would have made a very interesting juxtaposition for those nightly news reports, but probably the shrine would have had to live it down for months afterward as conservative supporters complained about allowing a *gaijin* such access to the Kami that protects the *Japanese* people and region. The issue is moot, however, because the TV crews stopped paying attention about ten minutes into the ritual and are outside at this moment, lounging on the shrine's steps, smoking cigarettes and chatting, waiting to be called in for the *real* photo opportunity.

The actual cleaning and exorcism of the Susu Harae is no-nonsense work that even the Gūji is involved in. He and several of the senior priests—Oka, Ureshino, and two more—as well as all of the junior priests and *miko*, have their billowing sleeves tied up as they choose a length of bamboo and take their respective places, all according to their various ranks. Uesugi-san (as chief priest) and Oka-san (as the most senior) are the only ones who can ascend the steps to the Inner Sanctuary. The other priests begin striking the lower walls with their bamboo branches and strain to reach into the corners along the stairs, over by the little kitchen, and on the level of the photographers and cameramen. One young newspaper photographer who rarely misses a public event like this tentatively places his foot on the steps to improve the angle for what he hopes will be an eye-catching photo, but he is frozen in his tracks by a curt "*Damé!!*" (meaning "bad," "forbidden," "out-of-bounds," and "you can't do that!" all in one) from the ever-vigilant Matsumoto-san. Like a docile pet who has just been scolded, he slinks away to focus on one of several *miko* gently wiping up the fallen leaves after the Gūji has passed.

As the bamboo whisk brooms move around the chamber, the bright lights from the video cameras follow their path. The Gūji carefully shakes around the special tablet inscribed with a golden character for "Kami" (神) presented to the shrine by the last of the Tokugawa period emperors himself. The soft, gauzy, pink silk banners that serve as dividers between priests and audience are also dusted, as are the spearlike poles holding standards bearing the shrine's oak leaf crest. When the group moves back to the Hall of Worship, the upper walls of the walkway encircling the ritual area are suddenly illuminated by the video lights and, as if for the first time, reveal an eclectic array of objets d'art, commemorative plaques, and artifacts (one of which is the propeller from an early biplane), which must all be cleansed. Oka-san has exchanged his long pole for a shorter wooden stick with a tuft of white paper streamers at its top, somewhat resembling the *haraigushi* used before all shrine events to purify participants, and he now busily attacks the white cloth banners around the ritual space as cameras and lights focus in on this new variation in the use of sacred tools.

There is no formal ending to the ritual—rather, a general dispersal of priests and photographers (and, one assumes, *susu* impurities).

The younger priests and *miko* will spend the rest of the morning and part of the afternoon doing a thorough cleanup of the fallen bamboo leaves scattered throughout the two tiers of the shrine accessible to them, as well as wiping every surface and polishing every gleaming bit of lacquer and gold or silver plate. It is the only conceivable way the shrine can be ready for the crush of rituals it will perform for those corporations, organizations, families, and individuals that desire to end the old year and start the new one petitioning the Kami for guidance and assistance. These will be in addition to the tens of thousands of people coming informally to worship and pay their respects on New Year's Eve and the following five days. As Ureshino-san comes down to the front entrance of the Hall of Worship, I see he is winded and ready for a break. "I felt guilty watching you all work so hard. Did you sweat?" I ask him as he lays down his bamboo pole. "Like a horse!" is his panting reply.

203
*Three
Rites for
Ending and
Beginning
the Year*

THE FAITHFUL HOLIDAY HORDES:
DECEMBER 31 TO JANUARY 3

"All right now, let's go through the checklist and make sure we've got everything ready." The intensity of the faces gathered around the large table of the meeting room could be matched in any corporate boardroom, but this is the pre–New Year's Eve synchronization of preparations and personnel at Suwa Shrine. In a few hours, nearly 3,000 people will converge on the shrine at one time—all hoping to begin the New Year by presenting their petitions for health, success, and good fortune to the three Kami they believe are sequestered deep in shadowy stillness.

"Tanaka, you've contacted all the high school and college students who are to be hired help and made sure they're to be here at six o'clock this evening, right? And they all have proper robes and costumes so they look like shrine staff and not students? Good. Mori, is the contractor in charge of erecting the temporary stalls for selling amulets and talismans almost finished? All right, fine. And what about the stalls of the vendors and hawkers along the steps leading up to the shrine? Are they well off the path? Niwa, how about the supplies of sake and the giant golden cup that will give people their first drink for the New Year? Are the tables for that all in place near the steps of the Hall of Worship? Remember, it's one thousand yen per cup. Oh yes, Suzuki, have you got the canvas in place at the front of the Hall of Worship to catch the tossed coins? What about the protective netting to keep flying objects from going into the shrine proper as we conduct services? Fine. Be sure it's firmly secured because don't forget how two years ago someone threw a full bottle of sake! Now, let's see, is there anything else? The security and police have their supply of sake and tea in their information room. The families and companies who have contracted rituals have all been told when to arrive and where to go so we can keep things moving smoothly. Everyone knows which ritual they're participating in and at which time, I hope. And, well, that's about it. I hope no one has any questions."

If you can imagine a holiday that merges the anticipation of Christmas, the feasting of Thanksgiving, and the benign glow of the first day of a New Year, then you are close to understanding what Oshōgatsu means for the Japanese. Before the accelerated pace of postwar modernization began to dominate individual lives, this celebration lasted a minimum of two weeks, and in some places, where snow and cold abound, as long as a month. Today, people will tell you that it is important to start the New Year with all accounts settled and one's emotional slate wiped clean of arguments, feuding, and disappointments, but the holiday has its origins in the folk beliefs of agrarian times reaching back to China. If a community wanted a bountiful harvest in the autumn, it was up to the people to create a warm, unhurried atmosphere for the year to "grow into" despite the cold of the winter season. In Japan, the communal ties fostered by ritual activities at the local shrine were important of course, but so were the interfamily bonds strengthened during this holiday from work and obligations, when even the women of the household were freed from the chore of preparing food so as to give the Kami of fire a "rest." Stimulated by a variety of alcoholic beverages, considerable merrymaking and sexual licentiousness went on as well, since this too was seen as amenable to the fertility of the year's growing season.

Time and social change have altered many things about the holiday, but it has managed to retain its communal and family-centered characteristics. As during the Buddhist-based Obon observations of late summer, when people return to their birthplaces to care for the graves of their departed ancestors (who are thought to return for a brief visit), the trains, highways, and airlines during the three days before Oshōgatsu are jammed with refugees from the urban jungles. On television and in the printed press as well, the virtues of rural life are romantically extolled as reports about the varieties of festivities, special foods, and local charms of southern Kyushu's palm trees or northern Tohoku's crystalline snows flood popular consciousness. And while many young people find the holiday noteworthy only because of a few days' school holiday, the monetary gifts they receive from relatives, and a license to eat as many *omochi* rice cakes as they want, they are largely bored by the go-slow pace of the actual holiday, beginning on the first, and the constant drone of cultural and singing shows on television targeted for the adult viewing audience. Nearly any feature film lucky enough to be playing in the theaters at this time is assured of enormous profits.

205
Three
Rites for
Ending and
Beginning
the Year

Socially, the end of December before Oshōgatsu is frantic with activity. During the day, businessmen of all miens and guises rush to settle accounts and deliver goodwill gifts to important clients, while housewives, innkeepers, and restaurant chefs (who have also delivered gifts to cement or nurture their own networks) converge on street markets and stores for the freshest produce and fish products used in the staggering array of New Year's dishes they will create. And as we have seen above, the large and small shrines of a community are busy as well cleaning and preparing for thousands of visitors, who will provide a substantial portion of the shrines' operating revenues for the coming year.

From the fifteenth till the twenty-fifth of December, nearly every restaurant with a banquet hall is solidly booked with *bonenkai* (literally, "forget the year parties"). To attend one of these is a cultural experience in itself because not only is a prodigious amount of food and drink consumed, but the members of a company or school or whatever institutional organization is "forgetting the year" that night often seem equally intent on forgetting all sense of status and propriety as well. After everyone is fortified (and "protected") by drunkenness, school principals, foremen, and departmental heads will join their subordinates in ridiculous skits about embarrassing topics or situations expressly designed to create laughter and a further blurring of status. In this sense, these parties approximate what anthropologists call "rituals of inversion," where the existing power hierarchy is temporarily reversed or neutralized, giving subordinates the chance to say what they wish and act in ways that would instantly be censored in any other context. At the same time, however, these parties are also very much in the Shinto/Buddhist tradition of exorcising "demons" before undertaking the new venture of the coming year. As a colleague told me, "If you can survive several nights of *bonenkai* and still manage to conduct your affairs during the daytime, you are *ready* for the three days of doing nothing that Oshōgatsu affords."

While we have read about a few of the activities occupying the Japanese at the end of the year, the holiday would not be complete without the visible signs and symbols popping up in front of home and business entryways, on automobile grills, and even in front of the neighborhood police "boxes." Suddenly it seems as the population of the entire nation has been seized with a Shintoesque fervor, because the primary decoration is a *shimenawa* rope, the same symbol found at any shrine and used to designate sacred from profane space. Coming in all shapes and sizes—from skinny little pieces of rough twine that can be purchased at discount stores for several hundred yen to the silky ropes of family heirlooms twisted thick as a man's arm—they show that *this* household or business is starting the year free of the troubles of the past and that the Kami of the community (and, in the eyes of a Shinto priest, nation as well) have been enlisted as allies. Often, these *shimenawa* have ferns and the stems of bitter oranges (called *daidai*, or "from generation to generation") entwined in their strands. They show up everywhere, from the handlebars of noodle-shop delivery bicycles to the license plates of *bosozoku* hot-rodders, from the ticket windows in train stations to school and office entrances, and especially in front of hospitals and governmental offices. Though it might have been someone playing a practical joke, I even saw one attached to the public-announcement bulletin board of a Christian church!

For those willing to pay anywhere from $20 to $200 for the display, another symbol resonating with contemporary Shinto perspectives found in front of dwellings and stores is the *kadomatsu*, or "gateway pine." Three differing lengths of bamboo (whose ends have been diagonally sliced), with their messages of strength and vitality, are the prime feature of the *kadomatsu*, but as the name implies, pine boughs (*matsu*) are also prominently featured behind the bamboo. Though interpretations vary, most people versed in Japanese traditions agree not only that the pine symbolizes constancy, morality, and resiliency but also that its needles can be used to ward off evil spirits and ghosts. There should also be a plum branch somewhere in the arrangement, signifying the noble courage to bloom when conditions are austere and cold. And as if this symbolization of the qualities a virtuous Japanese is supposed to embody is not enough, the entire arrangement is encircled with a *shimenawa* festoon, from which hang green ferns and bitter oranges, as mentioned above.[2]

207
*Three
Rites for
Ending and
Beginning
the Year*

All of these preparations, while interesting in themselves, are leading to one major event. It is not the family reunions, the *osechi ryōri* delicacies arranged in lovely lacquered boxes, or even the gift-giving and socializing. For a majority of people, almost as if under a spell from their ancestors and traditions, the highlight and sine qua non of New Year's Eve is *hatsumōde*, the first visit of the year to the local shrine. How else can the gift of a new year from the Kami Toshi-gami-sama be properly sanctified and dedicated to worthy pursuits? As Uesugi Gūji said to the participants of the Dolls' Day festival back in March:

> The belief of we Japanese is that the new year is given to us from Toshi-gami-sama, or the Kami of years. Therefore, that fact alone makes it special and important, something that we can't waste. What comes from the realm of the Kami is inherently good, which is why we congratulate each other on having received such a precious gift as an entire new year to fill as we can. So, as we look out upon the possibilities of the new year, we want to purify our blunders and sins and cast off whatever evil influences we may have accumulated in the old year. This is really the belief of Japanese at the start of a new year, something I'm sure all of you shared in when you came to a shrine and prayed for a good beginning.

And although it is always a matter of caution when ascribing a single subjectivity to an entire community or group of people, one may venture that most Japanese coming to a shrine (or in some cases a temple) on New Year's Eve (or any time from January 1 through 5) do share in the basic premise of the Gūji's words.

This is not to say that they cannot turn the occasion into a jolly good time, especially as the excitement builds in waiting for the clock to tick away the last few seconds of the old year. Pushing to be closer to the top of the steps leading to a brightly illuminated Hall of Worship (thanks to Otaguro-san's last-minute replacement of a spent bulb on one of the spotlights), as soon as the shrine's drum pounds out its unmistakable rhythm, people laugh and shout out greetings of "*Akemashite omedetō gozaimasu!* [Congratulations on the New Year!]" and then throw a coin into the canvas sheets (as both an offering and a casting out of impurities) before turning inward for a fleeting instant when they bow their heads over joined hands. Many pray in the Buddhist style—rubbing their palms together as if a Buddhist rosary were between them—while others demonstrate what seems a hundred variations on the basic Shinto style of hand claps and two bows. Most of these people will then flock to the crowded area near the Hall of Worship where they can purchase new charms, amulets, and talismans (they will later get rid of the old ones, whose efficacy is now spent). Of particular interest to the shrine's accountants is that as many people as possible buy one of the long white arrows (the *hamaya*) that, for the very reasonable average price of only ¥800, are thought to dispel and destroy malevolent forces.

The fact that so many people have come out in the cold air of midnight to engage in a brief ritual display of acknowledgment of the Kami as part of their New Year celebration is, even if they would not say so, a deeply significant, even possibly "religious," gesture— but not in the Western sense of assigning to religious activity a single type of collectivity to which an individual owes a singular allegiance. It is certainly not the institution of shrine Shinto that is the object of the silent prayers of the visitors, nor is the nation or community particularly important. Instead, one must understand that part of what it means to be a Japanese at New Year's is signified by Shinto cosmologies, which, in spite of high technology and rapid social change, continue to orient millions of individuals during important periods of transition (such as the New Year, baby dedications, the "seven-five-three" festival, and weddings) or during periods of crisis (school entrance exams, sickness, childbirth, house construction, travel, and so on). To return to one of the opening themes of this book, publicly subscribed-to festivals having their roots in religious systems are one of the principal ways "employed" by a culture "to interpret a people's own situation to themselves" (Ortner 1978, 7). From aged merchants in traditional kimonos to long-haired rockers in chic leather jackets, the "set of scenarios" provided by what goes on at a shrine during a holiday such as New Year's may or may not be used to "stage daily life" (Fox 1990, 11). But the fact that these symbols, practices, and concepts are socially accepted as being *available* seems an important part of both one's general cultural gestalt and one's particular and ever-expanding "tool kit" for building a meaningful existence.

Are you one of those people worried about the coming year's un- 209
*Three
Rites for
Ending and
Beginning
the Year*
predictable combinations of good and bad fortune? You attended
the Great Purification ritual on the last day of the old year, made
your pilgrimage to the shrine just after midnight to be there when
the New Year began, and have bought the sacred arrows, new tablets
for inside the family shrine, and talismans to protect your car from
accidents, your house from fire, and your son's wife from a difficult
delivery of your second grandchild. But if you are still not quite sure
you have set off on the right foot, Suwa Shrine has just the ritual for
you, in which a magical potion, as pure and simple as seven herbs
collected from the nearby hills, will be distributed to all and will
cover all possible maladies that afflict human life.

Just inside the front gate, not far from the information and amulet
counter, a rather familiar looking black cauldron (see chapter 10 on
the Yutate ritual) has been placed at the center of a sacred space
delimited by four tall bamboo linked by a *shimenawa* rope. Even before the ritual begins, one can tell this is not going to be just any old
potion, not with a fire that is stoked by the lucky New Year's arrows
of last year; the spent *shimenawa* ropes that once adorned doorways,
children's bicycles, and the grills of cars; and the extremely combus-
tible *ofuda* (wooden tablets) from within family Shinto altars that
have been replaced by freshly charged ones from Suwa and Ise (conveniently sold year-round at Suwa Shrine's amulet counter).

No Gūji or senior priests are present today. Two of the younger
men and two *miko* watch the cauldron's broth begin to boil while
a sizable crowd mills around the periphery of the sacred space. At
3 P.M., a drumroll carries forth from within the shrine as one of
the priests steps forward, bows to the cauldron, and begins chanting the opening prayer of purification. His voice is loud and clear
and sends a hush over those even in the back rows. The other priest
then steps forward and shreds the air above the mightily steaming
cauldron with the white paper streamers of the wand of purification,
then turns and purifies his colleague and the *miko* (swish to the left,
woosh to the right, whish back left, stop, and bow). He steps behind
them to the slightly bowing crowd of children and their mothers,
old men and women, a few students on their way home from school,
and an assortment of businessmen, foreigners, and the usual surly
photographers, who dare not follow protocol and bow like everyone

else, for fear of missing a prize shot. They, along with everyone else, are now purified to receive the potion that will soon be ready.

The two *miko* have brought with them their bell-wands for a dance around the cauldron. But with no music to accompany their movements, the silence is a little strained, accented only by the ching! of the bells and the popping white pine of last year's lucky arrows as they feed the flames burning blue and orange beneath the charred kettle. By now the broth is ready—physically, spiritually, and thermally—for one of the *miko* to chop up the leaves from the seven magical herbs and, before dropping them into the boiling liquid, lead the crowd in this little prayer: "The drink of seven herbs will prevent a thousand illnesses."

One by one the herbs are dropped into the cauldron: dropwort (*seri*), shepherd's purse (*nazuna*), cottonweed (*gogyo*), chickweed (*hakobe*), henbit (*hotoke no za*), turnip greens (*suzuna*), and radish greens (*suzushiro*). A Shinto-style rendering of a folk tradition (or is the folk tradition derived from religious practices?), the gruel serves as a sedative against the overindulgence of the New Year's feasting, drinking, and inactivity. Matsumoto-san appears with a long ladle and stirs in the first leaves, then other baskets full of the herbs materialize and are also carefully commended to the billowing clouds of steam. A few minutes pass while the whole concoction cooks. More old arrows are added to the fire, someone asks just exactly what the powers of these particular herbs are, and a few drops of rain splatter down.

I wonder how different this "medicine-making" would have been a hundred or two hundred years ago. Would the lighthearted atmosphere of today's rite have been preceded by more serious concern for a precise rendering of the ancient recipe, that it might truly promote long life and enable one to avoid sickness in the coming year? Would the priests have stood around and joked with members of the crowd? Would this many people have come (I estimate around seventy), or would there have been whole neighborhoods of pushing and shoving parishioners, all anxious for a few sips of potion?

A young reporter from the local newspaper steps forward and asks Matsumoto-san, "Can we have a taste yet?" not worried about his health and good fortune but about the five o'clock deadline for tomorrow's early edition. "No," the answer comes, "we have to serve it to the Kami first, and if it is deemed acceptable, then we'll pass it around." One of the younger men dishes up the first sampling of the brew, ladling it into three separate white-porcelain dishes—one for

Suwa-no-Kami, one for Morisaki-no-Kami, and one for Sumiyoshi-no-Kami—before he puts them on a tray and carries it high into the shrine. Good manners and the still-growing crowd prevent me from following him, but I imagine that he enters the Hall of Offerings, places the three dishes on the same table that holds the *tamagushi* branch offerings, then performs his bows, hand claps, and final bow. And since the earth does not shake nor do the heavens send lightning or a flock of crows into the shrine grounds, the seven-herb drink is pronounced efficacious for all.

Its taste is hot, bland, and a little smoky, but to wash it down the shrine has also brought out a large wooden tub full of warm *amazake*, a thick and very sweet sake that is roughly refined, with small chunks of rice floating in the whitish, soupy liquid. There is plenty for everyone; even the children are allowed a small cupful of the drink because it too has medicinal, as well as sacred, properties. The young reporter seems especially happy to exchange his portion of the seven herbs for a paper cup of *amazake*, though perhaps it is the pretty *miko* he has been talking with for the past few minutes that gives his face its glowing countenance. Not surprisingly, his notebook stays in his pocket since he has already decided how the headline of tomorrow's edition will read: Shrine's Herbal Potion Brings Health and Romance. What better way to start the New Year?

21

TO BE
AN
ADULT

PART I: COMING OF AGE AT THE SHRINE

Mika Yoshida, a motivated twenty-year-old college student, is skipping school obligations today with the full consent of her teachers. She'll do a little shopping in the afternoon and meet her boyfriend in their favorite coffee shop later, but at the moment she is listening attentively to Matsumoto-san as he explains how to hold the sacred sprig of *sakaki* leaves for the Coming of Age ritual (Saiten-sai) that she and seven others will soon participate in. Recommended by her neighbor, who belongs to the Suwa Shrine women's group, Mika thinks it is an honor to have been selected. But with the many instructions and points of proper etiquette she is now hearing, she isn't too sure this is what she had in mind when told it was a *matsuri*. "Be sure to reverse the stem so that it points to the Inner Sanctuary, because by doing so, you link your heart and spirit to that of the Kami," the priest says. She nods and, like the equally talented and intelligent young woman beside her, practices the movement with an invisible sprig, trying it first with the left hand on top, then with the right, unsure of how it is supposed to go. Will the television cameras that Matsumoto-san has arranged to film the event for the local news catch her indecision? What a disaster that would be for her family and herself, as thousands of people she doesn't even know see her make a fool out of herself. "But if you forget because you're too nervous," Matsumoto-san continues, "that's all right. It's not easy the first time."

The first time? Most scholars familiar with comparative religious practices would be amazed to learn how the young men and women selected for this ritual have had virtually nothing to do with the "life" of their community's shrine other than visiting it at New Year's. Unlike the Catholic Church's first communion or the Jewish bar mitzvah—which are rites performed after a designated period of instruction has imparted to young people their sacred and secular responsibilities of being an adult in the community at large—these twenty-year-olds have come inside the shrine by-and-large ignorant (or perhaps "innocent" would be preferable) of the entire socio-cultural linkages between Shinto practice and themselves. Yes, they know about the yearly Okunchi festival, and maybe one of the young men hopes someday to participate as a portable-shrine bearer or one of the women as a dancer, but for them, what happens inside the shrine on a regular basis and how this could possibly have resonance for their own aspirations and lives might just as well have been taking place on another planet.

The previously mentioned NHK poll (1984) showed that, when asked about religion, nearly two-thirds of respondents between the ages of seventeen and thirty-four associated it with "something dark, oppressive, and restricting." Yet these were individuals born and educated *after* the war, in the most liberal intellectual climate Japan has ever known. Did they base their negative impression of religion on what they learned in history classes about the complacent role of Shinto and Buddhist institutions in fomenting a nationalism that resulted in war? Or is the media's representation of the various phe-nomena associated with the "new religions" to blame? Incidents such as the shocking mass-suicide of eight women after the death of their spiritual leader or the Aum Shinri Kyo sarin gas attacks in Matsu-moto and the Tokyo subway may have contributed substantially to a sense of antipathy on the part of younger people.

We will return to this discussion in the latter half of this chapter, but for now let's again visit the twenty-year-olds as the ritual begins, honoring their new status as adults. As promised, not one but two television crews are adjusting their cameras and microphones from the walkway around the Hall of Worship while the four women and four men sit in a single row, nervously awaiting the entrance of the priests. Nothing prepares one for that first heart-stopping explosion from the drum which formally begins the worship service. Unfor-tunately the cameras are not rolling at this point, otherwise they would have captured eight human beings actually levitating an inch off the floor! The women giggle behind their hands and the men laugh openly, though they immediately become somber with the en-trance of the chief and senior priests.

Step-by-step the ritual proceeds in its stately, regulated rhythm, captured by the bright lights of the cameras for the approximately

200,000 households that will see this evening's news. The opening purification, bows, and beginning of the procession of offerings are all filmed before the crews have their footage and tromp out of the building. When the chief priest delivers the *norito* prayer, asking the Kami to guide and protect these "fine young men and women as they set off into adulthood," only a few of their parents and late-arriving curiosity-seekers are present. The *miko* perform an abbreviated dance to full *gagaku* accompaniment, and then the moment arrives when the special guests must follow the example of the Gūji and make their leafy offerings. From where they sit on the grass mats in front of the slightly raised stage, a mere fifteen feet separates them from the eight-legged table reserved for their branches. But for several of the group, this will be the longest distance they have ever crossed.

Instructed to go up in pairs of the same sex, two of the young men—one a baseball star and the other a budding scholar—struggle to rise after thirty minutes of sitting in the *seiza* style (with their legs neatly tucked underneath their posteriors). This is the only proper way to sit during a Shinto ritual, but for young people accustomed to the chairs and informality modern life affords, it is a painful and unsettling experience. The two young men stretch for an awkward moment until they are sure of their balance and then plod toward the little table where they must again assume the *seiza* position in order to present their *tamagushi* branches, make their bows, and clap their hands to the "alpha" and "omega" of the Kami's influence. As they rise to return to their seats, Mika and her partner are given the cue from Matsumoto-san to rise and take their turn.

Mika stands with all the quiet dignity she can muster, but, to her horror, she collapses back to the floor with a little yelp of surprise! What's happened to her legs?!? Her partner, equally shaky and off-balance, has struggled to make it into an upright position and now offers Mika her hand. Slowly, like an old person stepping out of a wheelchair, Mika stands up and begins shuffling across the polished wooden stage to the little table, each step an agony of embarrassment and humiliation she somehow manages to conceal with a charming smile. After going to her knees again to make her presentation of the branch (she will tell me later that at least she didn't drop it), she once more requires the assistance of her partner to stand and make it off the stage, though it seems Matsumoto-san is ready to leap to her rescue. One of the next pair of men also totters and almost falls, and so it goes for three more presentations until the last person has plunked down on the tatami with a little exclamation of triumph, "*Dekita!* [I made it!]." The relief of the group is tangible, like a sigh of relief breathed after a suspense movie has finally been resolved.

"I want to thank you all very much for coming today." The Gūji begins his formal speech of greeting not from the stage but on the same level as the students. His tall black hat gleams silver, reflecting the light outside the hall, and he holds by both hands the wooden scepter no priest would be without. "Today is the day when you can change your feeling about your position in society for the rest of your life. In the old days, one's twentieth birthday was even more significant than today because, then, you received a new name! This was symbolic of the person you had become in the eyes of society and reflected the responsibilities you assumed as a full-fledged member of that society. Today, on this happy occasion, your parents and ancestors are waiting for you to fulfill your position as an adult. Please, have a safe way of living and become a splendid member of society. Good luck to all of you."

The new adults all bow deeply to the Gūji and begin gathering up their coats and talking when he suddenly interrupts. "Oh, and by the way, let me show you a secret about sitting through long and boring Shinto festivals!" Everyone laughs. "It's hard for us too, even though we practice all the time. The trick is to keep your legs moving and awake by periodically rocking up to sit on your heels and flexing your toes against the tatami. This way, you can keep the blood circulating and your legs won't rebel against your desire to stand." A couple of the young men try it. His broad smile and fatherly tone of voice indicate that whatever transgressions of ritual etiquette that may have occurred during the offering of the *tamagushi* branches are nothing to be concerned with. "Please have the *miko* serve you a cup of *omiki* as you go out, and don't wait until your wedding before you come to see us again."

Despite the Gūji's pleasant remonstrations, today's ritual will very likely be the only one conducted within the shrine they attend before marriage—and most may choose to forgo a shrine ritual in favor of one held in a wedding hall or, more radically, in a chapel, the way Europeans and Americans usually do. At issue here is not so much whether the coming generation is "religious" in the same way their parents were but whether Japanese society since the war has changed in such a way as to make the earlier beliefs and practices irrelevant. To be sure, Shinto is threatened in an urban-industrial setting since its ritual observances and orientations to the world are basically defined by the seasonal rhythms of the agricultural cycle (Earhart 1983, 199). Buddhism as well has undergone major changes as the increasing migration from rural to urban areas has upset its parish system and undermined many of its ties to family rites honoring ancestral forebears. But does this social restructuring, based on the needs of a postindustrial economy, necessarily doom these two traditions to the dinosaur graveyard of dead ideologies and languages? A closer look at contemporary Japan, and how changes in public values since the 1970s are making themselves felt in the workplace, schools, and home, will bring a clearer understanding of the relative "health" or "sickness" of this new phase for Shinto's symbols, beliefs, and practices and lead us to some final conclusions.

PART II: A SOCIETY COMES OF MODERN AGE

Like countries in the West since the end of the war, Japan is seeing the children of the first postwar generation — those self-sacrificing individuals responsible for rebuilding a shattered nation — begin to move into society and the workforce in large numbers. The efforts of their parents have placed this new generation in a private haven of security forged out of the hardships of the postwar years. These hardships caused by the destruction of a nation and the ground-zero of poverty were *absolutes* for their parents, providing a haunting perspective from which to see the future and shape individual purposes and identity. But due to inadequate lessons on recent history at school and often highly biased documentaries on television, their children received little knowledge of the past except as a time of injustice and ordeals. Because of this gap in understanding and ages, many young people feel no need to structure their identities and future upon the same culture of work as their parents did.

With the majority of the population now self-described members of the middle class, a growing feeling emerged that current society, although created by the processes of industrialization, was no longer amenable to management by principles of industrialization alone (Yamazaki 1983, 14). For the new generation, the values of self-sacrifice, endurance, and loyalty to the higher cause were still part of the common meaning of Japanese society, but even among the vast middle class there was no longer a consensus about the degree to which these values were to be manifested. All along, cultural constructions of common meaning had preceded and framed Japan's technological progress by way of informing its ideology and thus granting it power, but that the culture now generated contests about the meaning of this economic advance is something few leaders or social architects had anticipated (Najita 1989, 5).

The "buzz words" of the late 1970s and 1980s became "relativization," "diversification," "differentiation," and "internationalization" (Nishibe 1986, 39). Many people in general but youth in particular began to seek cultural compensation to balance those strictures cloaking (some would say "choking") the socially sanctioned achievements they were expected to strive for. They would still be students, salarymen, office workers, and spouses, but the degree to which their identities depended on these roles became more and more obscure. An anecdote by Chikushi Tetsuya, who created the term *shinjinrui*, or "new breed," illuminates just this point:

> Just when the company was entering an extremely busy period, a new breed employee decided to go on vacation. He returned tan and fit, and when his superior learned that he had taken off to go skiing, he was scolded roundly for his lack of consideration for his fellow workers who had to shoulder his share of the work in his absence. But this scolding made the superior highly unpopular, since the employee, as well as the other workers, saw nothing wrong with going skiing. To them that was more important than any amount of work in the company. (Chikushi 1986, 294)

With "traditional" values in question and with the lack of a distinct social context (as had been provided, for example, in the States by the student movement, Vietnam protests, and Lockheed scandals), the new generation in Japan turned increasingly to the media for a sense of identity. Terms like "the local era" (in vogue at the end of the 1970s to emphasize the diversification of control), "moratorium person" (someone who yearns for an illusory simplicity of a romanticized past—early 1980s), the "Peter Pan syndrome" (used for men who refuse to cut maternal ties and to assume responsibility for their lives—early 1980s), and "schizo kids" (those persons split between traditional values and the need for self-discovery—mid- and late 1980s) all serve as "mirrors to reflect a social context in an age that doesn't create its own" (Field 1989, 172). Although many of these concepts were gleaned from highly literate texts—such as the subheadings of whiz-kid Asada Akira's essays on French postmodern philosophers—the books were rarely read by those bandying about the latest jargon. Like anything else in a youth culture based on style and appearance, knowledge (or its representation) could also be a commodity (Field 1989, 172). With its nonthreatening means of easing loneliness and alienation, the Japanese media assumed the role of a constant companion, always ready to capture and hold individual attention via a wide array of comic books, magazines, radio programs, and television shows. Today, even advertisements in magazines and especially on TV serve a mirroring function for this age group, often gaining instant popularity although the products they are pitching can rarely compete with the "message's" style, vividness, exoticism, or excitement.

Despite obvious differences in external *social* values between the generations—a conservative respectability for married couples versus the new generation's fads and fashion trends, mini-skirts, new-wave chic, and continued fascination with foreign ideas—is it also the case that many of the underlying *cultural* values have also changed? Accustomed to comfort and security, the new generation of the 1980s and 1990s has little of the revolutionary leftist leanings that many students and workers (now parents) of the late 1950s, 1960s, and early 1970s displayed. In fact, if the voting records of recent elections are any indicator, their lack of interest in politics has allowed a resurgent conservatism from the silent but economically powerful majority. Practically the only place one sees any kind of rebellion is in the choice of clothing they wear, but even here is an ironic twist. With style fluctuating like a barometer during typhoon season, it takes money to rebel in a convincing manner since a new jean jacket will cost $100, a *bleached-out* jean jacket perhaps $200 or $300, and a leather jacket with a few metal studs at least $500. As a result, to keep up with the latest styles, as well as accumulate those commodities which enhance individual worth and shape identity, the youth of today place equal, if not greater, emphasis on money than did their parents (Chikushi 1986, 292). Work is still important for individuals, but the only progressive ideology it holds is how quickly they attain immediate and tangible rewards. Forty-year-old managers complain that "talking to young people is like talking to foreigners. You've got to explain everything. Tell them to do a job and they'll do it, but when they're finished, they'll read magazines." Or, as a trading company executive laments, "Our younger generation is definitely a new breed. They're only willing to give 100%" (Clugston 1987, 26–30). We can also look back to the comments of Chief Priest Uesugi about the necessity of teaching new *miko* how to serve guests, anticipate requests, and, in general, refine their awareness of serving the public if they are ever to serve the Kami in a ritual.

But is this to say the common meanings of postwar Japanese social and work ethics are slowly deteriorating within the gleaming skyscrapers of Shinjuku or within rooms lit only by the dull glow of a television? The older generation still holds fast to the belief that human beings are honorable as long as they strive for an objective based on transcendent ideals. Whether this was the "Greater Co-prosperity Sphere" of the war years, the good of the company, or winning the women's marathon in the Olympics, it was part of human nature to be goal oriented. For many of the new generation however—grounded as they are in a reality dominated by multinational corporations, the nuclear threat, and the speed and replication of computerized information (what Marilyn Ivy calls the "extremity of the contemporary moment" [1989, 24])—many of their elders' concepts lack relevance because the world they describe no longer exists. A new milieu has emerged in which the individual desires to relate to a group, company, or ideal while maintaining a certain distance, identifying with it on a "more rational multivalent basis" (Yamazaki 1983, 12). From this stance an individual can go about realizing his or her identity, turning it into a kind of accomplishment (Blumenberg 1987, 456) or, as the news demonstrates nightly, a kind of pathology. The fact that you are born in a certain place no longer affiliates you with the neighborhood shrine, nor does the fact that your family have been parishioners of the local Zen temple for the past three hundred years bind you to supporting it if your destiny is to be found in Osaka or Tokyo.

Many of the older generation in Japan (as well as in other First World countries, especially those "neoconservative defenders of capitalist democracy") believe the acceptance of self-interest as the operating principle of life extends far beyond the pursuit of material goods. It is feared that the current emphasis on wealth and individual autonomy (once so valued as Lockean fundamentals at the heart of capitalism) has suppressed the important virtues of self-restraint, concern for the general good, and a certain amount of patriotism needed to sustain the system (Griffin 1989, 7). As I have already mentioned, in the past these social "virtues" were lived, not treated as indeterminate styles, and people's belief in them made society function smoothly and gave worth to individual endeavors.

To try and arrest this trend of dangerous individualism and "diseases of civilization," a movement in both popular and scholarly writing in Japan has revived early cosmological constructs that delineate notions of separateness, uniqueness, and "essences" that make up Japan and its citizenry. Called *nihonjinron* ("theorizing on the Japanese"), these new writings have attempted to create a kind of civil religion of "Japaneseness" from which few can escape (Lock 1987, 50) and which, in effect, denigrates Western ideas of political self-assertion, individual worth, and logical consistency (van Wolferen 1989, 266). Not only do the ideas behind *nihonjinron* emphasize the notion that the Japanese are different, but because of the uniqueness of the Japanese, an intrinsic superiority is claimed over what the rest of the world has to offer. As high technology becomes more affordable and diffused, bringing the Information Age to everyone's desk or lap, one of the fears of greater internationalization is that it will lead to an ambivalence toward Japanese culture that will paralyze its institutions (Aoki 1988, 50; see also Aoki 1990).

Prime Minister Ohira was one of the first to officially recognize the need to stem the tide differentiating individuals from their contemporaries and alienating them from the predominant social and cultural norms. In a 1979 speech he stated that "the unprecedented freedom and abundance (afforded by Japanese economic success) has stimulated reflection on the important side of human character, which had been lost sight of under the regime of industrialization and modern rationalism . . . which disregarded our traditional culture and fixed for us progress and standards and goals pursued by others" (Harootunian 1989, 80). What he and his brain trust proposed was an "affirmative culture" rooted firmly in the "reified values" of family, group, and community. Notions of the individual as ideally disengaged from natural and social worlds are countered by stressing the centrality of one's participation in a larger social and cultural complex. Concepts such as *ki*, the "essence" of life that is embedded in human relationships, *bun*, the participatory aspect of the individual in groups, and *en*, "binding ties," became catchwords in the affirmative culture's ideology. But none is as strong as the revitalized notion of *ie*, "household," a term that permits an "imaginary Japanese" in discourse by eliminating the usual distinctions of gender, class, and regional affiliation (Harootunian 1989, 91). Serving as a kind of "Mr. and Mrs. John Doe," this Japanese can be ascribed a stereotypical identity whose education, taste, psychology, and, most importantly, his or her social and cultural values absorb "deviant" variations from a postulated norm the way a white blood cell does bacteria.

The obvious argument is to see the rhetoric of affirmative culture as a reaction to the postwar period of breakneck industrialization and material affluence and to dismiss it as hopelessly out-of-date and nothing more. But Japanese politicians and industrialists (most of whom were educated before or during the war) continue to see the world as a dichotomy of beneficial and controlled "inner" essences and threatening but tantalizing "outer" forces which have their roots in Western systems of knowledge. Several of the Nakasone government's ministers in the mid- and late 1980s (most notably Education Minister Fujio) were forced to resign after they publicly voiced opinions (such as how Korea "assented" to its own annexation in 1910) informed by "national essence" ideology. In 1987, though under a new head, the Ministry of Education explained to textbook authors writing about the constitution the need to shift emphasis from how individual rights are guaranteed to social and national responsibilities (van Wolferen 1989, 291).

The year 1987 also brought the adoption by the Nakasone government of the Fourth Comprehensive National Development Plan, or Yonzenso, which had the noble task of creating less congested urban areas by redeploying Tokyo-based industries throughout the country. But instead of developing these regional capitals to handle their own international affairs and cultural exchanges, the administrators of Yonzenso, influenced in part by *nihonjinron* writings about eroding social values, intend to limit direct foreign contact to the national and corporate levels. Not only did this policy slow and possibly even prevent regional prefectures in Japan from becoming truly international (as, say, Bremen is in Germany or Edmonton in Canada), it also limited the competitiveness of redeployed companies in the international marketplace. With millions of people and trillions of yen affected by such policies, one can hardly dismiss the "inner/outer" demarcations of *nihonjinron* ideology as anachronistic and illusory.

If Japan's leaders are to preserve the substantial gains of the last forty years, it will take far more than a subtle campaign of indoctrination that persuades their constituents to withdraw behind barriers of culture and "national essence." They will need courage and foresight to address such pressing domestic problems as the high cost of food and housing (twice as much as in the United States), the long work hours routinely observed by Japanese salarymen (500 hours a year longer than in the United States), the family time that companies deprive their workers of (an average of 36 minutes a day is spent with children), the discontent with the school system (75,000 dropouts at the middle school level in 1992), and the tidal wave of elderly retirees in the coming two decades. Those other concerns mentioned earlier in this chapter—value formation, fulfilling expected roles, and establishing an authentic identity—must also receive attention and be the object of studies that are free of ulterior motives.

The leaders of Japan, until very recently, have never had any need to explain their objectives in a satisfying way, so thoroughly did their military clout shape social realities. They have communicated with their own people and with the world community through several manifestations of the same coercive ideology, via "things, not words" (Inouye, 1989, 122). But as the philosopher H. G. Gadamer observes, since technical and ethical know-how both imply a practical knowledge fashioned to the measure of the concrete tasks before them, an honest awareness of history can instruct the Japanese in the ultimate failure of overriding ideologies as a means of motivating a populace. The historical consciousness characterizing contemporary people is "a privilege as well as a burden, the likes of which have never imposed on any previous generation" (Gadamer 1987, 119). But it should help the Japanese see how the Meiji and Showa eras brought unity and industrialization at the cost of millions of lives throughout Asia and devastation at home, and lead them to ask what are the costs, both overt and hidden, of the nation's current economic expansions.[1] For Japan, as for postindustrial societies worldwide, new conceptual frameworks are demanded that require flexibility and foresight if a pluralistic democracy of values and social codes is to nurture, instead of alienate, the coming generations.

CONCLUSION

It is perhaps unavoidable that a book on a contemporary Shinto shrine ends up in an obligatory waltz with issues of nationalism, ideology, and the social and cultural values of coming generations. After all, these concerns have been with Shinto since its earliest formulations, right from the time of the *ujigami* and *ujiko* and their assimilation into the hegemony of the Yamato clan. Shinto has always been attentive to the maintenance and protection of communities from unpredictable human and divine forces, imbuing its ritual practices with techniques and strategies to aid human life in all its variety. (If the reader needs reminding of the scope Shinto aims for, please turn to the listing in Appendix 1 of what goes on during the yearly cycle.) Rather than speculate about the specific future of Suwa Shrine, I will instead keep my comments at a more general level concerning the directions in which Shinto might be heading.

Opportunities to "seize the day" and provide spiritual leadership have rarely been as clearly present and accessible for the leaders of Shinto shrines at both local and national organizational levels as they are today. As evidenced by the phenomenal growth of the new religions, never have so many people been searching for direction and guidance, nor have they ever been as free of old constraints and hierarchies as today's mobile and fast-paced society permits. As an outside observer who experienced only a portion of what actually occurs at a shrine, I am perhaps being somewhat hasty in making judgments and recommendations, yet I am not alone in my observations. The mere mention of the word "Shinto" still evokes a powerful emotional reaction among many Japanese intellectuals as well as common individuals, who see an alarming correspondence between today and the 1930s, especially in the removal of the 1 percent ceiling on military spending and in the Ministry of Education's insistence on schools singing the national anthem and displaying the flag before ceremonies, although this is reportedly in the interests of "internationalization" rather than nationalism. There are similar movements by conservative groups aiming to restore the Ise shrines to their former status so as to enable government financial sponsorship, to revise the constitution so as to safeguard the position of the emperor as head of the nation, and to restore Yasukuni Shrine's legal position as a place worthy of national veneration because it commemorates millions of people who gave their lives for Japan's "sacred" wars. Strong stuff indeed, the mere mention of which can set off demonstrations and riots in China and Korea, both of which suffered so greatly at the hands of Japanese militarists.

Even with these controversial issues grabbing headlines when they appear, it is at the level of individual shrines where a remarkable courage and integrity have been shown in standing up to powerful political pressure and asserting control over their own fates. As mentioned by Ueda (1979), Hokkaido Shrine in Sapporo fought off the government's broadcasting giant, NHK, when plans were announced to build a TV relay tower on top of the shrine's sacred mountain. Road building that would have violated the precincts of shrines has been successfully defeated or postponed at the Meiji Shrine in Tokyo, Suwa Taisha in Nagano Prefecture, and a celebrated case at Tōshōgū Shrine in Nikko, which saved "Taro" the tree. There are even those shrines that resist the in-house pressure originating from the Central Association of Shinto Shrines in Tokyo. Much to the dismay of the association, Ikuta Shrine in Kobe built and continues to maintain a very lucrative parking garage on shrine property and led the way for many other shrines to convert some of their extensive landholdings into financially sound investments. We saw in the case of Suwa Shrine how the efforts of its chief priest forestalled already-approved plans to replace the old decaying shrine with a ferroconcrete structure, and how he led the way to create financing allowing a magnificent reconstruction using mostly natural materials. In additional acts of resistance against conservative traditionalists, motivated for reasons of economy as well as public relations, shrines have changed their festivals to Saturdays and Sundays to allow more participation when people are off work, and concerted efforts are being made to attract as many visitors as possible by means of advertising and brochures placed in the offices of travel agents nationwide. All of this points to a healthy trend to keep shrines in pace with the changing times.

The greatest problem, as I see it, is for the leaders of shrines to guard against the simplistic interpretations of *nihonjinron* theorists and to realize that whatever changes are occurring in Japanese society do not replace the old models of ethic or moral standards as much as they supplement them with new combinations of Japanese and Western perspectives. Rather than focus on the "loss" of what many hold as the guiding principles of Japanese society, it is important to broaden and shift one's focus to see that, especially when considering religious observances, "loss" is often "reformulation," a necessary phase that precedes "rejuvenation." Since a sense of their society and culture as unique will most likely persist in the socialization of Japanese at home and school for generations to come, Shinto must resist the easy rhetoric of the past and turn instead to what has always been its saving grace and source of longevity: a focus that addresses the realities of *this* world and the problems human beings have with daily life. One of the ways for local shrines to gain increased public respect would be to reaffirm their commitment to the sanctity of environmental concerns, education, and community preservation, even if this risks alienating powerful supporters who just happen to be realtors, closet fascists, or politicians. They must also overcome centuries of male domination and broaden their appeal to encourage women's issues and rights as well as actively promote the entry of more women into the priesthood. Finally, they must continue to make changes in their "traditional" rituals so as to allow greater participation and understanding not only about what is going on but about what relevance a ritual might have for an individual's life. The challenges of hierarchy and habit are indeed great, but a number of priests, both young and old, have already realized that there is a battle to be won against the old guard's outdated perspectives. If, through its rituals and celebrations, Shinto can help Japanese renew themselves in an age of technology and material wealth, it will play an important part in the realignment of modern men and women to their environment and their own spirituality.

APPENDIX 1:

THE RITUALS AND FESTIVALS

OF SUWA SHRINE (1987)

JANUARY

1 Hatsumode: First worship of the New Year. (Chapter 20)

3 First Ebisu festival: Worship of the Kami of Good Fortune and
Wealth.

5 Chinka-sai: A ritual to control fire and protect local fire
departments.

7 Nanakusa-sai: A ritual in which a drink is prepared from the
sacred seven herbs to prevent illness. (Chapter 20)

10 Kagami buraki-sai: The ritual breaking of the New Year's
rice cakes.

15 Saiten-sai: The Coming of Age ritual for twenty-year-olds.
(Chapter 21)

19 Kenae-sai: Song-poems performed by members of the shrine
and community to extoll and entertain the Kami.

FEBRUARY

3 Setsubun matsuri: The "change of seasons" exorcism famous
for its use of beans as weapons against demons. (Chapter 7)

11 Kenkoku kinen-sai: Acknowledgment of the mythological
origins of the Japanese nation.

15 Yutate-sai: Exorcism and purification via scalding water.
Observed monthly on or around the fifteenth, save for January,
July, and August. (Chapter 10)

17 Kinen-sai: One of the first of the many spring festivals; prayers
are offered for a bountiful harvest.

28 Tsukinami-sai: Bimonthly worship service for members of the
shrine's Fujin-kai (Women's Club) and open to the general
public; also observed on the ninth of every month.

MARCH

3 Hina matsuri: Dolls' Day festival, in which living o-hina-sama
dolls (ikibina) participate in a procession and worship service
wearing Heian period costumes. (Chapter 9)

12 Jichinsai: A ground-breaking and sanctification ritual before building construction; held by individual request at construction sites throughout the year. (Chapter 19)
21 Shunbun-sai: Worship service in observance of the vernal equinox. (Chapter 5)
Sore-sai: Commemoration for ancestral spirits at an auxiliary shrine near the main buildings.

APRIL

8 Morisaki taisai: Great Festival for the deity called Morisaki, associated with fertility and farming; one of the three Kami of Suwa Shrine. (Chapter 11)
15 Otaue-sai: Rice-planting ritual, held at the field dedicated to this year's production of rice for the Suwa Kami.

MAY

5 Kodomo-no-hi: Children's Day. Children visit the shrine on this day. The shrine has organized a race up the seventy-three steps leading to the main gate below the Hall of Worship. Individuals recording the best times are presented with certificates.

JUNE

1 Koya-iri: Literally "Entering the Hut." First purification and worship by neighborhoods participating in this year's Okunchi festival of October.
15 Ko-yagi: Shrine visit and purification by the children participating in Okunchi.
28 Koto-hajime shinji: Ritual for New Beginnings, also connected to the Okunchi cycle.
29 Sumiyoshi taisai: Great festival for the deity called Sumiyoshi, guardian of fishermen and travelers.
30 Ikizakana ho no gyōji: Offering of living fish to the deity Sumiyoshi.
Oharae: Ritual of Great Purification. Also observed on December 31. (Chapter 12)

JULY

5 Festival for Kami dwelling within the shrine's seven wells. Originally, Suwa Shrine had seven wells that took their water from deep within the mountain behind the shrine.

SEPTEMBER

21 Shūbun-no-hi: Worship service in observance of the fall equinox.

Sore-sai: Commemoration for Ancestral Spirits.

OCTOBER

1 Misogi: Seawater purification for portable-shrine bearers who will participate in Okunchi. (Chapter 15)

3 Yogoto-sai: Opening shrine visits for all Okunchi participants. (Chapter 15)

Kori-shinji: Pondside ritual of supplication to the deities Suwa, Morisaki, and Sumiyoshi in preparation for Okunchi. (Chapter 15)

Juretsu mizoroi: Public procession circumambulating the shrine. (Chapter 15)

6 Naijin gyōji: Preparation of sacred objects (*go-shintai*) for removal to portable shrines and the two nights they will spend in an external, temporary shrine at Ohato pier.

Mikoshi kioharai: Purification of the portable shrines.

Karimiya kioharai: Purification of the external shrine at Ohato pier.

7 Senryō-sai: Installation of the three deities within the portable shrines. (Chapter 15)

Gohonsha-hatsugyō: Ritual for preparation of external, temporary shrine where from this day the portable shrines will be housed.

Karimiya onchaku-sai: Welcoming ritual for the deities to the temporary shrine at Ohato pier. (Chapter 15)

8 Hatsugyō-sai: A "good morning" worship service for the deities.

Reitai-sai: Ritual for the reception of offerings from the Central Association of Shinto Shrines.

Tokubetsu keisha kioharai: Special purification ritual (*yutate*).

Keishin fujin-kai kencha ho no gyōji: Tea and sweet cake offerings to the Kami, presented by the shrine's lay women's groups.

All the above are repeated on the ninth.

Yumikei-sai: A consolation ritual for deities on their second night away from the main shrine.

9 Honsha onchaku sengyō-sai: A "welcome home" service for the returning deities. (Chapter 15)

13 Naorai kai shinji: A ritual of transition back to secular life for Okunchi chairpersons and sponsors and for the priests. Noteworthy for its food and drink. (Chapter 15)

30 Rōjin kekkonshiki: A wedding ritual for a couple of advanced age (listed here to exemplify one of the shrine's ongoing public services).

NOVEMBER

15 Shichi-go-san no matsuri: A coming-of-age ritual for girls aged seven and three, and for boys aged five. (Chapter 16)

23 Shinkoku kansha-sai: Festival of New Rice, to give thanks for the harvest; also called Niiname-sai. (Chapter 17)

DECEMBER

20 Momote shinji: Purification and blessing of the sacred arrows (*hamaya*) available to the public at New Year's.
Mukade shinji: "Centipede" festival, so called because of the arrows carried by the guardian figures, the Zuijin, and the multiple ways they protect the shrine.

25 Tenmangū shinji: Ritual in honor of the Kami of Learning and Scholarship, Tenjin.

29 Susu harai shinji: Ritual cleansing of the shrine at year's end. (Chapter 20)

31 Oharae: Ritual of Great Purification for the end of the year.

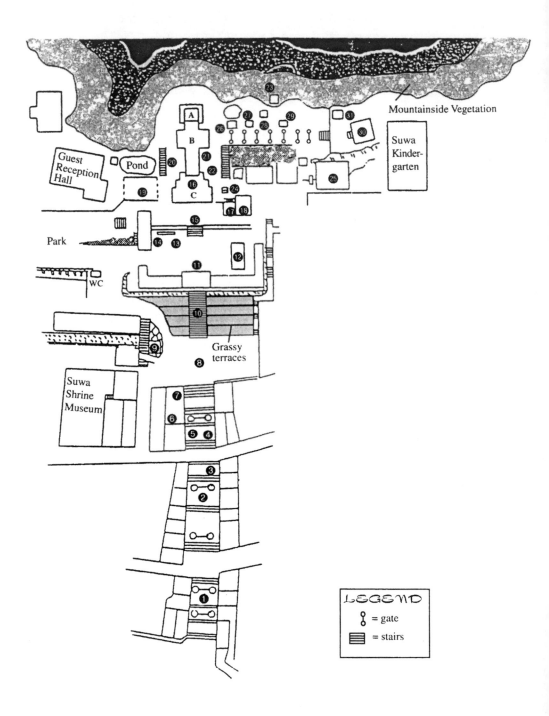

Map of the precincts of Suwa Shrine, Nagasaki, Japan.
The numbers on the map correspond to the numbered descriptions in the
Appendix.

APPENDIX 2:
MAP AND GUIDE TO THE
SHRINE PRECINCTS

The numbers below correspond to those on the map on the facing page. Acknowledgment is made to Mr. Norman Havens for many of the facts and dates which supplemented my own literal translations of signs on the shrine grounds:

1. Yin-yang stone: Representing the male force, "yang," from old Chinese cosmologies of Daoist origin, this stone is located between the two torii at the base of the shrine's central walkway.

2. Yin-yang stone: Together with its male counterpart, this female stone representing the principle of "yin" is thought to be efficacious for people wishing for happiness, safe childbirth, or success in marriage. A visitor should step on these stones with the right foot when arriving and with the left foot when leaving.

3. The Post for Lost Children: During the Edo period's festivals, children were frequently lost in the huge throngs of people attending shrine events. This post was erected by Meiji period police and shrine authorities in 1879 to assist parents in finding their children. The north side of the post was used for posting messages by parents looking for their children, and the south side was designated for notices of children found.

4. Memorial to Shimomura Hiroshi, a poet of Nagasaki.

5. Memorial to Mukai Kyorai (1651-1704), a disciple of Basho. The poem on the memorial can be translated as, "Talking about precious things in Kyoto / I remember the moon over Suwa."

6. Memorial to Yamamoto Kenkichi, a Nagasaki writer.

7. Haraedo Shrine: A recent addition to the shrine grounds to be used for personal purification before entering the upper level.

8. Main terrace: Normally used for visitor parking, it becomes the stage for the Okunchi festival proceedings that begin at the shrine.

9. Hiyoshi Shrine: One of the dominant features of Suwa Shrine,

this old camphor tree is estimated to be between five and six hundred years old. Formerly enshrined within the tree, a Kami of Healing is now located beside it. The guardian lion (*komainu*) standing nearby was originally by the Hall of Worship and represents a deity who prevents smallpox.

10. Stone stairs. There are seventy-three steps.

11. Main gate: The guardians known as Zuijin or Yagoro are found on either side.

12. Purification font (*temizuya*): Visitors should purify their hands and mouths here before proceeding to the Hall of Worship. This is done by first taking the dipper in your right hand and pouring water into your left hand. Then, take the dipper and perform the same action for your right hand. Finally, holding the dipper again in your right hand, pour water into your cupped left hand and rinse your mouth, taking care not to swallow the water but to spit it out into the gutter below. It is considered poor manners to drink directly from the dipper. A final act of courtesy is to again fill the dipper with water and hold it upright so the water trickles down the handle, thus cleansing it for the next visitor.

13. Bronze Horse of the Kami: Created by Kitamura Seibo (who also sculpted the statue in Nagasaki's Peace Park) for the commemoration of the sixtieth year of the Showa emperor's reign. Horses are sacred in Shinto mythology and thus were given as offerings to shrines. Later this practice changed, and pictures of horses painted on votive tablets were offered instead; one can find present-day examples of this custom hanging on specially constructed racks located on most shrine grounds.

14. Votive offerings board: Called *ema*, or "picture of a horse," these small plaques are purchased at the shrine's amulet office and inscribed with whatever wish or prayer the purchaser cares to convey to the Kami. At certain times, these *ema* will be gathered up and burned in a special ritual, thus "freeing" their messages to travel with the smoke up to the heavenly realm.

15. United yin-yang stone: Visitors step on this stone. Because it is a unified symbol, it is thought to balance whatever opposing forces are within each worshipper, allowing an unimpeded course for their prayers and petitions.

16. A. Hall of Worship (*haiden*): Rebuilt in 1984, most of the shrine's worship services take place on this lower level.

Good weather prevailing, the doors are generally open for visitors.

B. Hall of Offerings (*heiden*): Reached by a long flight of stairs, this intermediary level is reserved for special rituals of central importance to the shrine and its Kami.

C. Inner Sanctuary (*honden*): Uppermost of all the shrine buildings, the Kami are enshrined within this sanctuary. Only the most senior priests are allowed to approach this level.

17. Site for automobile purifications and blessings: Automobiles, both new and used, are purified and blessed in this location, after which a protective amulet is affixed to the vehicle's bumper or window. The service takes less than five minutes and, depending on the size of the vehicle, generally costs about ¥5,000.

18. Wedding Hall (*gokitoden*): Weddings are conducted in this elegant hall. A relatively recent addition to shrine services for the public, the hall (as well as priests and *miko*) is contracted by families well in advance to ensure an auspicious day for the ceremony. Private worship ceremonies are also conducted here.

19. Sacred Garden and "Stop Lions": Most shrine rituals begin in this space, where preliminary prayers of purification prepare the participants for entering the Hall of Worship. The "stop lions" are for people wishing to stop a bad habit; it is believed that tying thin paper strings to the lions' legs will empower one's desire to stop unwanted behavior.

20. Well of the Guardian Lions: Worshipped as a Kami of safe childbirth and wealth, this well has a wide reputation for its clean, fine-tasting water. To this day, proprietors of famous restaurants or bars come to the well to take water back to their establishments. It is thought that washing coins in the well will guarantee financial success and it is to this purpose that the bamboo baskets are placed nearby where the money may dry. The stone lantern standing nearby was dedicated in 1834.

21 and 22. Benzaiten and a Wishing Lion: The shrine closest to the wall is dedicated to Benzaiten, the Kami of music. The guardian lion has been the object of veneration by persons wishing some special favor. It is said that courtesans of the pleasure quarters turned the lion on its rotating pedestal so that its tail was turned toward the Suwa Kami, hoping this somewhat rude gesture would bring about a storm and keep

the courtesans' customers—the sailors—in port for a longer period.

23. Ebisu Shrine: A popular Kami who symbolizes wealth and good fortune.

24. Thorn-Pulling Lion: This guardian lion is the object of veneration by those people having emotional problems that need "removal."

25. Suwa-so: Originally built in 1920, this building was saved through a shrine campaign and relocated to its present location in 1988. It now serves as the shrine's abstinence hall and is used by the priests before important rituals and as a meeting place for various tea schools. As a point of architectural interest, no nails were used at the time of its original construction.

26. Hiruko Shrine and "Kappa" Lion: This shrine and its accompanying well are worshipped as a tutelary pair for the souls of dead children. The kappa is a mythical creature with a bowl-shaped head who must be kept wet and have water in his bowl else he perish. Local legends say that a ghost has been known to appear near the well.

27. Suwa Tenmangū: This shrine is dedicated to the deity of learning, Sugawara Michizane, an actual person of the early Heian period who lost favor with the ruling emperor. Banished to Kyushu, where he died, his vengeful spirit was thought to be responsible for a series of calamities that befell Kyoto; thus a shrine was dedicated in Kyoto to calm his spirit. It is especially popular with young people (and their parents) who hope for success in the all-important entrance exams to both high school and university. Special amulets dedicated to Tenmangū may be purchased on the shrine grounds, distinctive due to their five-corner shape known as *gokaku*, a homonym for "success in exams."

28. Itsukushima Shrine: A branch shrine affiliated in name only with the main shrine located at Miyajima, near Hiroshima, in the Inland Sea.

29. Yasaka Shrine: Home of the famous Gion festival in Kyoto, this is another of the many branch shrines.

30. Tamazono Inari Shrine: The main Tamazono Inari Shrine is located to the south of Kyoto. Inari shrines are distinguished by their red torii gateways and are thought to reward petitions for success in business. Branches of this shrine can be seen all over Japan.

31. Suwa "frog" stone: This stone is known as a "frog" (*kaeru*) because of its distinctive shape. Enshrined here since the seventeenth century, it is believed to guarantee a variety of "returns," ranging from money invested to the safe return from a trip. This association is based upon the homonym for "frog," which means "return." Miniatures are available for purchase at the shrine's amulet office.

NOTES

CHAPTER 1. *Frames and Focuses*

1. Cited in Ooms 1985, 283.

2. Representative works are Anesaki 1960 (originally published in 1930), Ono 1962, Ponsonby-Fane 1953, 1963, and Holtom 1965 (originally published in 1938).

3. See Kitagawa 1987, Ross 1965, Grapard 1992, Hardacre 1989, and Earhart 1984, to name only a few of the many works now available in English that deal specifically with Shinto. Schwade (1986) has published a useful bibliography of works in Western languages dealing with Shinto.

4. Even the eminent scholar Joseph Kitagawa (1987) begins his discussion on Shinto by following this trend, although it must be said that by the end of his first paragraph it is obvious he is aware that Shinto is decidedly not "indigenous."

5. Aikens and Higuchi's (1982) volume on the prehistory of Japan paints a more complete picture than that given by the classic study of Kidder (1959). Even more recently, Richard Pearson's edited volume (1986) adds a number of fascinating dimensions to the early formation of societies throughout the Japanese islands. Needless to say, the number of works on this topic in Japanese is staggering, but one of the more accessible is Kato Shinpei's (1988) attempt to answer the question of where the Japanese came from.

6. Isaacs 1975, 146, is the closest I can come to finding the source of this quotation. I would greatly appreciate assistance from a reader whose memory for quotations is more accurate than mine.

7. See the introduction to Hobsbawm and Ranger 1987. I have taken their three typologies and added an additional clause to each.

CHAPTER 2. *Historical Momentums*

1. The following summary draws from Boxer 1951, Cooper 1971, Hall 1977, Elison 1973, Matsubara 1983, Morita 1990, Nelson 1991, Perrin 1979, Okada 1955, Smith 1964, and Sansom 1961, as well as from conversations with local historians, such as Etchū Tetsuya.

2. This figure is taken from Hamazaki Kunio's 1978 book *Nagasaki Ijingai-shi* (A history of foreigners in Nagasaki), cited in Morita 1990, 20.

3. The Shimabara Rebellion is often cited as the climax of the persecu-

tion of Christians in Japan. In 1636, when governmental pressure against Christianity was increasing from all sides, armed resistance broke out among the peasantry of the Shimabara fiefdom east of Nagasaki. Though the nature of this rebellion was basically sociological, according to Sansom (1961), religious overtones soon provided the revolt's central themes since many of these peasants were indeed Christians. Starting from a single incident in which a farmer killed a tax collector who was said to have been abusing the farmer's daughter, the local peasantry armed themselves, formed alliances with masterless samurai as well as other peasant communities from the nearby Amakusa islands, and took refuge in an abandoned castle where they held off repeated attacks from December 1637 to April 1638. It is estimated that 20,000 defenders and government forces died in the final assault (yet, by the missionaries' standards set forth in the *Exhortations to Martyrdom*, issued in 1623, after the persecutions had begun, these Japanese were not martyrs, only poor peasants who died as Christians). Christianity did not vanish from the southern regions of Japan—it did what outlawed religions and political ideologies have done for centuries: sought concealment.

4. This was hardly a new idea of the times but rather one that had gradually gained credence over several hundred years. According to Muraoka Tsunetsugu's writings (1964), Shinto first took on a doctrinal meaning at the end of the Heian and the beginning of the Kamakura period (about 1192) as *ryōbu* (dual) Shinto, which fused elements of Buddhist doctrine with the Shinto Kami. Many scholars would push the date back even further. A reaction against Dual Shinto was initiated by Yoshida Shinto and the *yuitsu* school, which asserted that the Kami were primary, a theme later taken up and refined by both neo-Confucians and *suika* Shinto adherents. The principal theorists of these schools, Hayashi Razan and Yamazaki Ansai respectively, could be called anti-Buddhist, because they pushed for a monistic theory of heaven and man coupled with, in Yamazaki's case, absolute reverence for the emperor. By the time the Tokugawa government sought to settle the disturbances in Kyushu, there was no shortage of theoretical or theological justifications for whatever strategy they chose to employ.

5. The following information about Aoki Kensei is based on an account in Morita 1990, 20–22.

6. It is important to stress again that Shinto and Buddhism were, to use Grapard's term (1992), "combinatory" for much of Japanese religious history. Depending on which period and which school of thought one focuses on, Shinto Kami were either manifestations of Buddhist divinities or vice versa. Thus, from an administrative as well as a "traditional" point of view, it made perfect sense for Aoki's eldest son to be given this role in the new institutional framework. Needless to say, the Buddhist aspects of a shrine's history are not something most contemporary priests are particularly conversant about. To the credit of Suwa Shrine, however, a history sponsored

by the head office ("Suwa Jinja nenpyō"), currently in manuscript form, does include this information.

7. See Morita 1990, 23. More detail about the *kunchi* festival will be forthcoming in chapter 15.

8. A recent account of this fascinating story and some of its principal characters is Brian Burke-Gaffney's *Hana to shimo* (Flowers and frost) (1989) as well as the overview in the *Cambridge History of Japan*, vols. 5 and 6.

9. These figures are cited in the Kodansha *Encyclopedia of Japan*, vol. 1, and are based upon a 1977 study. Total casualties from the bombs are estimated at 270,000–280,000 people. See also Havens's *Valley of Darkness: The Japanese People and World War II* (1978).

10. One need only look through a number of anthropological works on village life in Japan to get a very clear picture of this process. Among these are Beardsley, Hall, and Ward 1959; Bernier 1975; Befu 1971; Dore 1978; Fukutake 1982; Norbeck 1976, 1978; Smith 1978, 1983; and Guthrie 1988. Similar discussions are to be found in Davis 1980b, Bellah 1970, Creemers 1968, Reader 1991, Sonoda 1988, and Ueda 1972, to name but a few of the works available in English.

11. I am thinking here of the land-calming rites of the *jichinsai* (see chapter 19), the end-of-summer return to ancestral graveyards of *obon*, and the controversial National Founding Day (*kenkoku kinen-bi*). Needless to say, all these events are open to multiple interpretations, yet they are frequently used by traditionalists eager to promote a sense of Japaneseness, national pride, and propriety. For a prize-winning overview of some of these writings, see Aoki 1990.

CHAPTER 3. *The Kami*

1. As has been demonstrated so persuasively by Matsunaga and Matsunaga (1974), Grapard (1983, 1992), Kitagawa (1966, 1987), Reader (1991), and Brown (1993), to name but a very few of the works in English alone, it is a grave mistake to think about early Shinto as being in any way an autonomous institution after the sixth century C.E. Instead, and with the full sponsorship of various successors to Imperial status, the Shinto deities were appropriated by the Buddhist universe by being given Buddhist names in addition to their already existing ones. While remaining powerful in their own right, they were, from a Buddhist perspective, subordinated to the greater, transcendental power of Shakyamuni (or other) Buddhas, who would eventually liberate even the most stubborn Kami so it too could enter Nirvana. Many scholars are quick to downplay the role of Shinto after the introduction of Buddhism into Japan. However, Delmer Brown (1993) reminds us that in 757 C.E., when Emperor Shōmu sponsored the construction of the Great Buddha of Tōdaiji in Nara, not only were the Kami consulted

beforehand via divinations at the Imperial shrines of Ise, but the powerful deity Hachiman was enlisted to guard the new statue from a higher vantage point on a nearby mountainside. Judging from the amazing persistence of such characteristic features as shamanism, animism, purifications, and, yes, even the emperor, one must not be overly hasty in assigning the earlier, Shinto-inspired cosmologies a subordinate status, especially concerning their importance in orienting both aristocratic and peasant societies to the forces of the surrounding world.

2. The later Meiji period saw the introduction of a system of examinations and certifications, and eventually most communities expected their priests to possess some kind of license as a verification of their legitimacy in the eyes of the state.

3. The campaign to get people to think about the doctrine that has just been outlined originates in a fortresslike, glistening black building (whose walls are fire- and rocket-proof) near the grounds of Meiji Shrine in Tokyo. Here, since the end of the war, the Central Association of Shinto Shrines, or Jinja Honchō, has doggedly pursued a systematization of Shinto doctrine that it is hoped will someday more closely resemble a unified, monotheistic theology that places the Sun Kami at the top, venerates the emperor as a descendant of this Kami as well as her intermediary, and wins the hearts and minds of the public in ways the prewar ideology never achieved (see Gluck 1985).

4. I am grateful to an anonymous reader of the manuscript for pointing out the role of the traveling *hijiri* in spreading originally localized traditions as well as myths about willfully mobile deities.

5. It is likely this earlier shrine reflected the cult of Suwa Taisha in Nagano Prefecture. See Kanai 1982 for a thorough study of the folk aspect of this cult.

6. See my article dealing with this theme as it relates to Kamo Shrine of north Kyoto (Nelson 1993b) and Czaja's *Gods of Myths and Stone: Phallicism in Japanese Folk Religion* (1974) for provocative discussions and photographs of fertility cult objects in Japan.

CHAPTER 4. *Ritual and Ceremony: An Overview*

1. One of the classic studies within this type of analytical framework is Kluckhorn's *Navaho Witchcraft* (1962). See also Morris 1987.

2. An attempt at clarifying this distinction in a secular direction can be found in Moore and Myerhoff 1977.

3. For a detailed look at purity from a folk perspective, see Namihira 1987.

4. See also Ashkenazi 1993, 36, for a summary of Judith Irvine's aspects of formality: increased communicative code structuring, the consistency of

this code, the invocation of social identities, and stress upon a central situational focus.

5. I will postpone discussing the other dimension necessary to any discussion of symbols, one that Talal Asad (1983) used to rightly criticize Clifford Geertz's 1964 definition of religion (reprinted 1973) for its avoidance of how symbols come to be symbols in the first place. Questions regarding what is considered meaningful, how meaning is constituted, by whom meaning is shaped, and at whose expense are all important questions that any detailed analysis of religious symbols must address. My intent in this book is not to tackle everything at once; but it is hoped that the reader will come to understand that there is most definitely a shaping process going on in a contemporary Shinto shrine. In brief, the strategic aspects of political power are never far from the institutional organization of *any* religious body. For a detailed discussion concerning this topic in relation to Shinto and other religious systems, please see my dissertation, "Enduring Identities: The Guise of Shinto in Contemporary Japan" (1993a).

6. The priests themselves will proudly say that a particular ritual *is* a thousand years old, as if the steady succession of head and subordinate priests who have enacted the rite has had no impact upon its present-day expression. I am not high-handedly denying the possibility that a particular ritual has managed to withstand the quirks and ideologies of the human beings that give it life, but as we will see in the case of several events at Suwa Shrine, one must exercise a certain degree of caution before wholeheartedly accepting at face value the statements of those whom Max Weber calls "religious virtuosos."

7. See Ohnuki-Tierney's chapter "Japanese Germs" (1984) for a fascinating look at the inner and outer cosmos of Japanese social life.

8. See Ellwood 1978 and his use of these categories for an event at Ise. These categories are quite different from those proposed by Japanese priests, who tend to focus on the calling, arrival, and sending off of the Kami as the three movements of every ritual. For more discussion of these variations, see Nelson 1993a.

CHAPTER 5. *Finding the Measure*

1. The drumbeats can be visualized like this (thanks to Bill Kats):

▬ ▬ ▬ ▬ ▬ ▬ ▬ ▬ ▮ ▮ ▮ ▏▏▏▏▏▏▏▏▏▏ ..... ▬ ▬ !!

This rhythm is used in many Buddhist temples, especially in Zen institutions to begin and end periods of sitting meditation.

2. Rather than burden the reader in the text with Japanese translations for each part of the ritual, I will give them here for purposes of reference. The opening purification, or *harae*, is called the *shubatsu*. Next, the Gūji's opening bow to the Kami is the *ippai*, immediately followed by the open-

ing of the shrine door, *kaihi*, and the accompanying "Kami call," *keihitsu*, which, despite what your ears tell you, is not performed by the Gūji. The dedication of food offerings is the *kensen*, which is intended to put the Kami in the proper mood to hear the prayer, the *norito sojo*. The sacred dance performed by female attendants is called *urayasu no mai*. Removal of the offerings is that part of the service called *tessen*, which precedes the door-closing *heihi* and the final bows, again called *ippai*. These terms may vary somewhat depending on the specific traditions of specific shrines, all of which are, it must be remembered, independently functioning institutional entities that are in no way legally obliged to follow the "suggestions" from the Central Association of Shinto Shrines in Tokyo.

3. When these syllables are sounded together, they become the Sanskrit "*a-hum*," or, as it is more commonly represented in English, "*aum*" or "*om*." See Ono et al. 1974.

4. The translation of the *norito* is not directly from the original text; I was never given permission to see and work with a copy, such is the veneration with which they are held even after being delivered in a ritual. But after having listened to so many, and through recording several, I have used Philippi's 1959 translations as a basis from which to work. Thus, while it is not a word-for-word translation, Philippi's poetic rendering sets a mood and tone appropriate for a Suwa Shrine *norito*.

CHAPTER 6. *Head Priest Uesugi*

1. This figure represents only those who perished on or immediately after August 9. It is estimated that over 200,000 people in Nagasaki alone have died between 1945 and 1993 of bomb-related injuries and radiation sickness.

CHAPTER 7. *Beans versus Demons*

1. I follow here Jean Herbert's categories (1967, 96).

2. Readers interested in further investigation of folk-related ritual practices have at their disposal such works as Hori 1971, Ishige et al. 1974, and Gorai et al. 1980 in Japanese, and well-written accounts in English by Blacker (1975), Sasaki (1990), Ouwehand (1964), Davis (1980a), and Reader (1991), to mention only a few. And while scholars of religion usually scoff at Lafcadio Hearn's work as being overly romantic and embellished by his own imagination, it serves nonetheless as a valuable compendium of many beliefs and folk practices at the turn of the century and makes for fascinating reading for those wishing to explore some of the roots of Japanese folk beliefs. Perhaps because of this, unlike many academic works, his books are still readily available and remain in print. Representative titles include

Kwaidan, Tales from Ancient Japan, and *Kokoro.* At a more theoretical level regarding the relationship between magical and religious practices, one could start with Evans-Pritchard's *Theories of Primitive Religion* (1965) and end with Brian Morris's *Anthropological Theories of Religion* (1987).

CHAPTER 9. *Backstage at the Dolls' Day Festival*

1. Jan Swyngedouw (1986) calls Shinto a "service religion" not so much because it meets the demands of the public but because its symbols and rituals provide people with the means to variously act out, acknowledge, and symbolize their principal concerns. I would add, however, that Shinto has always been extremely adaptable to varying situations and politics, due in part to the lack of a central body of teachings or ethics, so that it has "served" to further the political ambitions of any number of powerful men, ranging from the early Fujiwaras, to Hideyoshi, to Meiji, Taisho, and Showa era militarists. Borrowing the famous metaphor of Ishida Eichiro and conveyed by Professor Delmer Brown, Shinto is a "doll" that is dressed and then publicly presented in fashions that suit the "taste" of those holding political power at the time.

2. See Creemers 1968 for the dramatic changes in shrine Shinto after the war.

3. This is a classic statement, reflecting a number of important points. As the principal instigator of this new kind of "Dolls' Day," change is the bread and butter of Uesugi Gūji's tenure as the chief priest of the shrine. He has made alterations in any number of rituals, not to mention the shrine's architecture, its gardens, its financial base, and so on. Therefore, in his words to the young women, we see an example of the Japanese distinction between surface presentation (*tatemae*), actions or words done for appearance' sake only, and the essential substance of the matter (*honne*), which accurately reflects status, rank, political power, or a private situation that is, at all costs, not to be placed at center stage. In the words of Harumi Befu, "*honne* does not parallel behavior" (1980, 176). All societies and institutions have these distinctions, yet the degree of refinement with which individuals swing between them is perhaps nowhere as "artistically" well developed as in Japan. From a Western point of view, this frequently leads to charges of "insincerity" and "double-dealing." But for the Japanese, to consistently hang up one's private laundry to dry in public is to openly invite unwanted and potentially disastrous intervention. The head priest could easily have told the women that "it wouldn't look right" if everyone were to be given small seats to reduce the discomfort of the *seiza* position, but this would have detracted from the "historical" weight of the ritual he was trying to establish.

1. While a number of other shrines still observe this February purification ritual, the standard practice focuses on the scattering of drops by bamboo sprigs that have been dipped into the cauldron (the second part of the Suwa Shrine rite) (see Blacker 1975, 249; Iwata 1990). Suwa Shrine is the only place I have heard of where the priest still plunges his hand into the boiling water; thus, I have included the word "judgment" in the chapter title to evoke the judicial practice in seventh-century Japan and even earlier in China of determining guilt, innocence, truth, or falsity of an individual or his claims by plunging his hand into scalding water. See Nelson 1993a for an account of this practice.

2. For representative studies of Shugendō, see Blacker 1975, Earhart 1970b, Miyake 1971, Sakurai 1974, and Gojo 1983.

CHAPTER 11. *Festival for Fecundity*

1. The most recent rebuilding of Ise Shrine was completed in 1993 at a cost of $167 million. I recall seeing full-color posters announcing the rebuilding, which was sponsored by the Central Association of Shinto Shrines, as early as 1987. To raise money for this important and increasingly expensive rebuilding (called *shikinen sengū*), the shrine and the Central Association produced as mementos hand mirrors, two kinds of keyholders (one of a moon and the other of a star), a can of rubber stamps for the kiddies, telephone cards, a tape of songs—all of which were imprinted with a spunky-looking little rooster called the Ise Koko, or Ise Rooster. This creature is identified by a cartoon-style word-balloon over his head in which appears "Ise" in English letters and "*koko*" in the Japanese alphabet (*katakana*) usually used for words of foreign origin. For more information on the Ise rebuilding, see Casandra Adams's forthcoming work concerning its architecture, and Rosemary Bernard (also forthcoming) concerning the ritual process of the *sengū*.

2. According to the *Basic Terms of Shinto* (1985, 46), the oldest dance form is the *gosechi no mai*, so called because it consists of five movements. This style is said to have originated in the palace of Emperor Temmū at Yoshino, when he was playing his *koto* and an angel descended from heaven, raising her sleeves five times while dancing. The principal dances performed by contemporary *miko* are the *chihaya hibakama* and the *urayasu no mai*, the latter of which is said to commemorate the 2,600th anniversary of the foundation of the Imperial house. At the risk of sounding pedantic, one would be prudent not to stake one's life savings on a wager that this number reflects accurate historical information.

3. It all has to do with occasionally rocking forward so that one's feet are

flexed rather than flattened. After only a few seconds sitting like this, one is ready to again assume the more formal *seiza* posture.

CHAPTER 12. *Being Dirty, Getting Clean,*
            and the Ritual of Great Purification

1. See Donald Philippi's translation (1968).

CHAPTER 13. *"I Shouldn't Be Telling You This, But . . ."*

1. Readers who have been temporarily lulled by soothing pronouncements of the "harmony," "consensus," and "groupism" of Japanese society from a variety of writers ranging from Nakane (1970) to Benedict (1974) to Ishikawa (1987) are urged to take their medicine via more realistic studies of how social groups, and the institutions that serve as their vehicles, really operate in contemporary Japan. Along these lines, I would quickly recommend the following for a more historical approach: Befu 1980; Befu and Mannari 1983; Dale 1986; Moeran 1989; Yoshida (among others) in Krauss, Rohlen, and Steinhoff 1984; and van Wolferen 1989; plus Bix 1986 or Najita and Koschmann 1982. In brief, this latter group of writers stresses that conflict is endemic to Japanese society, and that when social coercion, conflict management, and attempts at mediation fail, the Japanese are as quick to express themselves emotionally as is (borrowing a stereotype) the most hot-blooded Sicilian, Greek, Jew, or Pakistani. The "group ideology" of the stereotypical Japanese shows him or her as self-sacrificing, all-enduring, and so forth, but the latter group of writers' emphasis on social exchange and reciprocity shows the Japanese as individuals to be as self-centered, pragmatic, and willing to be loyal because it "pays" to be loyal as the representatives of other cultural groups (Befu 1980, 180).

CHAPTER 14. *A Woman's Place Is the Shrine*

1. See Tsunoda and Goodrich's translation of "History of the Kingdom of Wei" (1951).
2. See Hardacre 1989 for a complete treatment of many of the dramatic changes that shrine Shinto underwent during the Meiji, Taisho, and Showa periods, including the Yasukuni Shrine controversies of the 1970s and 1980s. Her book covers nearly one hundred years of religious, political, and social history and is necessary reading for anyone wishing to understand the relation between ritual, politics, and power in a Japanese context. Kertzer 1988 provides examples of this theme from all over the world.

3. Walter Edwards's (1989) treatment of Japanese weddings makes the important point that society takes as its basic unit not the individual but "relational wholes, and demands that individuals be embedded in the most basic of these—the husband/wife unit—for valid participation in social life." He goes on to remind the reader of one of the essential differences between a Japanese way of looking at the world and, say, an American: for Japanese, the wider realm of social relations is founded on the principle of inter-dependence, a concept that "renders the individual incomplete as a social being" (116). Contrast this with the American value of an overly romanti-cized independence, where each man or woman stands alone and must make his or her own way in the world, relying on no one else. While this type of individual is not unknown in Japan, and frequently appears as a tragic hero in Japanese film, literature, television, and theater, the predominant mes-sage is that one cannot conquer the odds alone, or find fulfillment alone, without suffering terribly along the way. Ian Buruma (1984) explores this theme from a variety of perspectives in popular arts, finding a precedent in the *Kojiki* myths of Susa-no-o, the unruly Kami (see chapter 12), who settles down only when he enters into marriage, after which (according to Buruma) "nothing more is heard from him again."

4. In the pamphlet published by Kokugakuin University on the basic terms of Shinto, the description under *kegare* (pollution) is instructive of a loosening of interpretation about the prohibitions concerning participa-tion. "Until the middle ages, the death of humans and domestic animals, childbirth, menstruation, eating meat, and sickness, were all regarded as sources of pollution. Today emphasis is placed more on mental or spiritual pollution" (Shinto Committee for the Ninth International Congress for the History of Religions 1985, 29).

5. Please refer to Blacker's chapter "The Ancient Sibyl" (1975) for more detail on the *miko* archetype.

CHAPTER 15. *Okunchi: A City's Heart and Soul*

1. Emile Durkheim, the French sociologist and pioneer in the fields of both anthropology and sociology at the turn of the century, wrote eloquently of the need for public affirmations of the "sacred" principles upon which a particular society is based (1963). As a number of scholars have remarked, Durkheim saw society as a religious phenomenon, since it regenerated itself through the cosmologies and meanings promoted by reli-gion. While I do see aspects of this dynamic at work in Japanese society and have made it central to the following discussion, many factors compli-cate the picture considerably. Foremost among these is the problematic way in which Durkheim posits society and not the individual as the basic unit in which religion comes to life, as well as his overgeneralization of the various

conflicting strands within any religious tradition. For studies in English on contemporary Japanese festivals, see Sonoda 1975, 1988; Ashkenazi 1990, 1993; Bestor 1988; Gilday 1988; Littleton 1986; Aoyagi 1983; Inoue et al. 1979; Schnell 1992; Ueda 1972; Yanagawa 1988; and Sadler 1976, 1982; to name but a few of the many works available.

2. This notion of *genze riyaku* figures prominently in Ian Reader's 1991 assessment of religion in contemporary Japan. As he points out, *riyaku* was originally a Buddhist concept referring to the response of Buddhist figures to prayers, but it has come to signify any "intercessionary" act by divine powers on behalf of human beings (1991, 32). To quote Reader's definition in full: "The notion of *genze riyaku* affirms the responsive and fluid nature of the spiritual world and its powers and abilities to give succor to the living in response to human petitions and needs, and the importance for humans of acquiring solace and reassurance as well as guidance for living peacefully and happily in this life" (33). I am in full accordance with his view that, at the level of popular religious practice, *genze riyaku* is at the center of both Shinto and Buddhist popular religious observances.

3. According to some, the *otabisho* is the spot of original ritual significance, whereas the main shrine was built to house the portable shrines, the *mikoshi*. Although this may be true for other places, the amount of landfill around the harbor has all but erased the original coastline in Nagasaki. The possibility does exist, however, that since a small river enters the harbor near the site of the *otabisho* and since the conjunction of fresh and salt water was believed to be highly efficacious based on the old myths from the *Kojiki* (see chapter 12), perhaps by going inland some half a kilometer and beginning to dig, one could find the original sacred site.

4. The word *machi*, which dictionaries render as "town" or even "city," I use here as "neighborhood." They are, in fact, larger than the two- or three-block areas most Americans feel composes a "neighborhood" (and larger than the Japanese concept of *chōnai*), but they are generally small enough to foster a degree of intimacy among the people living within their legally recognized parameters. A *machi* may contain anywhere from 50 to 5,000 families, a disparity that does not enter into the selection process for Okunchi participants. A *machi* may decline the invitation when their turn arrives, but this appears to be rare.

5. At an exchange rate of ¥110 to the dollar, this would equal approximately $100,000.

6. Another character for "dance" is read as *mai*, meaning "to spin."

7. One of the explanations given to me about this arrangement stresses that even numbers can be easily divided and are thus "weak," whereas odd numbers resist easy division and thus deserve the yang attribute.

8. I am continually stunned by the ambivalent attitude of many Japanese toward trash. While keeping their personal dwellings and tiny yards spotless, many people are often extremely crass in violating public spaces with

litter. Sightseers will toss empty juice or beer bottles from excursion boats (though trash receptacles are abundant), dump garbage from their cars, and deposit the leftovers from lunches taken while hiking in sizable mounds of similar debris. Mount Fuji, one of Japan's traditionally sacred mountains as well as a dominant symbol of its peoples' alleged love of nature, is, by the middle of the summer, a huge litter heap. Similarly, many of the mountains I have climbed have, on or near their summits, monuments to human stupidity fashioned by discarded piles of juice, tea, or beer cans, as if the deities who formerly were thought to descend to earth via mountaintops might somehow make them disappear. Shrine Shinto could do much to shake the label of having become an "ossified" religion by revitalizing its fundamental ecological vision of the world into various kinds of social action directed at increasing public awareness of this staggering problem. See Earhart 1970a for a sadly ignored "call-to-arms."

9. It would be interesting to know the history behind the agreements worked out between the shrine and the city government and what percentage of the "take" is allotted to each, but unfortunately, my inquiries were never accommodated. If there is any topic more tabu to outsiders than the identity of the actual "sacred body" of the Kami (*go-shintai*), it would have to be the finances of the shrine. My study of Kamigamo Shrine of Kyoto (1993b) presents a more rounded portrait of a shrine's inner economic workings.

10. As a bit of evidence for what is to me an astounding fact, I offer the case of a Japanese computer specialist, originally from Tokyo but now living in the San Francisco Bay Area (Berkeley), who faithfully returns to Tokyo every year for the express purpose of participating in his neighborhood's major summer festival.

CHAPTER 16. *Children and Silk*

1. This refers to death by sickness rather than the economically motivated murder of unwanted children at birth (called *mabiki*).

2. Another possible dimension to the participation of children in seasonal and transitional rituals is outlined in Bernard Bernier's 1975 study of religion in a rural area. He finds importance primarily in the roles children serve as future descendants of a household or family, enabling them to function as mediators between rituals emphasizing life (such as the *shichi-go-san*) and rituals of ancestor worship they will be expected to perform later (144). The continuity between generations has already been mentioned as one of the reasons for distant families making the trek to Suwa Shrine, prompting me to again stress that while this book has been focusing on what happens at one shrine, the reader should not assume that the "loyalty" a family may feel to Suwa restricts its religious activities to Shinto ritual practices only.

Many Buddhist temples perform their own versions of *hatsumiyamairi* and *shichi-go-san* festivals, again, like Shinto, emphasizing the importance of children receiving blessings from powerful deities. Yet, with the historical tradition of *ujigami* so basic to the development of Shinto ritual practices, it seems safe to say that long before Buddhism made its official way to the Japanese islands in 538 C.E., a fairly systematic veneration of ancestors by their descendants was integral to a balanced cosmos. See Matsumae's discussion "Early Kami Worship" (1993).

3. My last comment, when seen on the evening news that night, caused a bit of controversy at the private women's college I was at that time employed by. Based upon the founding precepts of Presbyterian missionaries and known throughout Kyushu as one of the preeminent and oldest "mission" schools in Japan, the administrators found my comment "inappropriate" but of course chose to ignore the fact that many of the nonforeign faculty regularly attended school chapel, visited Suwa Shrine at New Year's, and had Buddhist altars in their homes to take care of their ancestors.

4. While there are many variations in style, the *gohei* used in this ritual symbolizes, according to Uesugi Gūji, the earliest form of a Shinto shrine (*himorogi*), where at the center of a cleared, sacred space was a tree or bamboo used as a kind of lightning rod to attract and provide a place for the deity to alight upon. The zigzag cut of the *gohei*'s gilded streamers may show the influence of yin-yang philosophy as well as representing actual lightning bolts, said to be one of the most dramatic of means used by the Kami to enact their will on earth. See *Basic Terms of Shinto* (1985).

5. One need only think of the highly detailed and goal-oriented rituals as outlined in works as various as Bastide's *The African Religions of Brazil* (1978), Danforth's *Firewalking and Religious Healing* (1989), Evans-Pritchard's 1937 classic *Witchcraft, Oracles, and Magic among the Azande*, Lienhardt's *Divinity and Experience* (1961), or Rosaldo's *Knowledge and Passion* (1980).

6. See Zuesse 1979, 27. In the same passage, he discusses the "prestige of the body" mentioned earlier in this book (see chapter 4).

CHAPTER 18. *On Spirit, Geomancy, and Sake*

1. For a sampling of works on these new movements, see Hardacre 1986, Davis 1980a, Earhart 1989, Murakami 1980, Guthrie 1988, and Inoue 1991. The quotation is from Reader 1991, 197.

2. The student of Japanese history will know that many symbols and rituals were appropriated and reinterpreted by the Meiji and later Taisho and Showa governments to form a "national essence" (*kokutai*) revitalization movement that fueled Japanese modernization and militarism and that eventually led to the war. However, this was possible only with a massive program of educational and religious indoctrination (backed up by military

and police sanctions) lasting many years and which met with varied success. See Gluck 1985, Fisher 1987, Anderson 1983, Gauntlett 1949, and Hardacre 1989 for more on the subject.

3. Unlike the job requirements for Protestant ministers or Catholic priests, however, people do not call him on the phone and make appointments for counseling, nor, except in special cases, does the Gūji make calls on people at home or when convalescing. While he may do this as a private citizen, he would not go in an "official" capacity, especially to a place as full of impurities and pollution as a hospital.

4. More accurately, the direction is northeast. This tradition extends back to continental China, where, as in the Japanese case, the northeast was home to "barbarian" invaders who threatened the imperial realm.

5. See Ellwood 1978 for a full description.

6. Though slightly dated, Holtom's (1931) study on tree worship and Kishimoto's (1958) work on mountains are among the first studies published on these fascinating topics.

CHAPTER 19. *Sanctifying the Earth*

1. See Kidder 1959 for photos of a Japanese "stonehenge" in the northern, Tohoku region.

2. In spite of the profound changes industrial societies have imposed on the customs that initially and traditionally validated cultural meanings, the proper orientation of an individual dwelling to the universe remains important in most of Asia even today. It also seems to be a part of the construction process in southern Germany and parts of Austria, where a custom survives of laying an evergreen branch atop the roof of a house only partially framed.

3. See also Hori 1972 for his views on the phenomenon of *onryō* and *goryō*, the vengeful spirits that are thought to be the result of the anger of human beings who were somehow wronged during their lifetimes.

4. See Hardacre 1989, 149. Also see Iisaka 1971, Hiro and Yamamoto 1986, Nishimura 1988, Shimojima 1986, and Hata 1986. Ueda (1979, 307) points out that while the Tsu case was making its way through the courts, other regional governments were happily sponsoring Jichinsai—such as those conducted for the Kyoto Prefectural Assembly building and the Osaka International Exposition—with no challenges from opposing groups. Hardacre makes the additional point that the Supreme Court ruling opened the door for visits to the shrine of Japan's war dead, Yasukuni, by members of the ruling party's cabinet and even by Prime Minister Nakasone himself. Veterans associations, the Central Association of Shinto Shrines, and other interested groups had been lobbying for this shift in legal policies for years, and although they have not yet succeeded in having an amendment made

to the constitution, one can assume that their future efforts will be made easier by this Supreme Court ruling.

CHAPTER 20. *Three Rites for Ending and Beginning the Year*

1. Although I do not describe the December 31 ritual of Great Purification, it is structurally similar in every way to the June observance, save for the absence of the sedge grass woven into a ring, which the priests and assembled participants walk through. Although the different steps of the ritual do not change, the December purification coincides with a transition between years rather than between seasons, and so one might assume that its emphasis is more pragmatically personal than that of June. I might also add, however, that in his closing remarks in December, the Gūji gave greater attention to the welfare of the nation, with the Kami's aid enlisted to guide the emperor and the elected representatives during the coming year.

2. See also Casal 1967 and Brandon 1994 for additional details on the New Year, as well as a popular account by Donald W. George in the *San Francisco Chronicle*, January 7, 1990.

CHAPTER 21. *To Be an Adult*

1. As a final sobering note, it is rare to find a Japanese who actually studied the last fifty to eighty years while enrolled in a public or private high school. The problem is not that textbooks lack information about this period (although there is an ongoing debate about how this information is presented); instead, the curriculum is so weighted with information about earlier eras that a year-long class in Japanese history simply cannot accommodate more recent periods. Teachers tell their students to "study on your own," but it appears few actually do. The result is a woefully ignorant generation of young people who, when compared with their counterparts in Germany, Italy, or the Soviet Union, have very little grasp of not only the manipulations involved in preparing a nation and its people for war but also what actually happened in the last world war. Since the national history curriculum systematically fails to educate students about the events of the last eighty years and since this curriculum is dictated by the Ministry of Education in Tokyo and *not* by the prefectures, is it any wonder people ask if there is a concerted effort at the highest levels of government to keep Japan's recent historical "skeletons" in the closet?

GLOSSARY OF JAPANESE TERMS

ah あ

The initial sound of "ah-uhn," adapted into Japanese from the Sanskrit "aum." The *koma-inu* guardians at the front steps of shrines are thought to make this pronouncement concerning the alpha and omega of the phenomenal realms governed by the Kami.

Amaterasu Ōmikami 天照大御神

The ancestral deity of the Imperial house and tutelary deity for the Yamato lineage. Created from Izanagi's left eye as a result of a purification, she taught humans how to make clothes and dwellings and is the source of food and peace. The Grand Shrine of Ise is dedicated to this Kami.

aramitama 荒霊

All Shinto Kami are thought to have two aspects: a rough one (*aramitama*) and a benevolent one (*nigimitama*). Many rituals are held in an attempt to bring this duality into balance through pacification and appeasement.

bakufu 幕府

Military government, used particularly to describe the Kamakura government (1185–1336) and the Tokugawa government (1603–1868).

bon 盆

As one of the two primary holidays of the year for the Japanese (along with New Year's), it justifies a break from work routines that permits individuals to return to their ancestral homes. It is celebrated in July in some parts of the country and in mid-August in others. The spirits of the dead are believed to return to earth at this time of year. Grave sites are cleaned, offerings presented, and prayers said on behalf of the departed ancestors.

bugyō 奉行

A magistrate of the central government. Nagasaki was a highly sensitive political arena to work within, so it sometimes had dual postings of administrators.

daikan 大寒

The period in early February when the coldest weather of the year occurs and during which time the Setsubun festival is held.

danka seido 檀家制度

This is the term given to a system of administration devised by the Tokugawa military government whereby family households were required to register with local Buddhist temples. This served to register the families for tax and census purposes in most parts of the country, but in areas once controlled by Christians, it officially forced families to affiliate with Buddhism.

eboshi　烏帽子

The type of hat worn most often by Shinto priests. The other style is the *kanmuri*.

gagaku　雅楽

Originating in the Imperial household and court, this ceremonial music has served as entertainment for aristocrats and deities since at least the Nara period.

gohei　御幣

Cloth or paper strips attached to a wooden stick and offered to a Kami. Also called *heihaku*.

goriyaku　御利益

Thought to be originally a Buddhist term, it now signifies those efficacious benefits bestowed by divine entities upon human beings in this lifetime. A sincere petition must be made to the deity, either by the individual alone or with priests serving to expedite the request. Whatever benefits are received must then be acknowledged with an expression of gratitude before the same deity at a later date. Failing to do so invites the possibility of divine retribution, called *tatari*.

go-shintai

See *shintai*.

gūji　宮司

The highest rank of Shinto priest, usually translated as "chief priest." Below him are the *gon-gūji* (associate or assistant chief priest), the *negi* (senior priest), and *gonnegi* (junior priest). These ranks can be grouped together under the term *shinshoku*, signifying the Shinto priesthood.

haiden　拝殿

The Hall of Worship, usually the most public and accessible part of a Shinto shrine. Most rituals are conducted here.

hakama　袴

These silk pantaloons are worn over a priest's formal robes. Their color signifies the rank of the priest, with purple and insignia reserved for chief priests, plain purple for assistant chief priests, and light blue for everyone else.

hara　腹

Literally the abdominal region of the body, but culturally it signifies the center of one's life force and emotions.

harae, harai　祓

Shinto purification rituals. They are thought to eliminate defilements, impurities, illness, evil, misfortune, and other impediments hindering the renewal of life energy emanating from the Kami.

haraigushi　祓串

A wooden stick to which paper or cloth streamers are attached. The use
of this ritual tool begins most formal worship in Shinto practice. It is
waved first to the left, then right, then back again to the left.

hatsumiyamairi　初宮詣り

This is the custom of taking a newborn infant to a local shrine for its
first visit. For boys, the visit is conducted thirty-three days after birth;
and for girls, thirty-two days.

hatsumōde　初詣

First visit to a shrine during the new year.

heiden　幣殿

Hall of Offerings. Used for the staging of rituals, this is the closest the
general public and junior priests can come to the Inner Sanctuary (*honden*).

heihaku

See *gohei*.

hijiri　聖

These itinerant priests did a great deal to spread religious teachings. Reflecting the centuries-long amalgamation of Buddhism and Kami worship, they were primarily Buddhist in orientation and learning but also
performed rituals to access the power of regional and local Kami.

himorogi　神籬

Originally a clearly delineated plot of land upon which an altar is erected
and around which *shimenawa* or other boundary-marking symbols are
placed. The *himorogi* is often discussed as being the "first" shrine. Next
to or behind the altar is a *sakaki* tree, the very spot which the descending
Kami are thought to infuse with their august presence.

hinoki　ひのき

A type of fragrant and fine-grained Japanese cypress wood from which
Shinto structures have traditionally been constructed.

hitogami　人神

Literally "person-deity." A term favored by Hori Ichiro to explain the
end product of the process of deification for important human leaders
within a clan.

hitogata　人形

Literally "person-shape," it signifies the kimono-shaped paper cutouts
used in the Great Purification ritual of June 30 and December 31.

honden　本殿

Inner Sanctuary. Within the confines of the *honden* rests the sacred
essence (*go-shintai*), which the Kami are thought to temporarily occupy
during their brief visitations to a shrine. Only the chief and associate
chief priests may enter the *honden*.

honne　本音

One's true intentions, which may not always correspond to surface presentations (*tatemae*). Other English translations for this dichotomy are "true wishes/expected behavior," "self-interest/public good," "practice/ideology," and so on.

iwasaka 磐境

An open-air enclosure in which rituals to a Kami may be held. It is a clearly demarcated rectangle of sacred space, marked with *shimenawa* ropes and stones, which priests and participants cannot enter until they are purified.

Izanagi (no mikoto) 伊邪那岐神 and Izanami (no mikoto) 伊邪那美神

In the seventh generation of celestial deities, this couple married and Izanami gave birth to the earth. Izanami died giving birth to fire and descended into the land of Yomi. Izanagi went to visit her, broke a tabu, and encountered pollution, and thus became the first practitioner of purification upon his return to the surface. The creation myths can be found in the *Kojiki* and *Nihon-shoki*.

jichinsai 地鎮祭

Land-calming and land-claiming rituals held before the construction of buildings.

jinja 神社

A Shinto shrine. Other words signifying the temporary residence of Kami are (in descending order of importance) *jingū*, *miya*, *oyashiro*, *hokora*.

jōe 浄衣

Usually made of white silk, this garment is worn by Shinto priests during rituals.

kadomatsu 門松

A New Year's decoration composed primarily of pine boughs, bamboo stalks sliced diagonally at the end, and (less commonly) a plum branch. Each of these represents various qualities and characteristics especially valued at the beginning of a new year.

kagura 神楽

A performance of music and dance within the shrine which is thought to pacify and entertain the Kami. Its origin stems from the mythological incident in which Amaterasu Ōmikami hid herself in a cave and was enticed to come out with music and a dance performance. *Kagura* is not restricted to shrines but may also be performed in the community (*sato-kagura*) and at the Imperial court.

kami 神

Divided into heavenly and earthly deities, the Kami are those numinous entities which Shinto rituals petition for protection, fecundity, divination, and so on, all of which are necessary for present-day concerns. Kami have beneficent and malevolent characteristics which must be propitiated and balanced if humans are to reap benefits (and not retributions) in their agricultural, commercial, social, or political endeavors.

kamidana 神棚

Shinto altar in a private home. Japanese homes frequently have both an altar for Shinto deities as well as a *butsudan* for worshipping the Buddha and honoring ancestral spirits. Shrines sell a wide variety of amulets that are then placed within the *kamidana*. Together, they serve to link the household to the shrine. Offerings of fresh leaves, water, and sake are traditionally made on the first and fifteenth of the month.

kanmuri 冠

Formal head attire for priests, distinguished by its springy "tail." Unlike the workaday *eboshi*, the *kanmuri* is reserved for more important ritual occasions. Like most Shinto priestly garb, its origins are found in the Chinese court.

kannabi 神名備

A site held to be sacred because it possesses the potential to attract Kami down from the High Plain of Heaven.

kannushi 神主

A common word (along with *shinshoku*) used in conversational Japanese to signify a Shinto priest.

kansha 感謝

Gratitude to the Kami for benefits received. Priests tend to see any respectful act performed at a shrine (such as hand-clapping, the tossing of coins, or simply bowing in the direction of the Inner Sanctuary) as an example of *kanshu*.

kasaboko 傘鉾

A portable shrine atop a pole which represents a particular neighborhood (*machi*). They are elaborately decorated, extremely heavy and awkward, yet are "danced" during the Okunchi festival performances.

kashiwade 柏手

The term given to the custom of raising one's hands to the level of one's chest and then clapping two or three times in succession. This is probably the most distinctive and representative gesture signifying an individual's public demonstration of respect for a Shinto Kami.

kaso 家祖

The practice in Japan of using Chinese-style geomantic practices to determine which auspicious and inauspicious directions, earth energies, and other unseen forces might impinge upon the safety and security of a dwelling, a place of business, or any structure occupied by humans.

kegare 穢

Depending upon the situation and its context, *kegare* may be thought of as either pollution, defilement, or the waning of vital life energy. Purification rituals are expressly designed to address and, it is hoped, eliminate the destructive effects of *kegare*. Also called *tsumi* or *imi*.

keihitsu

The eerie and extended single vowel sound uttered by a nearby priest whenever the door to the Inner Sanctuary (*honden*) is opened (thus "permitting" the Kami greater access to the participants' petitionings) or closed during a ritual. It is also performed outside during a land-calming ritual (*jichinsai*) to denote the comings and goings of the Kami.

kessai　潔斎

An act of abstinence performed by a priest in preparation for conducting a ritual. Also called *monoimi*.

kiai　気合い

A loud cry uttered to break through both spiritual and physical impediments. It is heard at Suwa Shrine during the *yutate-sai* and in martial arts at the moment of attack.

kimon　鬼門

The characters can be read as "demon's gate" and refer to the inauspicious northeast direction, from which malevolent forces are thought to wage their attacks on the happiness and harmony of governments, religious institutions, and individual dwellings. The concept has its origins in Chinese *feng-shui* geomancy and is still part of the traditions of building construction in a number of contemporary Asian countries.

Kōgakkan University　皇学館大学

Located in Ise, Mie Prefecture, it is the second most important training university (after Kokugakuin in Tokyo) for aspiring Shinto priests.

Kojiki　古事記

The "Record of Ancient Matters" is a vast repository of ancient ritual practices, customs, divinations, and taboos and has provided one of the bases for attempts to create a contemporary Shinto-centered theology. It was begun in 680 under the aegis of Emperor Temmu and completed in 712. Its purpose was to link the ruling clans to the deities that created the islands of Japan and thus to sanctify and legitimate their rule.

Kokugakuin University　国学院大学

Founded in 1882, Kokugakuin University has been at the center of a variety of government-sponsored movements, especially state Shinto (*kokka-shinto*) ideology. Today it offers a variety of undergraduate courses but is still the leading center for Shinto scholarship, priestly training, and cooperative efforts with the government regarding a number of conservative political agendas.

koma-inu　狛犬

At the entrance to every shrine is a pair of guardian beasts, most frequently the *koma-inu*, or "Korean dogs," which look more like lions than dogs. Inari shrines frequently have foxes as their guardians.

konusa　小幣

The *konusa* leaf (from the *sakaki* tree) is used to scatter drops of water to dispel impurities.

kotatsu　こたつ

A leg-warming table commonly used throughout Japan. The traditional *kotatsu* was heated by a brazier of coals and covered with a quilt. Most houses do not have central heating units and so today's electric *kotatsu* is, along with small portable heaters, one of the only sources of warmth in the winter.

kotodama　言霊

In many cultures worldwide, certain words were thought to possess innate spiritual energies that could alter the world. *Kotodama* belongs to this category, animating the words of a *norito* prayer delivered by the chief priest to the Kami during Shinto rituals.

kunchi　くんち

One of Japan's top ten festivals, the Okunchi *matsuri* of Suwa Shrine mobilizes thousands of people, requires vast financial resources, and occupies the city's attention for three days every October 7-9.

makoto　まこと

When an individual petitions the Kami, he or she must be sincere, truthful, and conscientious. These three qualities are part of *makoto*, thought to be one of the essential attitudes in Shinto worship and practice.

matsuri　祭

The word stands for festival-like events open to general public participation, such as the Okunchi, but *matsuri* also encompass in-house rituals conducted by the priests of a shrine. *Matsuri* most frequently are held to sanctify or commemorate certain critical moments of the yearly agricultural cycle (as in planting or harvest *matsuri*), but they may also honor a specific individual or event. In all cases, they require considerable organization and management, as the cooperative efforts of many people sharing a common purpose, residential area, or livelihood are harmonized to venerate and partake of the efficacy (*riyaku*) of a Kami.

matsurigoto　まつりごと

One of the most ancient of concepts of state rule in Japan, *matsurigoto* refers to a synthesis of politics and worship that was particularly in vogue during the Yamato ascendancy of the fourth to seventh centuries C.E. It is similar to notions of theocracy in other parts of the world (and to the Japanese notion of *saisei-itchi*) and stresses the need for political rulers to follow the will of the deities as conveyed to them by elite priests.

Meiji　明治

The Meiji period (1868–1912) covers the years of Japan's rapid modernization and social transformation from a feudal to a modern society. It is named after Emperor Meiji.

miki　神酒

When rice wine (*sake*) is offered to a Kami, it is called *miki*. After it has been consecrated upon the altar during a ritual, it is then shared with the participants in the postritual reception, the *naorai*.

miko　巫女

In many ways, the *miko*, or female shrine attendants, extend back to the earliest matriarchal rulers of Japan in the second and third centuries. Today, they perform a variety of functions at a shrine, ranging from serving tea in the shrine administrative offices, to selling amulets, to their more formal roles during a ritual when they dance and thus entertain the Kami.

mikoshi　みこし

These are the portable shrines (also called palanquins) used to convey the sacred essence of a Kami (*go-shintai*) outside the fixed shrine's precincts, sometimes to a temporary shrine, as during the Okunchi festival. In contemporary Japan, *mikoshi* come in a variety of forms and are sponsored not only by shrines and neighborhoods but also by companies and city governments as a way to bring people together and thus foster a sense of community.

misogi　禊

The act of purifying one's body and spirit by the use of water goes back to the deity Izanagi's purification after having escaped the land of Yomi. In contemporary Shinto practice, *misogi* may be complex rituals, such as the total immersion in seawater of ritual participants. Though not called by the same term, its principles extend to acts as simple as rinsing one's hands and mouth at the water font (*temizuya*) before entering a shrine for worship.

mochi　もち

Round "cakes" of pounded glutenous rice, most common at New Year's as a form of traditional treat eaten during the holidays. They are also frequently found among the food offerings to a shrine's Kami.

monoimi　物忌

Similar to the practice of *kessai* during a period of *saikai*, or abstaining from a variety of foods, habits, and encounters with defiling substances, *monoimi* is an essential preparatory obligation of Shinto priests before major ritual occasions.

Morisaki　森崎

One of the three principal Kami at Suwa Shrine, its efficacy concerns the renewal of fertility and life forces in general. Its shrine was destroyed by Jesuits in the mid–sixteenth century, but it is thought that its sacred essence was preserved and later incorporated into the altar of the church built to take the place of the shrine.

nagare-zukuri　流造

A term used for the prevailing architectural style of a shrine's inner sanctuary, the *honden*. Characterized by long flowing rooflines, its precedents are found in Chinese and Korean palace architecture.

Nakatomi　中臣

Probably the most powerful and influential of the early clans constituting Yamato rule, the Nakatomi were "medium diviners" directly responsible to the court. Their leader, Kamatari, helped overthrow the Soga rulers. The family became immensely wealthy and popular, controlling vast holdings and, through intermarriage, the Imperial line of succession as well. The Nakatomi are the forebears of the Fujiwaras.

naorai 直会

The reception held after a shrine ritual. Its purpose is to ease the transition from sacred to secular time and to allow the participants to share in the partaking of *omiki* rice wine and various delicacies (which may also have been sanctified on the altar).

negi 禰宜

One of the many words used for a Shinto priest. It is most commonly used by the priests themselves since it denotes the rank of a senior priest.

nigimitama 和魂

See *aramitama*.

Nihongi/Nihon-shoki 日本記 / 日本書記

Written in 720 in Chinese at the bidding of the Imperial court, the *Nihon-shoki* reflects strong influence from continental culture and yet encompasses many of the same stories as the *Kojiki* while extending its scope to more recent events and players. Its thirty volumes provide a wealth of information and detail about the ancient court and the state.

nihonjinron 日本人論

This term is used to describe writings on or about the Japanese or Japaneseness by native authors. It also denotes a certain problematic approach of these writings, since they tend to draw upon essentialized qualities, customs, or traditions. While having historical foundations, these essences serve to advance a political or ideological agenda about certain unique Japanese qualities (spiritual, cultural, social, etc.) not shared by the rest of the international community.

niiname-sai 新嘗祭

This fall festival is one of the oldest of all ritual occasions within Shinto. It can be traced back to the ancient Imperial court, where the emperor gave thanks to the deities for providing a bountiful harvest. Today, it is held on November 23 or 24 and is thought by many priests to be one of the rituals linking local shrines to the Imperial court, because in both places the event receives the full attention and participation of ritual practitioners, including the emperor.

norito 祝詞

The invocational prayer delivered before the Kami by the chief priest of a shrine. Stemming from a belief in the power of certain words to enact good results (*kotodama*), many *norito* are still delivered in an ancient style of Japanese. Priests at the training universities are schooled in both the performance and the composition of *norito*.

ofuda お札

These serve as a kind of talisman or amulet and contain the name of the Kami written within a protective cover of paper or cloth. Generally, they are placed within the household's *kamidana* and serve to incorporate the household into the deity's benevolent graces.

ōharae 大祓

Like the *niiname-sai*, the *ōharae* ritual is performed on behalf of and for the benefit of local and national communities. Originating from an invocational prayer by the Nakatomi diviners, it purifies the realm of defilements, impurities, and misfortunes. It is held on June 30 and December 31.

omairi お参り

This is the term given to formal or informal visitations to a shrine. Whether one does this every day or irregularly, or whether one is paying respects to a local Kami or to one far from home, any act of veneration or worship whereby a visitor enters into the shrine precincts to pray is called *omairi* by priests and practitioners alike.

oni 鬼

In Japanese myth and folklore an *oni* is a malevolent spirit that has entered a physical form. Some priests believe the concept is imported into Shinto from its long association with Buddhism, but the concept also occurs in Taoism, Shinto's other continental ancestor. Dispelling *oni* is the prime concern of the Setsubun festival of early February.

otabisho 御旅所

This may be thought of as a sacred spot outside the shrine's precincts where the *mikoshi* will rest during major festival occasions. During Nagasaki's Okunchi festival, the three *mikoshi* rest in a temporary structure erected at the edge of the waterfront.

otome-mai 乙女舞

When the shrine's female attendants (*miko*) dance during a ritual, it is called *otome-mai*. There are many varieties, of course, the most common being the *gosechi-no-mai*, or five-movement dance. The *miko* will typically use bell-wands (*suzu*) during the dance.

reikon 霊魂

A spirit, not necessarily divine, that must be pacified and kept in check so its influence does not impede the normal functioning of life energies. A ritual specifically designed to calm unsettled spirits is the *chinkon-sai*.

reisai 例祭

The annual or semiannual main festival of a shrine. This is one of the most important ritual occasions for the shrine, and the day is thought to have significance for the shrine's founding or to have a special connection with its principal Kami.

risshun 立春

The first day of spring. In agricultural areas, the yearly rice cycle begins on this day.

Ryōbu Shinto 両部神道

In many ways, it can be argued that Shinto and Buddhism have been fused to serve the interests of the state since the ancient period. The above term usually refers to the period of nearly one thousand years when religious institutions were centers for both Buddha and Kami worship.

saifuku 斎服

The white silk outer robes worn by priests during religious rituals.

saikai 斎戒

A period of abstinence for ritual participants observed either before or after the occasion. Depending upon the person's rank, duties in the ritual, and the event itself, the strictures can be quite demanding or rather relaxed. In all cases, they involve mental concentration and frequent bathing and avoidance of certain foods, the opposite sex, and death or sickness.

saisei-itchi 祭政一致

The characters signify a unity of ritual and government. The term is frequently associated with state Shinto (*kokka-shinto*) in the period before World War II when both the rituals within shrines and public education came under the control of the government. In the eighth and ninth centuries, *saisei-itchi* referred to both religious rituals and government as unified by the emperor's role in both.

saishu 祭主

Supreme Priest/Priestess at the Grand Shrine of Ise, ranked above even the *daigūji*. Since the end of the war, this position has been held by a female priest related to the Imperial family.

sakaki 榊

The leaves of this tree native only to Japan are used for purifying and blessing, as well as offerings (when they are called *tamagushi*), in Shinto rituals. The tree is green year-round, and its leaves are similar in shape and appearance to those of the camellia. Once used in a ritual, they cannot be used again, although they may remain as an offering beside the altar. See also *himorogi*.

sakoku 鎖国

Literally "closed country," or the period of forced isolation from international contact enacted during the Tokugawa shogunate's rule from 1603 to 1868. This policy was largely in response to the contact with Europeans during Nagasaki's "Christian century."

sakura 桜

The cherry tree or, depending on the context in which it is used, cherry blossoms.

seimei 清明

In contemporary Shinto ethics and thought, *seimei* stands for "purity" and "brightness" of heart. Along with honesty (*shōjiki*) and sincerity (*makoto*) it is among the most important of requisite attitudes for both petitioning and receiving the Kami's revitalizing powers. The word *seimei* occurs most frequently in Japan written with these characters 生命 and means "life" or "existence."

seiza 正座

Formal sitting, with one's legs bent at the knee and tucked under the body, the posture for Shinto priests during rituals. For the visiting participants, both men and women sit in this posture at the start of a ritual, but women will usually remain in the *seiza* position after the men have gone to a more relaxed, cross-legged posture.

sensei 先生

As one of the most commonly used words for "teacher," it implies both seniority and respect for the person who has knowledge to impart.

setsubun 節分

Once the day before the beginning of spring, it is the name of the Japanese festival when demons are cast out and happiness welcomed in.

shaku 笏

One of a priest's accessories, made of wood and carried in the right hand during rituals. It is thought to have been used as a prompter in the Chinese Imperial court.

shamusho 社務所

That part of a shrine housing its administrative functions. It is usually separated from the main compound of the halls of worship and Inner Sanctuary.

shichi-go-san mairi 七五三参

The festival for children aged seven, five, and three, held in November.

shidori

One of the titles for (usually) junior priests participating in a ritual.

shimenawa 注連縄

A rope marking the boundaries of an area that has been sanctified or purified, or an area to which the Kami might descend. Strips of paper called *shide* are hung from the rope.

shinji 神事

Another expression for a Shinto ritual. Also used are the word *matsuri* and the suffix *-sai.*

shinjinrui 新人類

A word coined by the social commentator Chikushi Tetsuya to describe the "new human beings" raised and educated after the hardships of postwar rebuilding had subsided. They are typically said to be selfish, independent, and materialistic and are frequently contrasted to the older generation, who are said to be frugal and self-sacrificing for greater goals.

shinsen 神饌

Food offerings presented upon an altar to the Kami. They always include rice, water, salt, sake, and food representative of the sea, mountains, and plains.

shinshoku 神職

Refers either to the entire Shinto priesthood or to an individual member thereof.

shintai 神体

Sequestered within the innermost sanctuary, the *shintai* (referred to by priests with the honorific prefix *go-*) is a material object that is a shrine's "holy of holies" because the Kami invest it with their presence during rituals. Although the general public may think the *go-shintai* actually *is* the Kami of a particular shrine, the priests point out that it is only the receptacle to accommodate the Kami's brief visitation.

shō 笙

A traditional instrument, originally imported from China, used in the performance of music for the court (*gagaku*). It resembles an upright panpipe.

shōgatsu 正月

The New Year's celebrations. In Japan, the holiday lasts from January 1 to 5 at most shrines. During this time, people make their first shrine visitations of the year to pray for health and prosperity.

shūkyō 宗教

The word in modern Japanese signifying "religion." It is a recent innovation, however, created in the early Meiji period to accommodate European-style concepts of "religion" as part of a theological and academic discourse. The two characters stand for "a sect's teaching."

Sumiyoshi 住吉

The name of one of Suwa Shrine's three Kami. Its efficacy extends particularly to fishermen.

susu 煤

Although this word means "soot," it also signifies lingering impurities or defilements within a shrine that lurk in ceiling corners and rafters as a result of allowing the public in.

suzu 鈴

The bell-wands used by a shrine's female attendants to bless or purify ritual participants.

tamagushi 玉串

A sprig of *sakaki* leaves between 20 and 30 cm in length. When paying one's respects to the Kami in a formal ritual conducted by priests, the *tamagushi* is laid upon a small table by the participant.

tamashii 魂

A "soul," "spirit," or sometimes even a "ghost." The word's meaning depends upon the context in which it is used. For example, it has different implications when used in a Christian worship service than when used to describe ancestral spirits. In Shinto, the word most frequently used is *tama* (霊), meaning "soul" or "spirit," which has both benevolent and malevolent aspects.

tatami 畳

Woven-grass mats that traditionally cover the floors of Japanese dwellings, temples, and shrines.

tatemae たてまえ

Usually used in conjunction with the word *honne*, *tatemae* indicates the
surface presentation or formal appearance that harmonizes (more or
less) with a particular situation or surroundings. It may or may not correspond with *honne*, which is one's true feeling or inclination temporarily
subordinated for the sake of "going with the flow."

temizuya 手水屋

At the entrance to every shrine is found the water basin where initial
purifications of the hands and mouth are performed by those wishing to
petition the Kami.

torii 鳥居

One of the most distinctive emblems of Shinto and often used to symbolize Japanese culture or the nation itself is the gateway found at the
entrance or along the approach to a shrine. *Torii* come in a variety of
styles and sizes, but they all serve as a kind of boundary marker between
the sacred and the profane.

toshibito 年人

This term signifies the group of individuals born under a certain sign
of the Chinese zodiac, which is still widely followed in Japan. The year
1995, for example, is the year of the wild boar, and so individuals born
in any of the years of this sign (1983, 1971, 1959, 1947, 1935, etc.) may
throw the magic beans to the crowd during Suwa Shrine's Setsubun festival for 1995.

tsumi 罪

Although the *Basic Terms of Shinto* published by Kokugakuin University's
Institute for Japanese Culture and Classics equates this term with the
English word "sin," the term appears to carry considerably more ambiguity and breadth when one considers what constitutes *tsumi*. It may
be anything from one's own experience of sickness, error, or calamity
to encounters with the death or misfortunes of others. For a listing of
"earthly" and "heavenly" sins, see the account in *Engi-shiki*.

uhn うん

The sound uttered by the close-mouthed guardian beast at the entrance
to most shrines. The "uhn" and the "ah" sounds represent the alpha and
omega of the Kami's influence.

ujigami 氏神

Once the deity of a particular family or clan, the *ujigami* came to represent a geographic area and thus protect all those in its precincts. Thus,
one can say that the *ujigami* of central Nagasaki is Suwa-no-kami.

ujiko 氏子

Those living within the precincts of a particular shrine, who are thus under the protection of its principal deity. At Suwa Shrine, the priests think of *ujiko* as both residents of the city (who may rarely interact with the shrine) and those who actively participate in shrine activities.

Urabe　裏辺

One of the clans serving the ancient Imperial court of the eighth century C.E. Their role was that of diviners.

wasshoi　わっしょい

A chant often heard by the bearers of portable shrines during *matsuri* processions as they wind through the city streets. It has no literal meaning but serves to unite energy and awareness to the sacred labor being performed.

yaku-yoke　厄除け

This term encompasses concepts such as defense against, protection from, and warding off a variety of misfortunes, calamities, or disasters thought to affect men and women at certain ages. The words also tend to remind people that a shrine's rituals are efficacious in protecting people from these misfortunes.

yamabushi　山武士

Wandering, ascetic priests who traveled from temple to temple by way of mountain paths. They were usually affiliated with Shingon-style ritual practices but also drew upon Kami worship as part of their ritual repertoire.

Yamato　大和

The name given to a confederation of formerly competing clans during the latter Yayoi period. Their hegemony in the Nara basin and surrounding areas formed the foundation for the Japanese state and Imperial court.

Yomi　黄泉

The land of the dead; the netherworld to which Izanami descended after giving birth to fire.

yutate　湯立

A dramatic ritual in which water is boiled in a cauldron, then sprinkled in the four directions to purify defilements and exorcise demons. Suwa Shrine is unique in that a senior priest will plunge his hand into the cauldron.

WORKS CITED

Aikens, C. Melvin, and Takayasu Higuchi. 1982. *Prehistory of Japan*. New York: Academic Press.

Anderson, Benedict. 1983. *Imagined Communities: Reflections on the Origins and Spread of Nationalism*. London: Verso.

Anesaki, Masaharu. 1960. *A History of Japanese Religion*. 1930. Reprint, Tokyo: Charles E. Tuttle.

Aoki, Tamotsu. 1988. Culture in the Age of Antirelativism. *Japan Echo* 15(1):44–51.

———. 1990. *Nihon Bunkaron no Henyō* (Changes in theories on Japaneseness). Tokyo: Chuokoronsha.

Aoyagi, Kiyotaka. 1983. Viable Traditions in Urban Japan: *Matsuri/Chonaikai*. In *Town Talk*, ed. G. Ansari and P. Nas. Leiden: E. J. Brill.

Asad, Talal. 1983. Anthropological Conceptions of Religion: Reflections on Geertz. *Man* 18: 237–59.

Ashkenazi, Michael. 1990. Festival Management and the Corporate Analysis of Japanese Society. In *Unwrapping Japan*, ed. E. Ben-Ari, B. Moeran, and J. Valentine. Manchester: Manchester University Press.

———. 1993. *Matsuri: Festivals of a Japanese Town*. Honolulu: University of Hawaii Press.

Aston, W. G. 1921. *Shinto*. London: Constable.

———. 1978. *Nihongi: Chronicles of Japan from the Earliest Times to A.D. 697*. 1896. Reprint, Tokyo: Charles E. Tuttle.

Basic Terms of Shinto. 1985. Comp. Shinto Committee for the Ninth International Congress for the History of Religions. Tokyo: Jinja Honchō (Central Association of Shinto Shrines) and Institute for Japanese Culture and Classics, Kokugakuin University.

Bastide, Roger. 1978. *The African Religions of Brazil: Toward a Sociology of the Interpenetration of Civilizations*. Trans. Helen Sebba. Baltimore: Johns Hopkins University Press.

Beardsley, Richard K., J. Hall, and R. Ward. 1959. *Village Japan*. Chicago: University of Chicago Press.

Beauchamp, Edward R., and Richard Rubinger. 1989. *Education in Japan: A Sourcebook*. New York: Garland Publishing.

Befu, Harumi. 1971. *Japan: An Anthropological Introduction*. San Francisco: Chandler Publishing.

———. 1980. The Group Model of Japanese Society and an Alternative. *Rice University Studies* 66(1):169–87.

Befu, Harumi, and H. Mannari, eds. 1983. *The Challenge of Japan's Internationalization.* Tokyo and New York: Kodansha.

Bellah, Robert N. 1957. *Tokugawa Religion: The Values of Pre-industrial Japan.* Glencoe, Ill.: Free Press.

———. 1970. *Beyond Belief.* New York: Harper and Row.

———. 1983. Religion in Japan: National and International Dimensions. In *The Challenge of Japan's Internationalization: Organization and Culture,* ed. H. Befu and H. Mannari. Tokyo: Kodansha.

Benedict, Ruth. 1974. *The Chrysanthemum and the Sword.* New York: New American Library.

Bernier, Bernard. 1975. *Breaking the Cosmic Circle: Religion in a Japanese Village.* Cornell East Asia Papers 5. Ithaca, N.Y.: Cornell China-Japan Program.

Bestor, Theodore C. 1988. *Neighborhood Tokyo.* Stanford: Stanford University Press.

Bix, Herbert P. 1986. *Peasant Protest in Japan, 1590–1884.* New Haven: Yale University Press.

Blacker, Carmen. 1975. *The Catalpa Bow.* London: Allen and Unwin.

Blumenberg, Hans. 1987. An Anthropological Approach to the Contemporary Significance of Rhetoric. In *After Philosophy: End or Transformation?* ed. K. Baynes, J. Bohman, and T. McCarthy. Cambridge: MIT Press.

Bock, Felicia G. 1970. *Engi-Shiki: Procedures of the Engi Era, Books 1–5.* Tokyo: Sophia University.

———. 1985. *Classical Learning and Taoist Practices in Early Japan.* Tempe: Arizona State University.

Bownas, Geoffrey. 1963. *Japanese Rainmaking and Other Folk Practices.* London: George Allen and Unwin.

Boxer, C. E. 1951. *The Christian Century in Japan: 1549–1650.* Berkeley and Los Angeles: University of California Press.

Brandon, Reiko. 1994. *Spirit and Symbol: The Japanese New Year.* Honolulu: University of Hawaii Press.

Brown, Delmer, ed. 1993. *The Cambridge History of Japan.* Vol. 1. Cambridge: Cambridge University Press.

Burke-Gaffney, Brian. 1987. Jaodori. *Harbor Light* 2(9):7.

———. 1989. *Hana to shimo: Groba-te no hitobito* (Flowers and frost: The people of Glover House). Nagasaki: Nagasaki Bunken-sha.

Burke-Gaffney, Brian, and Lane R. Earns, eds. 1993. *Crossroads: A Journal of Nagasaki History and Culture.* Vol. 1. Nagasaki: Showado.

Buruma, Ian. 1984. *Behind the Mask.* New York: Pantheon Books.

Cannadine, David. 1987. The Context, Performance, and Meaning of Ritual: The British Monarchy and the "Invention of Tradition," c. 1820–1977. In *The Invention of Tradition,* ed. E. Hobsbawm and T. Ranger. Cambridge: Cambridge University Press.

Casal, U. A. 1967. *The Five Sacred Festivals of Ancient Japan: Their Symbolism and Historical Development*. Tokyo: Sophia University and Charles E. Tuttle.

Chikushi, Tetsuya. 1986. Young People as a New Human Race. *Japan Quarterly* 33:292–94.

Clugston, Michael. 1987. The Oriental Dilemma. *Maclean's*, November, pp. 26–30.

Cooper, Michael. 1971. *The Southern Barbarians: The First Europeans in Japan*. Tokyo: Kodansha.

Creemers, Wilhelmus H. M. 1968. *Shrine Shinto after World War II*. Leiden: E. J. Brill.

Cuyler, Patricia L. 1979. *Sumo: From Rite to Sport*. New York and Tokyo: Weatherhill.

Czaja, Michael. 1974. *Gods of Myths and Stone: Phallicism in Japanese Folk Religion*. New York: Weatherhill.

Dale, Peter N. 1986. *The Myth of Japanese Uniqueness*. New York: St. Martin's Press.

Danforth, Loring M. 1989. *Firewalking and Religious Healing: The Anastenaria of Greece and the American Firewalking Movement*. Princeton: Princeton University Press.

Davis, Winston B. 1980a. *Dōjō: Exorcism and Miracles in Modern Japan*. Stanford: Stanford University Press.

———. 1980b. The Secularization of Japanese Religion: Measuring the Myth and the Reality. In *Transitions and Transformations in the History of Religions*, ed. Frank E. Reynolds and Theodore M. Ludwig. Leiden: E. J. Brill.

———. 1992. *Japanese Religion and Society: Paradigms of Structure and Change*. Albany: State University of New York Press.

De Vos, George A., and Takao Sofue, eds. 1984. Religion and Family: Structural and Motivational Relationships. In *Religion and the Family in East Asia*. Berkeley and Los Angeles: University of California Press.

Dore, Ronald P. 1978. *Shinohata: A Portrait of a Japanese Village*. London: Allen Lane.

Douglas, Mary. 1970. *Purity and Danger*. 1966. Reprint, Harmondsworth: Penguin Books.

Durkheim, Emile. 1963. *Elementary Forms of the Religious Life*. Trans. Joseph Swain. London: Allen and Unwin.

Earhart, H. Byron. 1970a. The Ideal of Nature in Japanese Religion and Its Possible Significance for Environmental Concerns. *Contemporary Religions in Japan* 11(1–2):1–26.

———. 1970b. *A Religious Study of the Mount Haguro Sect of Shugendo: An Example of Japanese Mountain Religion*. Monumentica Nipponica. Tokyo: Sophia University.

———. 1983. *Japanese Religion: Unity and Diversity*. Belmont, Calif.:
Wadsworth Publishing.

———. 1984. *Religion in the Japanese Experience: Sources and Interpretations*.
Belmont, Calif.: Wadsworth Publishing.

———. 1989. *Gedatsukai and Religion in Contemporary Japan: Returning to
the Center*. Bloomington: Indiana University Press.

Edwards, Walter. 1989. *Modern Japan through Its Weddings*. Stanford:
Stanford University Press.

Elison, Robert S. 1973. *Deus Destroyed: The Image of Christianity in Early
Modern Japan*. Cambridge: Harvard University Press.

Ellwood, Robert S. 1978. Harvest and Renewal at the Grand Shrine of Ise.
In *Readings on Religion from Inside and Outside*, ed. Robert S. Ellwood.
Englewood Cliffs, N.J.: Prentice Hall.

Embree, John. 1939. *Suye Mura*. Chicago: University of Chicago Press.

Evans-Pritchard, E. E. 1937. *Witchcraft, Oracles, and Magic among the
Azande*. Oxford: Clarendon Press.

———. 1965. *Theories of Primitive Religion*. Oxford: Oxford
University Press.

Field, Norma. 1989. *Somehow Crystal: The Postmodern as Atmosphere*. In
Postmodernism and Japan, ed. M. Miyoshi and H. Harootunian.
Durham, N.C.: Duke University Press.

Firth, Raymond. 1973. *Symbols: Public and Private*. London: Allen
and Unwin.

Fisher, Peter. 1987. Some Notes on Clergy and State in Japan. In
*Contemporary European Writing on Japan: Scholarly Views from Eastern
and Western Europe*, ed. Ian Nish. London: Paul Norbury.

Foucault, Michel. 1980. *Power/Knowledge: Selected Interviews and Other
Writings, 1972–1977*. Trans. and ed. Colin Gordon. New York:
Pantheon.

Fox, Richard G. 1990. Introduction. In *Nationalist Ideologies and the
Production of National Cultures*, ed. R. Fox. Washington, D.C.:
American Anthropological Association.

Frager, Robert, and Thomas P. Rohlen. 1976. The Future of a Tradition:
Japanese Spirit in the 1980's. In *Japan: The Paradox of Progress*, ed.
L. Austin. New Haven: Yale University Press.

Fujioka, Wakao. 1986. The Rise of the Micromasses. *Japan Echo* 13(1):
31–38.

Fukatsu, Masumi. 1987. A State Visit to Yasukuni Shrine. *Japan Quarterly*
34:18–24.

Fukutake, Tadashi. 1982. *Japanese Social Structure*. Tokyo: University of
Tokyo Press.

Gadamer, H. G. 1987. The Problem of Historical Consciousness. In
Interpretive Social Science, ed. P. Rabinow and W. Sullivan. Berkeley and
Los Angeles: University of California Press.

Gauntlett, John Owen, trans. 1949. *Kokutai no Hongi: Cardinal Principles of the National Entity of Japan*. Ed. Robert K. Hall. Cambridge: Harvard University Press.

Geertz, Clifford. 1973. *The Interpretations of Culture: Selected Essays*. 1964. Reprint, New York: Basic Books.

Gilday, Edmund T. 1988. The Pattern of Matsuri: Cosmic Schemes and Ritual Illusion in Japanese Festivals. Ph.D. diss., University of Chicago.

Gluck, Carol. 1985. *Japan's Modern Myths: Ideology in the Late Meiji Period*. Princeton: Princeton University Press.

Gojo Junko. 1983. *Shugendō no kokoro* (The heart of Shugendō). Osaka: Toki Shobo.

Goody, J. R. 1961. Religion and Ritual: The Definitional Problem. *British Journal of Sociology* 15:142–63.

Gorai Shigeru et al. 1980. *Kōza, Nihon no minzoku shūkyō* (Lectures on Japanese folk religions). Tokyo: Kobundo.

Graburn, Nelson H. H. 1983. *To Pray, Pay, and Play: The Cultural Structure of Japanese Domestic Tourism*. Aix-en-Provence: Centre des Hautes Etudes Touristiques.

Grapard, Allan. 1983. Shinto. In *The Kodansha Encyclopedia of Japan*. Tokyo: Kodansha Publishing.

———. 1992. *The Protocol of the Gods: A Study of the Kasuga Cult in Japanese History*. Berkeley and Los Angeles: University of California Press.

Griffin, David Ray. 1989. Introduction to *Spirituality and Society: Postmodern Visions*. Albany: State University of New York Press.

Guthrie, Stewart. 1988. *A Japanese "New Religion": Risshō Kosei-kai in a Mountain Hamlet*. Ann Arbor: Center for Japanese Studies.

Hall, John W. 1977. *Japan before Tokugawa*. Princeton: Princeton University Press.

Handelman, Don. 1990. *Models and Mirrors: Towards an Anthropology of Public Events*. Cambridge: Cambridge University Press.

Hardacre, Helen. 1986. *Kurozumikyō and the New Religions of Japan*. Princeton: Princeton University Press.

———. 1989. *Shinto and the State, 1880–1980*. Princeton: Princeton University Press.

Harootunian, H. D. 1989. Visible Discourses/Invisible Ideologies. In *Postmodernism and Japan*, ed. M. Miyoshi and H. Harootunian. Durham, N.C.: Duke University Press.

Hata, Ikuhiko. 1986. When Ideologues Rewrite History. *Japan Echo* 13(4): 73–78.

Havens, Thomas R. H. 1978. *Valley of Darkness: The Japanese People and World War II*. New York: Norton.

Herbert, Jean. 1967. *Shinto: At the Fountainhead of Japan*. New York: Stein and Day.

Hiro, Sachiya, and Shichihei Yamamoto. 1986. Yasukuni Shrine and the Japanese Spirit World. *Japan Echo* 13(2):73-80.

Hobsbawm, Eric, and Terence Ranger, eds. 1987. *The Invention of Tradition.* Cambridge: Cambridge University Press.

Holtom, Daniel C. 1931. Some Notes on Japanese Tree Worship. *Transactions of the Asiatic Society of Japan* 8:1-19.

———. 1965. *The National Faith of Japan: A Study in Modern Shinto.* 1938. Reprint, New York: Paragon Reprint Corp.

Hori, Ichiro. 1971. *Nihon no shamanism* (Japanese shamanism). Tokyo: Kodansha.

———. 1972. *Japanese Religion.* Tokyo: Kodansha International.

———. 1975. Shamanism in Japan. *Japanese Journal of Religious Studies* 2(4):231-87.

———, ed. 1968. *Folk Religion in Japan: Continuity and Change.* Chicago: University of Chicago Press.

Iisaka, Yoshiaki. 1971. The State and Religion in Postwar History. *Japan Interpreter* 8:307-20.

Inoue, Nobutaka, ed. 1991. *New Religions: Contemporary Papers in Japanese Religion.* Tokyo: Institute for Japanese Culture and Classics.

Inoue, Nobutaka, et al. 1979. A Festival with Anonymous Kami: The Kobe Matsuri. *Japanese Journal of Religious Studies* 6:163-85.

Inouye, Charles S. 1989. Do Non-Japanese Fear the Flame? *Nation,* January 30.

Institute for Japanese Culture and Classics. 1988. *Matsuri—Festival and Rite in Japanese Life: Contemporary Papers on Japanese Religion.* Tokyo: Kokugakuin University.

Isaacs, Harold R. 1975. *Idols of the Tribe.* New York: Harper and Row.

Ishige, Naomichi et al. 1974. Kami, tsukimono, hito: Shimabara-hanto no minkan-shinkō o megutte (Gods, possessions, and people: On the folk beliefs of the Shimabara Peninsula). *Kikan, Jinruigaku* 5(4).

Ishikawa Takashi. 1987. *Kokoro.* Tokyo: East Publications.

Ivy, Marilyn. 1989. Critical Texts, Mass Artifacts: The Consumption of Knowledge in Postmodern Japan. In *Postmodernism and Japan,* ed. M. Miyoshi and H. Harootunian. Durham, N.C.: Duke University Press.

Iwata, Masaharu. 1990. *Kagura* (Sacred dances). Tokyo: Meicho Shuppan.

Kageyama, Haruki. 1973. *The Arts of Shinto.* New York: Weatherhill/Shibundo.

Kanai Noriyoshi. 1982. *Suwa Shinkoshi* (A history of Suwa belief). Tokyo: Meicho Shuppan.

Kato Genchi. 1973. *A Historical Study of the Religious Development of Shinto.* Tokyo: Japan Society for the Promotion of Science.

Kato Shinpei. 1988. *Nihonjin wa, doko kara kita ka?* (Where did the Japanese come from?). Tokyo: Iwanami Shinsho.

Kertzer, David. 1988. *Ritual, Politics, and Power.* New Haven: Yale University Press.

Kidder, J. Edward. 1959. *Japan before Buddhism.* New York: Praeger.

Kishimoto, Hideo. 1958. The Role of Mountains in the Religious Life of the Japanese People. In *Proceedings of the Ninth International Congress for the History of Religions.* Tokyo: Tokyo University Press.

Kitagawa, Joseph. 1966. *Religion in Japanese History.* New York: Columbia University Press.

———. 1987. *On Understanding Japanese Religion.* Princeton: Princeton University Press.

Kluckhorn, Clyde. 1962. *Navaho Witchcraft.* Boston: Beacon Press.

Krauss, Ellis S., Thomas P. Rohlen, and Patricia Steinhoff. 1984. *Conflict in Japan.* Honolulu: University of Hawaii Press.

Kurihara, Akira. 1990. The Emperor System as Japanese National Religion: The Emperor System Module in Everyday Consciousness. *Japanese Journal of Religious Studies* 17(2–3).

Kuroda, Toshio. 1981. Shinto in the History of Japanese Religion. *Journal of Japanese Studies* 7(1):1–21.

Leach, E. R. 1968. Purity. In *Encyclopedia of the Social Sciences.* Vol. 13. New York: Macmillan.

Ledyard, Gari. 1975. Galloping along with the Horseriders: Looking for the Founders of Japan. *Journal of Japanese Studies* 1:217–54.

Lehman, Arthur C., and James Myers, eds. 1989. *Magic, Witchcraft, and Religion: An Anthropological Study of the Supernatural.* 2d ed. Mountain View, Calif.: Mayfield Publishing.

Lewis, Gilbert. 1980. *Day of Shining Red: An Essay on Understanding Ritual.* Cambridge: Cambridge University Press.

Lienhardt, R. Godfrey. 1961. *Divinity and Experience: The Religion of the Dinka.* Oxford: Clarendon Press.

Littleton, C. Scott. 1986. The Organization and Management of a Tokyo Shinto Shrine Festival. *Ethnology* 25:195–202.

Lock, Margaret M. 1980. *East Asian Medicine in Urban Japan.* Berkeley and Los Angeles: University of California Press.

———. 1987. New Japanese Mythologies: Faltering Discipline and the Ailing Housewife. *American Ethnologist* 15(1):43–61.

Matsubara Hisako. 1983. *Nihon to Yoropa no chishiki* (The Wisdom of Japan and Europe). Tokyo: Mikasa Shobo.

Matsumae, Takeshi. 1993. Early Kami Worship. Trans. Janet Goodwin. In *The Cambridge History of Japan,* vol. 1, ed. Delmer Brown. Cambridge: Cambridge University Press.

Matsunaga, Daigan, and Alicia Matsunaga. 1974. *Foundation of Japanese Buddhism.* Vol. 1. Los Angeles: Buddhist Books International.

Mitsui Rokuro and Doi Shinichiro. 1974. *Shin Nagasaki nenpyō* (A new chronology of Nagasaki). Nagasaki: Nagasaki Bunken-sha.

Miyake Hitoshi. 1971. *Shugendō girei no kenkyū* (Research on the rites of Shugendō). Tokyo: Shunjusha.

Miyoshi, Masao, and H. D. Harootunian. 1989. Introduction. In *Postmodernism and Japan*, ed. M. Miyoshi and H. Harootunian. Durham, N.C.: Duke University Press.

Moeran, Brian. 1989. *Language and Popular Culture in Japan*. Manchester: Manchester University Press.

Moore, Sally F., and Barbara G. Myerhoff. 1977. *Secular Ritual*. Assen and Amsterdam: Van Gorcum.

Morita Saburo. 1990. *Matsuri no bunkajinruigaku* (The cultural anthropology of Matsuri). Sekaishisō-sha: Kyoto.

Morris, Brian. 1987. *Anthropological Theories of Religion*. Cambridge: Cambridge University Press.

Murakami, Shigeyoshi. 1980. *Japanese Religion in the Modern Century*. Trans. H. Byron Earhart. Tokyo: University of Tokyo.

Muraoka, Tsunetsugu. 1964. *Studies in Shinto Thought*. Trans. Delmer M. Brown and James T. Araki. Tokyo: Ministry of Education.

Myerhoff, Barbara G. 1984. A Death in Due Time: Construction of Self and Culture in Ritual Drama. In *Rite, Drama, Festival, Spectacle: Rehearsals toward a Theory of Cultural Performance*, ed. J. MacAloon. Philadelphia: Institute for the Study of Human Issues.

Najita, Tetsuo. 1989. On Culture and Technology in Postmodern Japan. In *Postmodernism and Japan*, ed. H. Hartoonian and M. Miyoshi. Durham, N.C.: Duke University Press.

Najita, Tetsuo, and J. Victor Koschmann, eds. 1982. *Conflict in Modern Japanese History: The Neglected Tradition*. Princeton, N.J.: Princeton University Press.

Nakane, Chie. 1970. *Japanese Society*. Berkeley and Los Angeles: University of California Press.

Namihira, Emiko. 1987. Pollution in the Folk Belief System. In *An Anthropological Profile of Japan*, ed. M. Yamaguchi and N. Nagashima. Supplement to *Current Anthropology* 28(4):65–74.

Nelson, John K. 1987. Suwa Shrine: A Special Report. *Harbor Light* 1(2): 7–8.

———. 1986. Okunchi, Nagasaki's Festival. *Harbor Light* 1(9):3–6.

———. 1991. Myths, Missions, and Mistrust: The Fate of Christianity in 17th Century Japan. Unpublished seminar paper. University of California, Berkeley.

———. 1993a. Enduring Identities: The Guise of Shinto in Contemporary Japan. Ph.D. diss., University of California, Berkeley, Department of Anthropology.

———. 1993b. Of Flowers and Phalli: Sexual Symbolism at Kamigamo Shrine. *Japanese Religions* 18(1):2–14.

———. 1994. Land Calming and Claiming Rituals. *Journal of Ritual Studies* 8(2):19–40.

NHK Hōsō Seron-chosa-sho. 1984. *Nihonjin no shūkyō-ishiki* (The religious consciousness of the Japanese). Tokyo: Nippon Hoso Shuppankyokai.

Nishibe, Susumu. 1986. A Denunciation of Mass Society and Its Apologists. *Japan Echo* 13(1):29–34.

Nishimura, Hidetoshi. 1988. Flag and Anthem, Symbols of Distress. *Japan Quarterly* 35(2):152–56.

Norbeck, Edward. 1976. *Changing Japan*. New York: Holt, Rinehart, and Winston.

———. 1978. *Country to City: The Urbanization of a Japanese Hamlet*. Salt Lake City: University of Utah Press.

Ohnuki-Tierney, Emiko. 1984. *Illness and Culture in Contemporary Japan: An Anthropological View*. Cambridge: Cambridge University Press.

———. 1987. *The Monkey as Mirror: Symbolic Transformations in Japanese History and Ritual*. Princeton: Princeton University Press.

Oka Masao. 1979. *Ijin sono ta* (The stranger and others). Tokyo: Gensosha.

Okada Akio. 1955. *Kirishitan Bateren* (Japanese Catholics). Tokyo: Shubundo.

Ono, Sokyo. 1962. *Shinto: The Kami Way*. Tokyo: Charles E. Tuttle.

Ono Susumu et al. 1974. *Kogo jiten* (A dictionary of old words). Tokyo: Iwanami Shoten.

Ooms, Herman. 1985. *Tokugawa Ideology: Early Constructs, 1570–1680*. Princeton: Princeton University Press.

Ortner, S. B. 1978. *Sherpas through Their Rituals*. Cambridge: Cambridge University Press.

Ouwehand, C. 1964. *Namazu-e and Their Themes: An Interpretive Approach to Some Aspects of Japanese Folk Religion*. Leiden: E. J. Brill.

Pearson, Richard, ed. 1986. *Windows on the Japanese Past: Studies in Archaeology and Prehistory*. Ann Arbor: Center for Japanese Studies, University of Michigan.

Perrin, Noel. 1979. *Giving up the Gun*. Boston: David Godine.

Philippi, Donald L. 1968. *Kojiki*. Tokyo: University of Tokyo Press.

———, trans. 1959. *Norito: A New Translation of the Ancient Japanese Ritual Prayers*. Tokyo: Institute for Japanese Culture and Classics, Kokugakuin University.

Ponsonby-Fane, Richard. 1953. *Studies in Shinto and Shrines*. Ponsonby-Fane Society Publications, vol. 1. Kyoto.

———. 1963. *The Vicissitudes of Shinto*. Ponsonby-Fane Society Publications, vol. 5. Kyoto.

Preston, James. 1986. In *Magic, Witchcraft, and Religion: An Anthropological Study of the Supernatural*, ed. A. Lehman and J. Myers. Mountain View, Calif.: Mayfield Publishing.

Reader, Ian. 1991. *Religion in Contemporary Japan*. Honolulu: University of Hawaii Press.

Rosaldo, Michelle. 1980. *Knowledge and Passion: Ilongot Notions of Self and Social Life*. New York: Cambridge University Press.

Ross, Floyd H. 1965. *Shinto: The Way of Japan*. Boston: Beacon Press.

Sadler, A. W. 1976. The Grammar of a Rite in Shinto. *Asian Folklore Studies* 35:17–27.

———. 1982. Carrying the *Mikoshi*: Further Field Notes on the Shrine Festival in Modern Tokyo. *Asian Folklore Studies* 31:89–114.

Sakurai Tokutaro. 1974. *Nihon no shamanism* (Japanese shamanism). Tokyo: Yoshikawa Kobundo.

Sansom, G. B. 1961. *A History of Japan*. 3 vols. Stanford: Stanford University Press.

Sasaki, Kokan. 1990. Priest, Shaman, King. *Japanese Journal of Religious Studies* 17(2–3):105–27.

Schnell, Scott. 1992. Matsuri and Symbolic Opposition in Central Japan. Paper delivered at the annual meeting of the American Anthropological Associations, San Francisco.

Schwade, Arcadio. 1986. *Shinto-Bibliography in Western Languages*. Leiden: E. J. Brill.

Shils, Edward. 1981. *Tradition*. Chicago: University of Chicago Press.

Shimojima, Kyushiro. 1986. Facts and Fallacies about Yasukuni Shrine. *Japan Echo* 13(2):69–72.

Shisei hyaku-nen: Nagasaki Nenpyō (One hundred years of city government: A Nagasaki chronology). N.d. Manuscript copy, Suwa Shrine.

Smith, Bradley. 1964. *Japan, A History in Art*. Tokyo: Toppan Printing Co.

Smith, Jonathan Z. 1981. The Bare Facts of Ritual. *History of Religions* 20:34–47.

———. 1987. *To Take Place*. Chicago: University of Chicago Press.

Smith, Robert J. 1974. *Ancestor Worship in Contemporary Japan*. Stanford: Stanford University Press.

———. 1978. *Kurusu: The Price of Progress in a Japanese Village, 1951–1975*. Stanford: Stanford University Press.

———. 1983. *Japanese Society: Tradition, Self, and the Social Order*. Cambridge: Cambridge University Press.

Smyers, Karen. 1993. *The Fox and the Jewel: A Study of Shared and Private Meanings in Japanese Inari Worship*. Ph.D. diss., Princeton University.

Sonoda, Minoru. 1975. The Traditional Festival in Urban Society. *Japanese Journal of Religious Studies* 2:103–36.

———. 1988a. Festival and Sacred Transgression. In *Matsuri: Festival and Rite in Japanese Life*. Tokyo: Institute for Japanese Culture and Classics, Kokugakuin University.

———, ed. 1988b. *Shinto: Nihon no minzoku shukyo* (Shinto: Japan's folk religion). Tokyo: Kobundo.

Suwa Shrine Shamusho. N.d. Suwa Jinja nenpyō (A chronology of Suwa Shrine). Manuscript copy, Suwa Shrine.

Swyngedouw, Jan. 1986. Religion in Contemporary Japanese Society. *Japan Foundation Newsletter* 13(4):3.

Tambiah, S. J. 1968. The Magical Power of Words. *Man*, n.s., 3(2): 175–208.

Tsunoda, Ryusaku, and L. C. Goodrich, eds. 1951. History of the Kingdom of Wei (Wei Chi), c. A.D. 297. In Ryusaku Tsunoda, *Japan in the Chinese Dynastic Histories*, ed. L. C. Goodrich. Perkins Asiatic Monograph no. 2. Pasadena: P. D. & I. Perkins.

Tsunoda, Ryusaku, et al. 1958. *Sources of Japanese Tradition.* New York: Columbia University Press.

Turner, Victor. 1969. *The Ritual Process.* Chicago: Aldine Publishing.

———. 1973. Symbols in African Ritual. *Science* 179:1100–1105.

Ueda, Kenji. 1972. Shinto. In *Japanese Religion*, ed. Ichiro Hori. Tokyo: Kodansha International.

———. 1979. Contemporary Social Change and Shinto Tradition. *Japanese Journal of Religious Studies* 6(1/2):303–27.

Wagatsuma, Hiroshi. 1975. Problems of Cultural Identity in Modern Japan. In *Ethnic Identity*, ed. George De Vos and Lola Romanucci-Ross. Berkeley and Los Angeles: University of California Press.

Warner, Langdon. 1952. *The Enduring Art of Japan.* New York: Grove Press.

van Wolferen, Karel. 1989. *The Enigma of Japanese Power.* New York: Knopf.

Yamazaki, Masakazu. 1983. Signs of a New Individualism. *Chuo Koron*, August, p. 14. *Yomiuri Shinbun.* 1992. January 5, p. 2.

Yanagawa, Keiichi. 1988. The Sensation of Matsuri. In *Matsuri: Festival and Rite in Japanese Life.* Tokyo: Institute for Japanese Culture and Classics, Kokugakuin University.

Yoshida, Teigo. 1967. Mystical Retribution, Spirit Possession, and Social Structure in a Japanese Village. *Ethnology* 6(3):237–62.

———. 1981. The Stranger as God: The Place of the Outsider in Japanese Folk Religion. *Ethnology* 20(2):87–99.

———. 1984. Spirit Possession and Village Conflict. In *Conflict in Japan*, ed. Ellis S. Krauss, Thomas P. Rohlen, and Patricia Steinhoff. Honolulu: University of Hawaii Press.

Zuesse, Evan. 1979. *Ritual Cosmos.* Athens: Ohio University Press.

INDEX

CPSIA information can be obtained at www.ICGtesting.com

261166BV00002B/2/P